The New Housing 2 – building better communities

The New Housing 2

BUILDING BETTER COMMUNITIES

THE ROYAL INSTITUTE OF THE ARCHITECTS OF IRELAND

THE NEW HOUSING 2 – BUILDING BETTER COMMUNITIES

Published by the Royal Institute of the Architects of Ireland with the support of
the Department of the Environment, Heritage & Local Government

editors   James Pike, Kathryn Meghen

ISBN   978 0948037 405 (ISBN-10: 0948037 407)

Produced for the RIAI by Gandon Editions
design   John O'Regan (© Gandon Editions, 2009)
production   Nicola Dearey, Gunther Berkus
                 Susan Byrne, Niamh Butler
printing   Nicholson & Bass, Belfast
distribution   Gandon Distribution and its overseas agents

GANDON EDITIONS, Oysterhaven, Kinsale, Co Cork, Ireland
T +353 (0)21-4770830 / F 4770755 / E gandon@eircom.net / W www.gandon-editions.com
(Gandon Editions is grant-aided by The Arts Council / An Chomhairle Ealaíon)

cover / frontispiece – Alto Vetro, Grand Canal Quay, Dublin 2 by Shay Cleary Architects
pretitle – Kilkenny Western Environs LAP by O'Mahony Pike Architects

ACKNOWLEDGEMENTS

The RIAI would like to thank the members of the Joint RIAI / DoEHLG Sustainable
Communities and Housing Committee:

The opinions expressed herein are not necessarily those of the RIAI, its officers or
members. Every effort has been made to ensure the accuracy of this information, but the
publishers cannot be held responsible for errors.

Project descriptions were supplied by the architectural practices.
All drawings, illustrations and photographs courtesy of the architects.

THE ROYAL INSTITUTE OF THE ARCHITECTS OF IRELAND, 8 Merrion Square, Dublin 2
T +353 (0)1-6761703 / F +353 (0)1-6610948 / E info@riai.ie / W www.riai.ie

Comhshaol, Oidhreacht agus Rialtas Áitiúil
Environment, Heritage and Local Government

RIAI

Contents

Featured Housing

2 URBAN INFILL

Foreword

SEÁN Ó LAOIRE

The socio-economic context in which *The New Housing 2* has been published will no doubt present historians with a challenge. It is tempting to speculate that it might be simply seen as a footnote to the history of an era which saw this island produce an unprecedented number of residences. If it is thus, then the point of this book and its predecessors will have been missed, and will testify to the waste of opportunities a time of crisis offers. We now have time. Unless we critically and honestly interrogate how our society contrived to produce such a volume without evidence of demand in specific locations, or without any strategic connections to social and public transportation infrastructure. then we are fated as a country to pay a very heavy price indeed. While the 'shelter' function of Irish housing may have been augmented, this epoch dramatically illustrates systematic disconnection between public policy and a sustainable Ireland.

At the time of writing there is a palpable fear about the prospect of an Ireland of six million people in 2030, which eminent demographers predict. We still have one of the youngest populations in the EU, and a great repository of talent. What we arguably lack is a capacity to imagine that growth presents huge opportunities to revisit the settlement patterns we have created. Where and how we focus our collective talents is now our great challenge. This must centrally embrace a radical and imaginative approach to 'retrofitting' existing settlement and, with that, a requirement for an alliance between politicians, communities, policy-makers and the profession I represent.

In that capacity, I wish to pay special tribute to my colleague and predecessor James Pike who has given forty years of extraordinary commitment to the cause of housing in Ireland. As an architect and as the bridge between the profession and the Department of the Environment, Heritage & Local Government, his contribution has been enormous. I would urge my colleagues to build on his contribution, and energetically engage in the promotion of solutions that can make Ireland, yet, a model of sustainable living.

Beir bua is beannacht.

SEÁN Ó LAOIRE
President, Royal Institute of the Architects of Ireland

March 2009

Foreword

JOHN GORMLEY TD

This publication could not be more timely. We are caught in what is now an international economic maelstrom, which threatens the very fabric of our society and economy. The current crisis is real, and it is being felt in every corner of this country, in every sector, in every home. Thousands of people have lost their jobs, and a large proportion of those losses have been in the construction sector.

There is no doubt that the unprecedented levels of demand placed on our regulatory systems over the last decade have not always led to decisions that have sufficiently prioritised long-term social, economic and environmental sustainability. Moreover, the principal regulatory system in this context, the planning system – the key mechanism by which all forward-planning, development management and enforcement takes place – was asked to significantly diversify its functions while meeting the challenge of the Celtic Tiger years. The system has generally coped very well, but the sheer volume of construction activity at times threatened to compromise the ambition of the regulatory framework. Similarly, the degree to which the health of our public finances was linked to activity in the construction sector is now presenting major challenges, which will fall to all sectors to overcome collectively. In many cases, it is the communities that expanded the fastest, sometimes without having the necessary infrastructure and services in place to support their rapid development, that are suffering the most in this current down turn.

I believe we now have a once-in-a-generation opportunity to get things right. We have the opportunity at this time to put measures and policies in place to build the right buildings in the right place at the right time, and to ensure that when we do see economic recovery, future development in Ireland will be along a sustainable model where the long-term benefits for society are put ahead of short-term profit or revenue.

In my own department we are committed to this vision. I have been engaged in an ongoing and fundamental reform of our planning regime. Our new sustainable residential guidelines are now in place, alongside the Urban Design Manual. New flood-planning guidelines have also been produced and are in place. I will also soon be introducing new planning legislation, which I hope will see some fundamental reforms of our planning system. The measures ensure that planning schemes are evidence-based, and that they are consistent. The legislation will require core strategies in development plans, to ensure consistency between national, regional and local planning guidelines. The legislation will also require that such guidelines must be adhered to.

I hope that this new planning regime, combined with ongoing investment in public transport, social and environmental infrastructure, will offer an enormous opportunity for high-quality urban development. We owe it to the people who are now suffering to repair their urban communities, to make them more sustainable, to put in the proper infrastructure so we can make them attractive places to live, where jobs and business can be generated.

The essays and projects in this publication point out a path forward towards better urban development. They outline the problems and the challenges we face in improving our urban areas and creating sustainable communities. But they also highlight the fact that strong planning laws and rules should not be viewed as a cost. Strong planning rules impose high standards that, if met, can actually improve competitiveness. They ensure that developments remain viable throughout the economic cycle, and that the social, environmental and financial benefits of sustainable design and development greatly outweigh any initial financial or regulatory cost.

This publication is, therefore, very welcome as it shows the huge opportunity that is before us. We just have to seize it.

JOHN GORMLEY TD
Minister for the Environment, Heritage & Local Government

Sustainable Communities

JAMES PIKE

The collapse of the economy, crime wars in our cities, and failure to meet our Kyoto targets illustrate sharply that we are failing in all three areas of sustainable development – economic, social and environmental. A history of successful cities and small towns has been destroyed in the last forty years with the growth in the use of the motor car. For several decades our towns and cities became the domain of lower-income groups and social housing, while those with larger incomes departed for suburbia and the countryside. The last fifteen years of unprecedented boom has largely exacerbated the situation.

In Dublin city, in spite of the major development of social housing in the suburbs, those living in the inner city remained Corporation tenants or private tenants in rooming houses. Until about 1990, no private housing was built in the inner city and the population was declining. The last decade has seen a major reverse in this process, with the inner-city population expanding, and extensive new private apartment developments, particularly in Docklands. Families with children are returning to the inner suburbs, and new schools are being built or old ones extended. This is a pattern we must encourage in all our cities and towns if the current decline is to be reversed. This has reached crisis point in Limerick, where the Government has been forced to move in to try to stop social and economic meltdown.

With two-thirds of our population now living in our five main city regions, we need to discover patterns of urbanism which will attract people to live in towns again. People are already experiencing the problems of sprawl and badly planned suburban development, with long commuting distances and lack of facilities – shops, schools, recreational amenities and jobs – close to where they live. While this destructive trend has continued largely unabated, there are encouraging examples of good planning and urban development, some of which have won international recognition.

Each household needs to calculate the time it spends driving cars, which wastes productive time for work, family or social activities. It is possible to read or socialise on public transport, and walking or cycling can provide the exercise needed to keep reasonably fit. It has been calculated that two parents with two children at school, living fifteen to twenty miles outside a town or city, spend over 2,500 hours between them every year in their cars, when the average time at work is 1,750 hours. Our obligations under the Kyoto Agreement will require a reduction of 500,000 daily commuter trips by 2020 to reduce our rapidly rising transport emissions. The Department of Transport's 2020 Vision proposes a 60%:40% modal split nationally between public transport and walking and cycling to work, as against the use of private cars.

This book intends to show best practice in housing and mixed-use development through schemes which are planned, under construction or completed. It follows the full range of urban planning, from villages and small towns, through the extension of towns and cities, to regeneration of existing towns and cities. While there are fine examples from abroad which point to a variety of solutions, we will only persuade Irish householders to change their preferred way of life to a more urban form by building new developments and regenerating existing communities here at home.

The DoEHLG has been making major progress over the last few years in publishing guidance on planning, urban design and housing issues (as set out in the Minister's introduction). This publication relates particularly to the *Urban Design Manual*, published to accompany *Guidelines for Planning Authorities on Sustainable Residential Development in Urban Areas*. These guidance documents and *The New Housing 2* set out best practice, which all local authorities need to adopt for promoting good urban development. We also need strong Regional Development Plans and adoption across the board of good Local Area Plans, including costed infrastructure plans and urban-design master plans, so that this best practice will be a prerequisite for all new development projects (as set out in a recent letter to *The Irish Times* by Dublin City Councillor, Oisín Quinn). The adoption of good plans, supported by the community, will reduce the workload in the development-control section of local authorities, allowing more resources to be devoted to development planning and compliance. Above all, we need a consistent approach across all local authorities to the management of the planning system.

In this publication, there are four essays covering different aspects of the current situation; the projects are then grouped into four sections – villages and small towns, the urban fringe, urban infill and regeneration, and a special section on the regeneration of Ballymun.

Supported by reports from key State agencies, Tony Reddy sets out the scale of the challenges posed by a rapidly expanding population. He explores solutions tried elsewhere and current international trends, and proposes solutions for the Irish situation. He returns to the ESRI report of 2004 which states that the challenge of creating sustainable communities for the future is the greatest challenge facing Irish society – equal to the opening-up of the economy in the 1960s and the creation of Social Partnership in the 1980s.

Toal Ó Muiré describes how our planning system has developed, and the potential which recent planning legislation has created to solve our major problems of co-ordinating development. He highlights the lack of consistency across the many local authorities, particularly in the Dublin region. He refers to some planning initiatives (illustrated in the projects sections) which offer realistic best practice, which should be followed by all local authorities, and

the risks created if we do not impose a strong national policy.

The next two essays set out examples which attempt to show a way forward. The first is the regeneration of Dublin's docklands; the second is the planning of the Cork city region. John McLaughlin shows the progress made by the Dublin Docklands Development Authority with the direct powers to create Planning Schemes and carry them out in a disciplined and co-ordinated way. A major, high-class urban quarter is being created, which sets a strong example for our other cities.

Roddy Hogan writes about planning in the Cork city region, where successive regional plans have been created through collaboration between the City Council and County Council. He highlights, however, the potential lack of follow-through as the city's growth accelerates well ahead of predictions made in a period of relative stagnation, and the need for greater regional co-ordination if the plans are going to be successfully realised.

The introductions to the project sections discuss the particular issues related to those sections. Paul Keogh highlights the current problems in small towns and villages and the urgent need to reverse our attitudes to urban development. He reiterates the ESRI's call for sustainable communities, the need for strong policies from central government, and the will to carry them out.

The introduction to 'Town and City Edge / New Communities' by Seán Harrington presents a clear vision of how we should be creating new communities as we expand our urban centres. He points out that while the new projects illustrated do indicate the way forward, too many of them are largely residential, lacking a sufficient mix of uses to create fully sustainable communities, and pose major challenges if they are to prove successful in the long term.

Eddie Conroy's introduction to urban infill and regeneration describes a very positive picture of the progress being made and the quality of the schemes illustrated, but he does highlight a number of problems, particularly the need for high-quality urban design to help create the necessary variety of public space and a balanced mix of dwelling types and uses.

David Prichard, who was the project director of the original Ballymun master plan, reviews progress on this massive regeneration project. He highlights the many social, educational and managerial issues which must be tackled to create really successful and sustainable communities, particularly where those communities so abjectly failed in their previous form.

13

ModelWorks ARCHITECTURAL PRESENTATION T + 353 1 2899 0

Sustainable Urbanism: creating communities for the knowledge economy

ANTHONY REDDY

The challenge of 21st-century urbanism is to create sustainable mixed-use communities with a high-quality public realm.

UNDERSTANDING THE PROBLEM

The economic and social changes that have occurred in Ireland in the past two decades – the era of the 'Celtic Tiger' economy – are well documented. These changes were the catalyst for a spate of growth that has physically transformed our cities, towns and villages on a scale which is more profound and far-reaching than any in history. As recently as 2006, economic commentators were predicting an unsustainable future, with an increase in population, significant traffic gridlock, housing being less affordable, and the countryside covered in even more suburban sprawl.

The onset of recession as a result of the global financial crises has provided a temporary pause from this future scenario. One of the few benefits of the financial crisis and the recession is that it has created an opportunity for planners, architects and policy-makers to reflect on the development that has occurred over the past two decades, to learn from the mistakes made, and to take action to ensure that we plan a better future.

For the first time ever, the majority of Ireland's population now lives in urban areas. This trend will continue over the next twenty years. It is critical to Ireland's future that the cities and towns which evolve are more sustainable than our current models. An Italian philosopher once said, 'There is nothing more difficult to take in hand, more perilous to conduct, or more uncertain in the success than to take a lead in the introduction of a new order.' Trying to map out how we should create sustainable towns and cities is part of a new order of things.

UNDISTINGUISHED URBAN FORMS

Most of us, directly or indirectly, shape the built environment. A few have the mixed privilege of being architects, planners, engineers, developers or policy-makers who make direct decisions about the form of our towns and cities. The majority of people make more oblique, but no less consequential decisions regarding the environment through the selection of our political representatives. For the most part, we make these choices with particular interests in mind and with, at best, a general concern about 'community' or the 'environment'.

← Sustainable new town
– Adamstown, Co Dublin

However, all of us, and, in particular, the professionals and policy-makers involved with the built environment, have difficulty in fully understanding or interpreting the scale and character of contemporary urbanisation. Like other countries in the developed world, we see a society that is generating vast, undistinguished urban zones with the same array of road systems, electricity cables and satellite dishes. In summary, sprawl! As we look at the sprawl of nearly every city, town and village caused by our own Hibernian interpretation of the model, who can doubt that we need to do something about the vast undistinguished urban forms now being created?

THE CHALLENGE

Human destiny has been closely linked in history to the success or failure of urban and village life. Successful towns and cities have existed continuously for hundreds, even thousands of years; others have disappeared either as a result of devastating the local environment from which they drew their resources, or following major historic catastrophes. In the increasingly urbanised world of the 21st century, a major challenge is to find solutions to the problems facing our towns and cities – the control of sprawl, sustainable growth, integrated transport systems, and better-quality urban environments and public realms.

Cities and towns that are diverse, varied in use, walkable, human-scaled and identifiable by the high quality of their public realm can contribute to the process of creating sustainable urbanism. The challenge for all citizens is to make our towns and cities viable in the long term environmentally and socially, as well as economically. There will be no sustainable world and no sustainable country without sustainable cities and towns. Against the backdrop of a wider agenda – 'the need to meet the needs of the present without compromising the ability of future generations to meet their own needs' – sustainable urbanism is crucial to the future of our island and our planet

SEARCHING FOR SOLUTIONS

Current attempts to reform contemporary cities and towns continue a century-long response to the problems of the model urban form through architectural, planning and urban intervention. Some of the initiatives and reforms of the early 20th century have been responsible for the most significant urban problems of the past half-century.

In his famous diagram of the three magnets (1898), Ebenezer Howard brilliantly encapsulated the virtues and vices of the late-Victorian city and countryside. To summarise, the city had economic and social opportunity but overcrowded housing and an appalling physical environment. On the other hand, the

countryside offered open space and clean air, but little prospect of employment or social life. By creating a third magnet, 'Town-Country', it would be possible to combine all the opportunities of the town with all the qualities of the country.

Over one hundred years after the Garden City movement began, the countryside has now been transformed – to some extent under its influence. Electricity and the car make it easy to communicate. Television and the internet give access to entertainment, education and information. However, as the suburbs have become the dominant form of urban development, the weaknesses and problems associated with them have become more apparent. When the majority live in suburbs, the assumed advantages become disadvantages as communication and accessibility become more car-dependant and, hence, more time-consuming. In addition, the aspirations of most Irish suburban-dwellers to live near city and country, to own and control their property, including front and back gardens, to have constant freedom of movement and to cherish their privacy, all tend to work against establishing good communities. There are also vast areas where little thought appears to have been given to concepts such as urbanism and place-making.

SUBURBAN SPRAWL

Sprawl is commonly referred to as the low-density form of development of single-use pods (e.g. housing, office parks and shopping malls) connected by a few large roads and totally car-dominated. Typically, it consists of a series of private spaces with little public space. The dispersed nature of sprawl forces residents and users to depend on cars for mobility. Normal daily activities such as shopping and working are usually not accessible to pedestrians, and the densities associated with sprawl are too low to support public transport. There have been a number of primary reasons for the emergence of sprawl:

Lack of regional planning – The lack of co-ordinated planning at a regional level results in great ecological and economic costs which impact on city areas as well as surrounding suburbs and open space. Without a regional plan, it is difficult to direct growth to preserve land and natural resources, while encouraging urban and suburban infill. Public transport requires minimum population densities and compact development patterns, which are best encouraged and co-ordinated at regional level.

Lack of neighbourhood design – The lack of design and planning which focuses on the neighbourhood as the primary pedestrian-orientated unit of design is a major cause of sprawl. Contemporary suburbia has all the elements of a traditional town or neighbourhood, but dispersed in isolated car-accessible

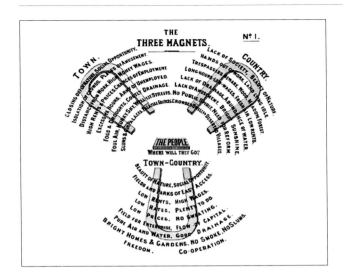

← The Three Magnets diagram by Ebenezer Howard (1898)

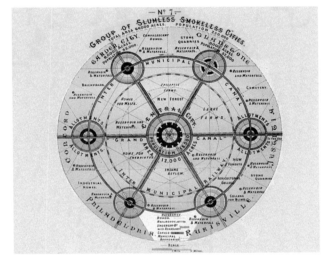

← The Social City diagram by Ebenezer Howard (1898)

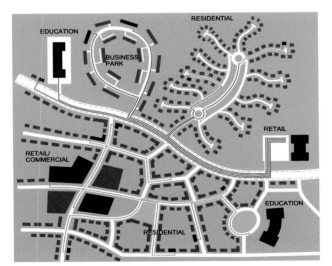

← Typical pod development

pods. There is a richness and complexity in the traditional neighbourhood pattern to be found in older suburban areas, such as the Victorian suburbs of Rathmines and Ranelagh and the early 20th-century suburbs of Glasnevin, Marino or Terenure in Dublin. This has been completely lost in the postwar suburban pattern consisting of isolated and dispersed forms of development.

Zoning policy – The original purpose of zoning – to separate industry from residential areas – is mostly unnecessary in Ireland's knowledge economy. As a result of zoning, the multiple uses that once co-existed in cities and towns are now separated and isolated from each other, connected by wide roadways. Current zoning principles are unable to accommodate different urban situations or densities, and contribute to a homogeneous building landscape.

Specialisation and standardisation – Increased specialisation in the built-environment professions has also contributed to sprawl; separate disciplines work to resolve problems in a particular area of expertise. Despite the fact that architects, engineers and planners are all involved in shaping our towns and cities, few receive training in how complex urban spaces work. Can we imagine if doctors were trained as specialists first? Patients would have great difficulty getting advice from any member of the medical profession. But that is how our built environment professionals are trained, and hence we have poor new urban spaces, suburban sprawl and the edge-city phenomenon.

The role of the private car and roads – The widespread ownership of the motor car has given citizens a new mobility and has enabled the rapid development and dispersion of suburbs. The tendency of modernist planning to give priority to the car has altered the forms of new and existing development so that the dominant image of our cities is of wide roadways, large setbacks for car-parking, and a vast network of roads.

ECONOMIC COST OF SPRAWL

A number of organisations, researchers and journalists have studied sprawl, and many conclude that there are serious social, financial and environmental implications to the current pattern of development. Recent studies have found an inverse correlation between density and municipal capital costs. In the United States and the United Kingdom, for example, the cost of providing infrastructure and services for low-density, non-contiguous development is estimated to be approximately twice the cost of providing for compact terraced development. The direct cost in time and money for the average family are enormous. Apart from housing costs, suburban dwellers spend more money on cars than any other expense category, including food.

We in Ireland are among the most car-dependent countries in the world. A particularly compelling argument against the current suburban patterns of development is that environmental costs are considerable and irreversible.

There are also many criticisms of suburbia as a place to spawn social isolation. The disconnected patterns of residential development discourage walking and have exacerbated the isolation of the very young, the old and the poor. The random encounters of many types of people, so necessary to urban culture, are less likely to occur in the isolation of sprawl suburbs where most human contact is planned and controlled.

The flight to the suburbs has created severe dis-investment in central-city and town areas, although urban-renewal legislation in Ireland has balanced this trend somewhat in recent years. The likelihood in the future is that there will be a continual threat to investment in our inner cities and towns because of increasing demands for services, schools, utilities, refuse collection, etc, in the ever-widening suburban periphery.

EMERGING TRENDS

Until the publication by Jane Jacobs, *The Life and Death of the Great American Cities* in 1961, the design philosophies of Modernism and the Garden City Movement had enjoyed an unassailable position as the dominant philosophies in modern city-planning. She initiated a critique of those philosophies which gradually led, in the 1980s and 1990s, towards a worldwide movement for sustainable urbanism.

The work of the Congress of the New Urbanism (USA), the Urban Task Force (UK), the Academy of Urbanism (UK), the Urban Forum and the Sustainable Communities and Housing Committee (Ireland) has been largely responsible for creating awareness among architects and planners of the principles required to achieve this form of urbanism. The aim has been to attempt to redefine the architectural and planning professions and their relationship with society, while simultaneously redefining urban-design theory. These movements exhibit a common theme of searching for alternative solutions for the future of our cities and towns based on the principles of sustainable urbanism.

The stated principles of all of the bodies monitoring sustainable urbanism has been consistent. In order to promote community, the built environment must be diverse in use and population, scaled for the pedestrian, and capable of supporting public transport as well as the car. It must have a well-defined public realm supported by buildings reflecting the architecture and ecology of the region. The underlying principles of these bodies and movements are:

↑ Sustainable new town
  – new town centre at Adamstown, Co Dublin

↗ Hammarby Sjöstad, Stockholm – aerial view

↘ Hammarby Sjöstad – integration of landscape
  and development

– to select and adapt from existing models in our towns and cities which have proven to be successful
– to support the restoration of existing city and town centres within coherent metropolitan regions
– the reconfiguration of sprawling suburbs into real neighbourhoods and diverse districts
– the conservation of natural environments and the preservation of our built heritage.

Bodies such as the Urban Task Force, CNU, the Academy of Urbanism and the Urban Forum recognise that physical solutions by themselves will not solve social and economic problems, but neither can economic vitality, community stability and environmental health be sustained without a coherent and supportive physical framework. These bodies advocate the restructuring of public policy and development practice to support the following principles:
– neighbourhoods should be diverse in use and population
– communities should be designed for the pedestrian and public transport as well as the car

– cities and towns should be shaped by physically defined and universally accessible public spaces and community institutions
– urban places should be framed by architecture and landscape design that celebrates local history, climate, ecology and building practice.

Publications including *The Charter of the New Urbanism*, *Towards an Urban Renaissance*, *The New Housing*, and this publication, *The New Housing 2*, set down these principles in detail in order to guide public policy, development, practice, urban planning and design.

SUSTAINABLE URBANISM: NEW SOLUTIONS

Ireland has been, and continues to be, distinguished by a high degree of home-ownership and a propensity to live in houses with gardens. Many architects and planners prefer to ignore the suburb, considering it to be as inconsequential as it is distasteful. Most built-environment professionals see themselves as urbanists, whose professional focus is on the opportunities provided by urban culture. As a profession, we tend to consider urban values as dominant in our culture and the suburbs an aberrant form of settlement. But, unless we confront the fact that the suburbs have a persuasive hold on the Irish imagination, it will continue to dominate developing urban forms in unsatisfactory patterns.

The formula for the successful and sustainable city seems to be constant: a permeable layout, a range of high-quality buildings to fill it, a series of successful public spaces, and sufficient density for the whole entity to be brimming with life. Over the past century, and, in particular, in the post-war period, most urban dwellers' way of life has changed profoundly. Apart from increasing car-ownership, the average family size has become smaller, our habits as consumers have been gradually altered, while our leisure patterns have evolved beyond recognition.

Best practice in the design of new settlement patterns is orientated towards minimising, but not eliminating, the need for cars and travel, and containing the low-density sprawl of the past decades. Compactness is therefore an important goal, but is also necessary to generate densities that permit such urban advantages as public transport, pedestrian activity and shared public space.

A number of models have been put forward in opposition to the conventional model of suburban planning. One of them is the traditional neighbourhood unit. The neighbourhood is described as 'a community sustaining a full range of ordinary human needs', whether districts, villages or towns. This neighbourhood is limited by the distances one can walk within five minutes (usually a quarter of

a mile in radius). The ideal traditional neighbourhood development contains a range of housing types, the town centre –often a square or plaza – places to work, places to shop, schools and civic or community buildings. Streets and blocks are the infrastructure of the new neighbourhood pattern. Connected street networks are once again employed in place of the cul-de-sac pattern of sprawl. This connecting network is advantageous because
– it reduces congestion by keeping local traffic, which comprises the majority of trips, on local roads instead of major roadways
– travel is more direct and flexible
– the town centre, accessible from all directions, can be concentrated in the centre rather than dispersed. Non-vehicle travel, including walking, cycling and public transport, becomes possible, safe and more enjoyable than travelling on distributor and main roads.

The building of new neighbourhoods and towns and the reworking of existing suburbs and cities require planning on a regional scale. Ideally, the region would comprise collections of neighbourhoods focused on public transport, or transit lines, called 'transit-orientated districts' (TOD). Limiting metropolitan sprawl is a regional issue, balancing urban and rural areas. A regional plan helps direct growth in appropriate areas, and can ensure the minimum densities necessary for shared services, including utilities, places of work, and other facilities.

These models propose principles for structuring settlement patterns that can be applied to cities, towns and villages equally. Their flexibility, popular appeal and ability to accommodate different scales and density of development set them apart from previous urban strategies. In the United States, Europe and Ireland, there are now architects and planners who are applying these principles and models in their work. There is a shared belief that the establishment of public space, pedestrian scale and neighbourhood identity are as applicable to the centre of our towns and cities as to suburban conditions. The challenge for architects and planners is to influence the design of our town and city centres and the vast area in which the majority of the population now live – sprawled between the centre and the open countryside. The major objective has been to reshape the form of our car-dependant suburbia into communities that make sense.

The human settlement pattern – and not just individual buildings and dwellings – is the crucial component in the environmental equation. The primacy of the settlement pattern is demonstrated by what can happen when it is overlooked. Much of the settlement pattern in suburban areas of Irish towns and cities has been of poor quality and is problematic in terms of its effect. In response, significant attempts have been made by a cross-section of architects, planners and other building professionals to arrive at solutions to current and future growth to provide a sustainable form of urbanism.

↖ Sustainable new town
– new town centre at Adamstown, Co Dublin

↑ Adamstown, Co Dublin – new residential development

← Sustainable village extension
– Newcastle, Co Dublin

The emerging patterns of sustainable urbanism in limited locations in our country – Adamstown, Clonburris, the North Fringe and Newcastle in south Dublin, and the Dublin and Cork docklands – hold out the prospect of indicating a new way forward. These exemplar projects all attempt to create new communities with a moderate density (forty to eighty dwellings per hectare) and greater public-transport provision.

Exceptional international models of sustainable urbanism include the Västra Hamnen and Hammarby Sjöstad developments in Sweden. The Västra Hamnen development on the waterfront in Malmö was given its initial impetus by an exhibition aimed at promoting sustainable urban development. The significance of this project is that it seeks to reconcile the goals of sustainable design with the demands of the market. The master plan has maximised the contrast between views of the sea and the green spaces encompassed by the residential units. Hammarby Sjöstad is a residential and mixed-use environmental and urban-planning scheme on a brownfield site in Stockholm. The project master plan sets high standards in respect of residential design,

landscape design, waste-handling, energy-generation and transport policy. The project includes approximately 11,000 apartments and 300,000m² of commercial space, with a population of 25,000. There is a high standard of design in the residential units and in the public spaces, including parks, canals, streets and pavements.

The personal and national choices this generation makes in respect of settlement patterns will determine the inheritance of our children and grandchildren. We need an increasing number of our political leaders and policy-makers to recognise the inherent sustainability of a walkable, diverse urbanism integrated with high-performance buildings and infrastructure

Both of these Swedish examples are characterised by an emphasis on creating communities with a high-quality public realm, streets and squares with an urban character, and a plan-form based on increased permeability to minimise car-dependency. The first phases of the developments are now reaching completion, and they promise to be a significant contribution to the debate on appropriate forms for modern architecture and urbanism in Ireland and Europe.

PARTICIPATION

An important aspect of sustainable planning is the principle of participation, and its benefits can be expressed in the following terms: the more stakeholders affected by an urban process are involved in decision-making, the more knowledge will be accumulated and the easier it will be to avoid possible conflicts, by identifying them and channelling them towards more constructive ends. Sustainable planning should be a bottom-up process which is based on the involvement of all stakeholders from the beginning of and throughout the process. The result of a participation process which incorporates the wealth of information held by the users will be richer and more diverse than any solution conceived in isolation. In addition, the effort of creating consensus will generally be rewarded by greater commitment to the final results from a wider group.

The task of implementing sustainable urbanism will require the participation of several generations of development professionals. Sustainable urbanism represents a generational shift in how human settlements are designed and developed. Its adoption as a planning norm requires all of the many participants in the process of planning and developing the built environment to work in unison towards a shared objective.

The material included in this publication is indicative of an increasing involvement of Irish architects and planners in urban design and good place-

21

making. It represents a fundamental challenge to society, and should be seen as an exciting move towards designing successful and sustainable communities, which may in turn become models for town extensions in Ireland and elsewhere.

VISIONS FOR THE FUTURE

The great parliamentarian Edmund Burke said, 'No-one made a greater mistake than he who did nothing because he could only do a little.' We have to begin to treat our cities and towns much more responsibly, and to recognise that they are more fragile than we realise. Each of us has a part to play, however small, in the process of creating future sustainable communities.

Since the foundation of an independent Irish state in 1922 there have been many national achievements, but none more significant than the great policy initiatives of the post-war era. These include:
– the opening-up of the economy in the early 1960s under the leadership of Seán Lemass and TK Whitaker
– the introduction of free second level education in 1967
– Social Partnership of the mid-1980s, which involved government, employers and trade unions in a long-term social and economic pact.

As Ireland entered the 1990s following a prolonged period of recession, few could have anticipated the impact that these initiatives would have for the future of the Irish economy. Having entered the European Economic Community in 1972, and with a young, well-educated workforce, Ireland was well positioned to take advantage of the opportunities which the following decade would bring. In 1989 Ireland had a total of 18% of its workforce in creative or knowledge economy activities. By 2002 this had risen to 33%, catapulting the Irish economy to top place in the International Creative Class Index. This change in the make-up of the workforce reflected the fact that in a short period Ireland had begun to attract investment, initially from American pharmaceutical and information technology companies, but also, at the fledgling International Financial Services Centre in Dublin's docklands, from a range of banks and financial investment companies.

Our new policy initiative for the next decade should be the creation of sustainable communities in our cities and towns to allow Ireland to continue to compete at the highest levels in the global knowledge economy. As a society, if we are to achieve success in this, a series of policies is required at national

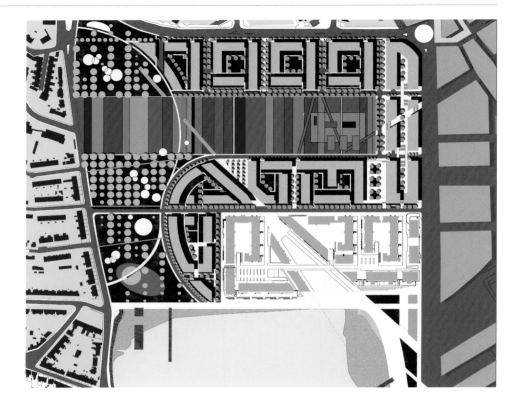

↗ Poolbeg Peninsula, Ringsend, Dublin – master plan
→ Poolbeg Peninsula – aerial view

regional and local levels.

- Recognising the importance of cities and towns to our future economic success, the Government should create a new department of urban affairs.

- Government policy, physical planning and economic strategies should ensure that the region becomes the fundamental economic and planning unit.

- Government policy should make the implementation of Regional Strategic Planning Guidelines mandatory.

- Government should publish an urban sustainability white paper, which addresses economic, social and environmental policy requirements for the planned growth of our towns and cities, co-ordinating the activities of all relevant departments and institutions.

- Government should establish an Urban Policy Board which will combine national, regional and local leadership to drive urban policy at all levels of Government.

- The Department of Education & Science should arrange for the introduction of undergraduate training in urban design and urbanism at all third level courses in architecture, engineering, town planning and the built environment.

- The DoEHLG and Department of Education & Science should establish a programme of international secondment with the aim of ensuring that a core of Irish professionals benefits from exposure to best European urban-design practice.

- The physical organisation of each region should be supported by a framework of transportation alternatives. Public transport, pedestrian and bicycle systems should maximise access and mobility throughout the region while reducing dependence on cars.

- The DoEHLG should ensure greater co-operation between local authorities in each region to avoid destructive competition for rates income and to promote national co-ordination of transportation, recreation, public services, housing and community institutions.

The changes in the Irish economy have created unparalleled opportunities and challenges for Ireland's policy-makers, architects and planners. The future development of our towns and cities must conform to environmental, socially uniting principles, striking a sustainable balance between economic, social, environmental and cultural issues. This is one of the major challenges of the coming century. These new challenges hold the key to our country's future. Environmental development opens up new perspectives, with significant potential for innovation, and brings new perspective to individual and collective endeavours. An environmentally friendly city with well-designed buildings and open public spaces will be a competitive city which can both maintain and attract business and citizens in the global knowledge economy.

This challenge bears comparison with each of the major policy changes that Ireland has faced in the last half-century. Responding successfully is essential to the social and economic future of our society. Let us hope that the next two decades can produce a similar success in the implementation of public policy for sustainable communities and integrated development in our cities and towns. To achieve this will require a more widely shared understanding and consistent implementation of the public-policy principles by Government, local authorities, planners, urban designers, architects, and all those involved in the development of our urban centre.

———

ANTHONY REDDY is a director of the Reddy Architecture & Urbanism Group. He is a director of the Academy of Urbanism, founder-member of the Urban Forum, and past-president of the RIAI. He has been involved in a range of new and regeneration works in projects in Ireland and central Europe.

Working with the legislation

TOAL Ó MUIRÉ

Author's note (March 2009) – This essay was written in 2007 when the coffers of local authorities, developers and households were full, and when the demand to expedite large-scale housing development was, accordingly, far greater than now, in 2009.

The National Economic & Social Council (NESC) report *Housing in Ireland: Performance and Policy* (2004) concludes that Ireland needs *a clear vision of the kind of high-quality, integrated, sustainable neighbourhoods that are worth building.* [All quotes from the NESC report or from legislation, etc, appear in italics.] That vision, according to the NESC, is

– *first, essential to the social and economic future of Irish society;*
– *second, requires a widely shared understanding and consistent action by numerous organisations, both public and private;*
– *third, challenges not only established behaviour but also the self-perception that underpins that behaviour.*

Planners, architects and developers are gratified that the Social Partners in the NESC have recognised that housing can do essential things for society. The 'vision thing', on the other hand, creates threats as well as opportunities, and so it raises questions as to how (and even whether) *shared understanding, consistent action* and *challenges [to] established behaviour can be achieved.* This essay reviews current legislation in the context of these questions.

– First, it examines law as a tool-kit, a resource available to help (or sometimes hinder) shared understanding and consistent action to provide high-quality housing and neighbourhoods. It mainly focuses on planning legislation, but also mentions Finance Acts, Roads Acts, etc, as these bear on the planning and delivery of housing and neighbourhoods.
– Next, it examines legislative approaches which affect or reflect our self-perceptions and established behaviour.
– Finally, it looks at legislative underpinnings for two key concepts – plan-led development and development control – and links the issues of tax incentives, planning risk and the trade-offs between these and housing quality.

THREE CONCLUSIONS ABOUT THE 'PICK-AND-MIX' OF MANDATORY AND ENABLING LEGISLATION

One conclusion is that DIFFERENT LAWS OPERATE ON DIFFERENT, AND SOMETIMES CONTRADICTORY, PRINCIPLES. Good housing is currently being planned and built, sometimes by following *mandatory* legislative provisions, and in other instances by taking advantage of *enabling* provisions. For example, the Adamstown SDZ exploits *enabling* provisions of the 2000 Planning & Development Act (PDA), originally envisaged to expedite planning in industrial zones. By contrast, the Dublin Docklands Development Authority Act is also delivering good housing under a *mandatory* legislative regime of design and planning, but the developers (and their customers) who comply with those demands get rewarded with tax incentives and with exemption from planning permission requirements.

← Adamstown, Co Dublin – master plan by O'Mahony Pike Architects

A second conclusion is that, by reason, sometimes it seems, of historical accident, PARTS OF OUR LEGISLATION REFLECT OR FACILITATE ESTABLISHED SELF-PERCEPTIONS WHICH MAY SERVE US BADLY in some instances, as the NESC implies. Similarly, other legislation (some of which has lapsed) contains principles, criteria and processes which could serve us well if applied more generally, or if they were at least still available as part of the 'pick and mix'.

A third conclusion is that, without new planning legislation yet to tackle the NESC challenges, and with an under-resourced planning system, some developers' architects and local authority planners (in Adamstown and other examples shown in this book) have, in the NESC's words, A NEW *SELF-PERCEPTION* WHICH IS HELPING IN SEVERAL PLACES TO PRODUCE *HIGH-QUALITY, INTEGRATED, SUSTAINABLE NEIGHBOURHOODS* THROUGH *SHARED UNDERSTANDING AND CONSISTENT ACTION BY ORGANISATIONS, BOTH PUBLIC AND PRIVATE*. This collaboration allows the private developer to get on with development, in return for planning, paying for and managing the infrastructure provision. That requires a huge trust between public and private sectors, in the absence of more explicit statutory controls, and the local authority still needs sufficient resources to control and retain ownership of the plan. A vacuum on the public side threatens failures of propriety as well as of neighbourhood planning. This book does not show those many failures, and legislation is surely required to prevent repetition of those failures in the future.

LEGISLATION AS A TOOL-KIT FOR PLANNING HOUSING AND NEIGHBOURHOODS

So, beginning with the legislation as a tool-kit for action, the first two columns in the accompanying tables compare two types of plan under the 2000 Planning & Development Act (PDA) – the Local Area Plan (LAP) and the Strategic Development Zone (SDZ) – with two other types of statutory local plan, both made under different legislation, and both of which involve tax incentives:
– Integrated Area Plans (IAPs) under the Urban Renewal Act 1998; and
– Master plans under the Dublin Docklands Development Authority Act 1997.

The tables compare these plan types under the headings of:
A – CONTROL AND POLICY
   who initiates the plan, and the criteria they follow in doing so
B – MEASURES AND PROCEDURES
   who adopts (and reviews) the plan, and after consulting with whom
C – APPEALS (against the plan itself, or decisions on planning applications
   made under it); the plan's STANDING (e.g. does it supersede the
   Development Plan); and its overall CONTENT

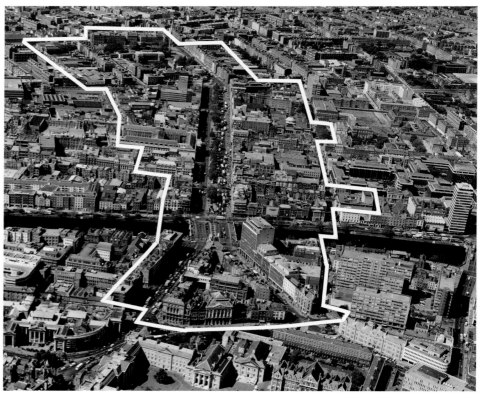

D – SPECIFIC CONTENTS

elements or objectives which must *or* may be covered in the plan.

The tables overleaf show that the last two categories of plans are not adopted by councillors, and are less subject to planning appeals against decisions made under them. DDDA master plans are adopted by the Minister for the Environment, Heritage & Local Government, who is also, by law, the person who sets the rules for IAPs, and is the only person who can initiate an SDZ. However, all three of these last plan types (SDZ, IAP and DDDA) involve extensive public notice and consultation, and statutorily must comply with a greater range of social and environmental objectives and criteria than the legislation requires for an LAP.

I asked some colleagues to check tables A to D after I showed them at an Urban Forum workshop in 2006. They found them reasonably balanced, yet the tables are neither exhaustive nor beyond criticism. For example, the *Specific Contents* shown in Table D for SDZs, IAPs and DDDA plans could be included in an LAP, though few LAPs do so. While Section 19 of the PDA requires no specific contents in an LAP, any of the many *purposes for which objectives may be indicated in a development plan*, in the First Schedule of the PDA, are presumably permissible in an LAP.

Unfortunately, much tax-incentivised housing now appears, at least along the River Shannon, to be mainly built in the absence of anything that involves real *planning*, less still *urbanism*. And tax reform has rightly reduced and focused the range of tax incentives generally.

THE LOCAL AREA PLAN (LAP)

The LAP is, therefore, the obvious legislative baseline in relation to neighbourhood plans for housing. The requirements and powers which underlie the LAP in many ways parallel the Development Plan much as it has existed since the 1963 Planning Act. The LAP, as the Development Plan writ small for 'suitable' areas, involves similar processes of preparation, consultation and adoption by elected representatives. It is subsidiary to the Development Plan, and planning application decisions made under it by the planning authority are equally open to appeals to An Bord Pleanála.

The centrality of such plans to the NESC agenda can be gauged from the Fingal County Manager's statistic that Fingal County Council has 128 actions (variations, LAPs, studies, ACAs, town plans, etc) to be completed within its 2005 Development Plan. One colleague describes each LAP as 'a tiring three-consultation, two-year process'.

↑ O'Connell Street Integrated Area Plan
– proposal for O'Connell Street
(Dublin City Council, 1998)

→ The Spire by Ian Ritchie Architects
– symbol of a rejuvenated O'Connell Street area, seen from Henry Street

opposite

↖ Michael Angelo Hayes
Sackville Street, Dublin [O'Connell Street],
c.1853
(National Gallery of Ireland)

← O'Connell Street Integrated Area Plan
– aerial view showing extent of area covered, from Parnell Squre to Westmoreland Street
(Dublin City Council, 1998)

(illus: Gandon Archive, Kinsale, unless otherwise stated)

■ Table A – Area Plan Types – CONTROL AND POLICY

Plan type and legislation:	1. LAP Planning & Dev Act 2000	2. SDZ Planning & Dev Act 2000	3. IAP Urban Renewal Act 1998	4. DDDA Act 1997
Legal requirement or authority for the plan	19(1)(b) CSO towns 2000+; excl. suburb or environs 'Suitable areas'	S.166(1) Government, through Minister for Environment (MEHLG)	S.7 Integrated Area Plans (IAPs)	S.18
Criteria or objectives for the plan	suitable; and in particular, area in need of economic, physical and social renewal	development of economic/ social importance to the State	social/economic renewal on a sustainable basis; improved physical environment	as for IAP + support for financial sector of economy
Who starts the plan ?	Planning Authority	MEHLG can choose agency	Planning Authority or authorised company at request of Planning Authority	DDDA, both master plan & planning schemes
Deadline for draft plan	2 years after Dev Plan	2 years after Min order		
Plan to be consistent with	Development Plan	MEHLG order	MEHLG rules: market conditions and impediments	

■ Table B – Area Plan Types – MEASURES AND PROCEDURES

Plan type and legislation:	1. LAP Planning & Dev Act 2000	2. SDZ Planning & Dev Act 2000	3. IAP Urban Renewal Act 1998	4. DDDA Act 1997
Land acquisition & disposal		by planning authority		S.18(1)(b): this is a key element
Agreements with landowners	S.49 levies?	agency can enter agreement		
MEHLG Regulations	e.g. classes of areas, certain circumstances			
Consultation public: public agencies: residents, etc: commercial/business:	yes yes yes yes	as S.169(1) yes, + prescribed authorities	S.7(7) 'with such persons as appear to be concerned with the matter'	promote co-ordination of programmes of State bodies and others
Notice to An Bord Pleanála public notice: report on submissions:	yes yes yes	yes yes yes	no	no
Council adopts	yes	yes	no	no
Implementation		yes, as S.177		
Review	6 years maximum	rescind at will	Department of Finance	5 years

■ Table C – Area Plan Types – APPEALS, STANDING AND CONTENTS

Plan type and legislation:	1. LAP Planning & Dev Act 2000	2. SDZ Planning & Dev Act 2000	3. IAP Urban Renewal Act 1998	4. DDDA Act 1997
Appeal allowed to An Bord Pleanála (ABP)	not on the plan, but yes on planning applications	yes on the plan, but not on planning applications		no
Supersedes Dev Plan	no	yes		
Detail of the objectives	*as planning authority may determine*	see below	see below, + renewal, etc	as for IAPs
Community facilities	*yes, and amenities*	yes, incl. schools & childcare	*yes, + social integration*	help people to work, shop or reside there
Design standards	*yes, of developments & structures*	yes, incl. items below	*yes, including co-ordination*	
Significant effects	'likely' effects	yes, incl. mitigation		

■ Table D – Area Plan Types – SPECIFIC CONTENTS

Plan type and legislation:	1. LAP Planning & Dev Act 2000	2. SDZ Planning & Dev Act 2000	3. IAP Urban Renewal Act 1998	4. DDDA Act 1997
Specific items to be in plan		type(s) of development	*objectives for conservation*	
		extent of development	*development of derelict and vacant sites*	
		overall design	*layout, building pattern, density*	
		building heights		
		exterior finishes	*shop frontages*	
		general design	*streetscapes*	
		public transport	*transport*	
		roads	*treatment of spaces between buildings*	amenity development, environmental improvement
		parking provision	*environment*	infrastructure
		traffic managment	*transport*	
		services/utilities	*infrastructure*	infrastructure
		waste management	*environment*	
			employment, training education especially for residents	
			extent of investment	co-ordinate investment

THE STRATEGIC DEVELOPMENT ZONE (SDZ)
AND TAX-INCENTIVISED LOCAL PLANS

A STRATEGIC DEVELOPMENT ZONE (SDZ) begins with the Minister for the Environment, Heritage & Local Government intervening to initiate it as a development of *economic or social importance to the State*. Provisions for public display and consultation are less fixed than for LAPs, and involve greater intervention by Government ministers. However, it should be noted that an LAP (or draft LAP) can be turned into an SDZ by ministerial intervention, as happened in Adamstown.

LEGISLATIVE APPROACHES

The examples of legislation above show that varied approaches to planning law need not be mutually exclusive, and that contradictory approaches survive in current legislation. I try below to list and illustrate these approaches roughly in historical sequence:

THE *PUBLIC WORKS* APPROACH is as old as cities and towns, and their streets, drains and parks. Naxos in Sicily was levelled around 300 BCE, leaving its grid of streets and drainage, clearly not a product of *one-off* housing. Lord Drogheda began the development of Sackville Street, a place that people could walk across between horse-drawn vehicles, long before Dublin Corporation covered it with bitumen and white lines. The recent retrieval of O'Connell Street as an icon of Irish urbanism for *the people* – including those not in cars – shows the potential to apply legislation (including Roads and Traffic Acts) to public works in a considered and strategic way, rather than in the formulaic and fragmented way seen in so many of our suburban streets and roads.

THE *PUBLIC HEALTH AND WELFARE* APPROACH has origins in Victorian-age industry, philanthropy and municipal engineering. One legacy of this sanitising *self-perception* was the segregation of uses through development-plan zoning under the 1963 Planning Act, despite Ireland having few heavy or dirty industries, least of all in urban and suburban areas. Use-zoning contradictorily separated housing from 'light industry', defined as industry compatible with housing. The environmental and social damage increasingly caused by commuting between work and living has required us to rediscover that work and living (and schools and shops and recreation, etc.) should be near each other, as several projects in this book illustrate. Unfortunately, non-access distributor roads built since the 1980s in many cities and towns will remain for decades to come as a legacy of the impoverished *public health and welfare* approach which is still too prevalent in planning (especially of roads) outside our older urban cores, discriminating in the name of road safety against the many

↑ Peter Coyne, former CEO of DDDA, with a scale model of the Dublin Docklands area
(The Irish Times)

↓ Spencer Dock – master plan by Kevin Roche (with the National Conference Centre in the foreground)
(SDCC / Gandon Archive)

(especially the young and old) who do not own a car or have access to public transport.

THE *VETO* APPROACH of the 1963 Planning Act, requires planning permission for most types of building development. Initially the system granted most owners permission, except where a proposed development conflicted with a Development Plan *specific objective* (as public works projects came to be called), or with a Development Plan constraint. This is what I characterise below as *lean development control*.

THE *EIS* APPROACH shifted some of the burden of proof – which had been on the planning authority if it vetoed development by refusing permission – on to the applicant instead to show that a planning application deserves a grant of permission. An environmental impact statement (EIS) is *a statement ... of the effects, if any, which proposed development, if carried out, would have on the environment*. There is, nonetheless, an element of advocacy on behalf of the applicant in most EISs, and architects for applicants can often choose the issues to highlight in an EIS so that the planning authority finds that it makes its Environmental Impact Assessment (EIA) on grounds chosen by the applicant. However, EIA has shifted our design and construction culture back somewhat to the *public works* approach, in that (like 18th-century private developers, whether of Sackville Street or of canals) large-scale 21st-century private developers are forced to justify their projects by reference to public policy and the public good – i.e. to the notion of housing, especially large-scale housing, as public works.

THE *IAP* APPROACH: As already noted, tax-incentivised housing in most designated areas required only the same planning permission as any other development. However, Integrated Area Plans (IAPs) and Dublin Docklands master plans incorporated detailed master-plan objectives and criteria, or (as with the former Temple Bar Renewal Ltd) compliance with statutory criteria and project-by-project scrutiny by a Government-appointed board.

LEGISLATION AS A FRAMEWORK FOR ACTION... AND INACTION

I proposed at the outset to examine legislative tools which may also sometimes hinder *shared understanding and consistent action* on providing high-quality housing and neighbourhoods. It may seem superfluous to mention that the legislation can provide a framework for inaction. Yet belief in *laissez-faire* has led some commentators to the self-perception that it is downright unpatriotic to 'herd people into towns', which is how they characterise action to consolidate urban areas and villages. The *laissez-faire* opponents of

the NESC agenda see no harm in a disintegrated housing environment, and see a demand for shared understanding and consistent action as a threat to their liberty. A leading politician has remarked that sustainability does not resonate with Irish people.

The 1963 Planning Act certainly allowed plenty of *laissez-faire*. Most development plans under it demanded little or no *shared understanding and consistent action* on housing. At the other extreme, we had in Temple Bar Renewal Ltd a Taoiseach-appointed board, representative of many interests, to micro-manage the allocation of uses to buildings in Temple Bar.

So the final third of this essay looks at legislative underpinnings for two key concepts – *plan-led development* and *development control* – and links the issues of tax incentives, planning risk and the trade-offs between these and housing quality.

BEHAVIOUR AND PERCEPTION: TYPES OF PLAN-LED DEVELOPMENT

Adamstown and the Dublin docklands show, in contrasting ways, that Irish developers have begun to share the appetite which planners, architects and community and neighbourhood groups have always had for a *clear vision* and for *consistent action by numerous organisations, both public and private*. Unfortunately, an older set of *established behaviour* and *self-perceptions* also survives in Irish planning, for example in the barely concealed free-for-all of Government rural housing policy, and in 'decentralisation' (in reality, the fragmentation without devolution) of Government departments. This book shows many examples of good housing, apartments and mixed-use neighbourhoods, but the sad reality is that most new Irish housing is poor or mediocre when measured by criteria either of sustainable neighbourhood planning or of the art and craft of construction.

A key difference between older and newer behaviours and perceptions is in how we use the word *plan*, especially in the phrase *plan-led development*. A *Development Plan*, as in the 1963 Planning Act, can facilitate a free-for-all – for example, by not listing any protected structures or by vastly over-zoning existing agricultural land for residential development. A test for *plan-led development*, as noted by one commentator, is whether the *plan* describes (or even is) a *project* in the way that the Adamstown Local Area Plan (LAP), and the Dublin Docklands Master Plan, each clearly describes a *project*. Where the words *plan* and *project* are not so interchangeable, development is usually not *plan-led* in any real sense.

BEHAVIOUR AND PERCEPTION:
THE LAW AND DEVELOPMENT CONTROL

The Adamstown SDZ – and particularly the public oral hearing on it – illustrates a similar duality in what the words *development control* may mean. At its leanest, *development control* under a development plan means compliance with set formulae (e.g. plot ratio, set-backs, garden lengths) or with known preferences of the planning authority, whether in the Development Plan or not. For example, a Kerry architect told me some years ago that planning permission for a large building in or near Tralee is easier to obtain if the façade, at least at ground-floor level, is clad in stone (even uncoursed limestone rubble) and the roof is double-pitched. While *development control* is equally prescriptive in the Dublin docklands, DDDA prescriptions by contrast are drawn from a carefully wrought master plan whose parameters are clearly documented, and are adopted after scrutiny by a variety of stakeholders.

At its best, *development control* reflects what statisticians and management gurus mean by *control* – i.e. to mean *the process of comparing actual outcomes with a norm or objective*, as is the case in the DDDA. In Adamstown, under less prescriptive legislation, phasing and sequencing of physical and social infrastructure were made part of the LAP, and a planning application in Adamstown therefore gets measured against a range of criteria and planned outcomes which have been agreed in advance – as in the DDDA, but in Adamstown not because the legislation so strictly required it – between the planning authority, the developer and many other stakeholders.

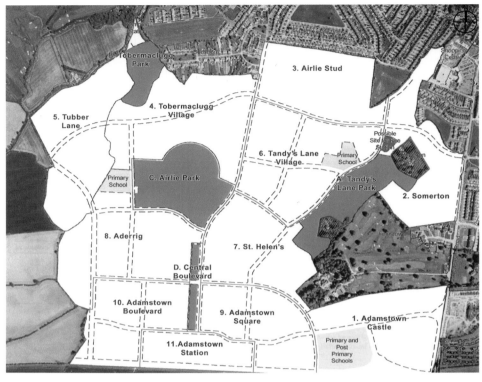

↑ Adamstown, Co Dublin
– Strategic Development Zone Planning Scheme by O'Mahony Pike Architects

↗ Clongriffin, Dublin 13
– master plan by Conroy Crowe Kelly Architects

↘ Royal Canal Park, Pelletstown, Dublin 11
– proposed marina by McCrossan O'Rourke Manning Architects

BEHAVIOUR AND PERCEPTION:
TAX INCENTIVES, UNCERTAINTY & TRADE-OFFS WITH QUALITY

The NESC's preamble to its call for *vision*, referred to at the start of this essay, says that a general finding which informs its recommendations is that *the instruments that can address the core challenges [for housing] are to be found more in the areas of planning, urban design, infrastructural investment, land management and public service delivery, rather than in manipulating tax instruments to alter the supply or demand for land or housing.*

Tax incentives for housing and urban renewal were first introduced in the mid-1980s, at a time of national and government stringency, which suddenly curtailed local authority house-building. Tax incentives represented the furthest shift away from the interventionist and CPO-driven urban renewal policy advocated in US town planner Charles Abrams' advice to the Government 25 years earlier, before it drafted the 1963 Planning Act. There is now, in the new millennium, a broad political consensus to reduce (and end) most of the 1980s tax incentives.

But the 1980s urban-renewal tax incentives had unrecognised benefits in removing old uncertainties and the planning blight those uncertainties had caused. The tax-designated areas put a final nail in the coffin of plans to widen Dublin's Liffey quays which, like other inner-city roads projects, had been 'half-abandoned' by Dublin Corporation's Roads and Planning departments. The tax incentives for particular districts were a signal – or forced planning authorities finally to give a signal – as to which plans were current and which were defunct.

Arguably, some redevelopment which was tax-driven might have been made to happen with a less tax-based but equally clear legislative signal – for example, an SDZ (like Adamstown) or a master plan for Dublin's medieval core. The enthusiasm of developers for Adamstown and for the Dublin docklands – where public participation takes place before the master plan is adopted – is understandable, given that elsewhere An Bord Pleanála overturns 30% or more of the local authority planning decisions appealed to it. The resulting uncertainties hamper (in the words of the NESC) *urban design, infrastructural investment, land management and public service delivery*, or at least they delay them.

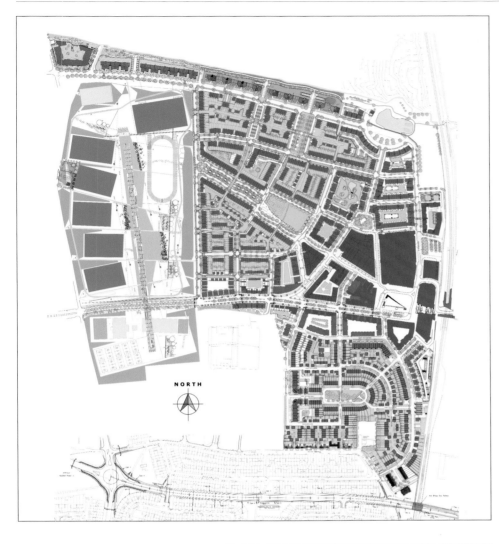

NORTH

The greater certainties of the DDDA and of the SDZ have allowed imposition by central and local authorities of higher requirements for housing floor areas, etc, compared with, for example, general guidelines for tax-designated areas. This shows that a publicly driven plan ultimately can secure more developer and investor *buy-in* than can the *laissez-faire* approach, and so can secure better housing and neighbourhood quality.

SO... WHERE NEXT ?

The essay title 'Working with the legislation' is ambiguous: it can mean either doing what can be done WITHIN THE LEGISLATION, or doing what can be done to AMEND THE LEGISLATION. This essay, like the rest of this book, emphasises what can be done WITHIN THE LEGISLATION. I hope it shows how the legislation, and the existing structures which implement it, afford opportunities to build housing and neighbourhoods *that are worth building*, as the NESC says.

But our planning legislation clearly has too light a touch in many respects. The lack of 'teeth' in many key elements of Departmental guidance to planning authorities on planning and housing development is frequently raised by the RIAI in submissions to the Department of the Environment, Heritage & Local Government (DoEHLG). Architects, both inside and outside the public service, fear DoEHLG deference, in the name of local autonomy, to planning inaction which delays LAPs, or to unsustainable inconsistency between neighbouring planning authorities' planning and housing policies. The fear is that this could frustrate what the NESC report demands: and to permit instead *low-quality, disintegrated, unsustainable neighbourhoods; inconsistent action by numerous organisations, both public and private; and failure to challenge established behaviour and the self-perception that underpins it.*

It is good to celebrate the achievements in Irish housing illustrated in this book. But among the lessons to be learned is that our achievements are still patchy, and that legislation may be needed so that standards and procedures being implemented through the enlightenment of our best planners, developers and architects are given greater mandatory effect. Now that we have improved policy at national level for sustainable housing and neighbourhoods, and through the examples of good work in this book, the challenges are all the clearer for resources – including legislation – which can help to overcome obstacles at local government and project level.

TOAL Ó MUIRÉ is a former partner in OMS Architects and past-president of the RIAI. He co-chairs the RIAI / DoEHLG Sustainable Communities & Housing Committee. He holds degrees in architecture, housing research and business administration, and diplomas in arbitration and in construction law.

Urbanism: high-density development

JOHN McLAUGHLIN

I n 1956, a Newark entrepreneur welded a steel frame onto the deck of a war-surplus tanker called the *Ideal-X* and created the roll-on/roll-off container ship. It was to have massive implications for logistics and industry over the succeeding decades as containerisation led to a huge increase in global trade. It dramatically hastened the decline of traditional dock areas of port cities as dockers jobs evaporated and the ports themselves moved towards deeper water to meet the berthage requirements of the huge container ships. Rail-borne freight also declined rapidly as more and more goods went by road, and the reduced transport costs meant that domestic industries suffered stiff competition from imports.

By the 1980s, the dockland areas of most ports had been decimated, and many cities began to think of strategies for regeneration. In Ireland the Urban Renewal Acts of 1986 and 1987 led to the foundation of the Custom House Docks Development Authority, which, over the following decade, through a combination of tax incentives and fast-track planning powers, redeveloped the area around George's Dock – from the Custom House to Commons Street – as the new International Financial Services Centre. This first phase of the IFSC urban renewal involved building offices for financial services companies on sites around Mayor Street and North Wall, with new apartments around the inner dock bounded by Harbour Master Place and Commons Street. It was phenomenally successful. The effect of deregulation of stock exchanges on international financial markets was similar to that of containerisation on logistics, and the new IFSC was well positioned to benefit from the tide of globalisation. By the mid-1990s the area had been fully developed, and more space was required to facilitate further expansion.

→ Dublin Docklands – aerial view, 2005

← Grand Canal Square, Dublin
 – computer perspective of completed scheme at dusk, with hotel by Manuel Aires Mateus; theatre by Daniel Libeskind; office building by DMOD; and landscaping by Martha Schwartz (DDDA)

THE DUBLIN DOCKLANDS DEVELOPMENT AUTHORITY

In 1997 the Government passed an act to create the Dublin Docklands Development Authority (DDDA). This act was broader in its goals than the earlier urban-renewal acts and explicitly required the new Authority to secure three things:
– the social and economic regeneration of the Dublin Docklands Area on a sustainable basis
– improvements in the physical environment of the Dublin Docklands Area
– the continued development in the Custom House Docks Area of services of, for, or ancillary to the financial services sector of the economy.

The geographic area of the docklands is defined by the rivers Liffey, Dodder and Tolka, the Royal and Grand canals, and the Loopline railway bridge which severs the area from the rest of the city. It is very close to O'Connell Bridge, and is spatially layered parallel to the Liffey. The areas of North and South Lotts, which were reclaimed for warehousing in the late eighteenth century, were substantially derelict, whereas the residential villages of North Wall, East Wall, City Quay and Ringsend have strong residential communities with historic links to the area and the traditional economic activities along the river. When seen from above, it appears as a quadrant of the rounded inner city, bound by the canals.

The Docklands Authority works to a master plan which sets overall policy and social objectives that are developed with the DDDA council, made up of representatives of the local community, Dublin City Council, and other stakeholders. The objectives set in the master plan form the basis of the planning schemes which are the statutory urban-design framework plans for the various physical areas. Planning schemes are plans for comprehensive redevelopment of an area, and there are currently three of these – the IFSC, Grand Canal Docks and North Lotts. A fourth planning scheme, for the Poolbeg peninsula, is currently under preparation. In addition to the planning schemes, there are a number of Area Action Plans for the more intact areas of docklands, such as East Wall.

The population of the area in 1997 was just over 15,000 people, concentrated in the existing urban villages. By the time the docklands project is complete in 2015, the population of the area should have grown to around 45,000 people. One of the most radical social policies adopted by the DDDA council in 1997 was to require that 20% of all new residential development be provided by the private developer as social and affordable housing. (This initiative that was taken up in the 2000 Planning & Development Act.) In Docklands these units must be provided on-site and must be designed and built to an equal standard to the market units.

↑ The Liffey quays – looking east towards Dublin's docklands
(Dublin City Council)

↓ Dublin Docklands – map showing the 1,300 acres under the control of the DDDA
(The Irish Times)

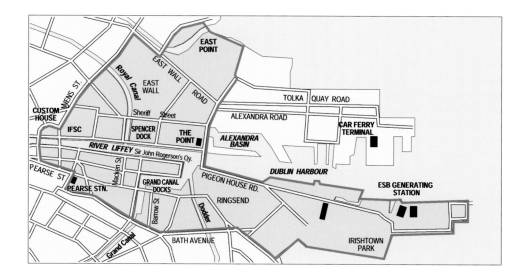

↑ Custom House Docks – original 1987
competition-winning proposal by
Benjamin Thompson & Associates
(Gandon Archive)

→ Relationship betweeen urban density
and fuel consumprtion
(*Towards an Urban Renaissance* (DETR, 1999))

↓ Clarion Quay apartments –
competition-winning proposal by
Urban Projects
(Gandon Archive)

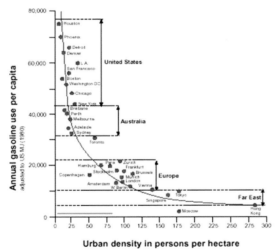

Urban density in persons per hectare

The Government bestowed fast-track planning powers on the Authority to facilitate comprehensive redevelopment, and these powers are governed by Section 25 of the DDDA Act. In summary, the process is as follows: the Oireachtas designates an area of docklands as a Planning Scheme area, and the Authority prepares a draft Planning Scheme for that area. The Authority then consults the public and interested parties, who may make submissions or observations on the draft scheme. Having regard to submissions made, the Authority amends the draft and submits it to Minister for the Environment, who approves or amends the Planning Scheme as he deems appropriate. Development in accordance with the approved Planning Scheme then becomes exempted development, and developers can apply to the Authority for certificates of compliance with the Planning Scheme.

The Planning Schemes define the nature and extent of the proposed development, the proposed distribution and location of uses, proposals in relation to the overall design of the development, including maximum building heights, proposals relating to the development of amenities and conservation of heritage, and proposals relating to transport and traffic management.

In parallel with the physical regeneration, the DDDA social-regeneration team work on a huge array of educational and community projects to help the indigenous population benefit from the economic regeneration, with the goal of attaining social and economic sustainability. The effect of this work on the docklands area is shown in social statistics:

	1997	2005
education – school drop out rate (before 15 years) *	65%	30%
– sitting for Leaving Cert *	10%	60%
unemployment **	26%	9.8%

* source: ESRI   ** source: Census

The second phase of the IFSC was developed between 1997 and 2002, and a more mixed-use approach to urban form was adopted than in the initial phase of the IFSC, with residential development over ground-floor commercial uses mixed in with the financial services offices. The general urban model of perimeter blocks with enclosed courtyards was maintained as a basis of urban form, and building heights were carefully controlled.

More architectural variety was achieved than in the first phase of the IFSC by having numerous architectural practices design different sites, and the design for Clarion Quay – a site that the Authority owned – was procured through an architectural competition. Clarion Quay was the first scheme to apply the principles of mixed tenure with 20% of units being social and affordable

housing. The Authority undertook the development to demonstrate to the market that private purchasers would buy into a mixed-tenure scheme. The architectural competition was won by Urban Projects, a consortium of three smaller practices (DTA / Derek Tynan Architects, GCA / Gerry Cahill Architects and McGarry Ní Éanaigh Architects). It was completed in 2003, and has been very successful both in architectural terms and in convincing developers that the 20% social and affordable requirement is quite viable economically.

One shortcoming of the mixed-tenure model, which emerged after occupation, is the potential dominance of management companies by the private apartment owners. In Clarion Quay this prevented proper play space for children being provided in the development. The Authority has since addressed this problem by drawing up mandatory play-space guidelines for all new residential developments, and making these a condition of planning.

The residential densities permitted in the planning scheme areas are up to 247 units/hectare (100 units/acre), with 325 units/ha permissible in certain locations. A broad residential mix is also required, in line with the new Dublin City Council guidelines. The overall development density objectives are extremely ambitious by any European standard – up to 25,000 people per km^2 – a range that is higher than the density of Tokyo.

GRAND CANAL DOCK

As the entire Docklands area had been home to chemical, industrial and recycling industries over the years, the ground has generally been contaminated and remediation is usually necessary. For example, the Bord Gáis site in Grand Canal Dock had been used for making town gas (gas from coal), which leaves significant levels of contamination in the ground. The Authority bought the gasworks site, remediated the ground, reduced the levels, prepared a planning scheme, installed the infrastructure, and sold the prepared sites on the market. With the risk of contamination removed, and the benefits of a fantastic waterfront location close to the city centre, enjoying excellent transport links, the area is developing very rapidly. The Bord Gáis site was only part of the wider planning scheme for the Grand Canal Dock area, which covers 29.2 hectares (72 acres). The plot ratios permitted are generally in the range of 2.5:1 to 3:1. General land-use mix is generally 60% residential and 40% commercial. On this basis, a projected yield of 3,300 apartments and 430,000m² of non-residential space is expected in this Planning Scheme area.

The general urban building model in this planning scheme is a four-to-eight-storey perimeter block, though there are a number of tall buildings proposed for key sites. These include the site next to Grand Canal DART station, the

↑ Grand Canal Dock – aerial view from the south, 2006
(Peter Barrow Photography / DDDA)

↓ Grand Canal Dock – aerial view from the north, 2008
(Peter Barrow Photography / DDDA)

Millennium Tower on the corner of the dock, and the U2 tower at the confluence of the Liffey and Dodder rivers. A new square was built at the western end of the dock, and a theatre designed by Daniel Libeskind is planned, along with a hotel designed by Manuel Aires Mateus. An office building by DMOD (Duffy Mitchell O'Donoghue) has recently been completed. The opportunity to re-route traffic off Grand Canal Quay allowed the square to be increased from 4,000m^2 to almost a hectare, and the reconfigured design by Martha Schwartz optimises the public space and the relationship with the water.

One of the first sites to be taken was the corner of Sir John Rogerson's Quay and Macken Street, which was purchased by McCann Fitzgerald Solicitors. They commissioned Scott Tallon Walker Architects to design a headquarters, which was completed and occupied in 2007. It is one of STW's finest buildings, and works very well in the wider urban context to mark the corner. The glazed oculus over the central atrium, seen from the Custom House, reads at the same scale as one of the city's 18th-century copper domes.

The Docklands Authority ran an architectural competition in 2001 for a major residential development, which was jointly won by Benson & Forsyth and O'Mahony Pike Architects. Both practices were commissioned to design new mixed-use developments, which were worked up to scheme design and tendered for developers to deliver. Both of these schemes have been completed, and they have set new standards for high-density urban living. There was a very strong take-up by owner-occupiers buying into the area, and record apartment prices were achieved. As with everywhere in the docklands, 20% of residential development is required for social and affordable housing, and many of these were provided as duplex units with their own front doors and private patios to the rear, linked to the communal courtyards at the centre of the blocks. The duplex units, which are five metres wide, establish a grain of frontage at street level which is similar to the grain of residential areas in the historic city. In O'Mahony Pike's Hanover Quay scheme, the architects have, by means of a clever sliding/folding system of glass panels, created winter gardens on the waterfront balconies, which allow them to be used all year long and afford protection on windy days.

The area also has a number of tall landmark buildings. The first one of these is Millennium Tower on Charlotte Quay, also by O'Mahony Pike, a seventeen-storey residential tower which marks the south-east corner of Grand Canal Dock. The second is Alto Vetro, a sixteen-storey residential tower by Shay Cleary Architects, located beside the General McMahon Bridge at the intersection of Grand Canal Quay and Pearse Street. Alto Vetro has a very small footprint, just 9 x 20 metres, which gives two compact apartments per level, either side of a stair- and lift-core. This makes the tower very slender when viewed from the north, acting as a visual termination of the north-south axis set up by Forbes

Street and continued across Grand Canal Square towards Pearse Street.

URBAN FAMILY LIVING

The social sustainability of the newly regenerated docklands will depend on achieving sustainable communities. A number of recent British city-regeneration projects are suffering from a process of 'churn', where twenty-somethings move into studios or one-bed apartments in regeneration areas until they meet a life-partner, at which stage they move on to a house in the suburbs. This is having a number of negative effects, including an increase in anti-social behaviour in city centres and a lack of social cohesion and social capital. The Residential Guidelines from the DoEHLG give minimum apartment sizes and minimum mixes of units, which goes a long way towards preventing these problems. However, there is also a cultural inertia to be overcome to encourage people with housing choices to remain in the city, especially in the context of unsustainable low-density, car-based urban sprawl.

The Authority is looking closely at the provision of civic infrastructure across the docklands – schools, parks, play spaces, sports facilities and community resources – to ensure that the full needs of all age groups are met in the area. The recent dramatic expansion in the economy and population means that part of the Irish population will have to evolve to urban living if we are to maintain family bonds.

LAYERS AND CONNECTIONS

The docklands project was driven by the recent sustained buoyancy of the property market, and as the physical development of the area became more secure, the Authority began to focus more on other layers of use and connections. One of the principal challenges to the geographic area is the historic severance from the rest of the city due to the Loopline railway bridge, which reduces permeability. The Docklands Authority worked with Dublin City Council to extend the Liffey Boardwalk along Eden Quay from O'Connell Bridge to the Custom House, and is now looking, with Dublin City Council and the Office of Public Works, at ways to improve the setting and environs of the Custom House itself, in the context of reduced traffic on the quays, in order to improve connections. On the north side of the Custom House, selective landscaping would renew its relationship with the surrounding Georgian streets and squares. On the south side of the Liffey, proposals to open Trinity College's frontage with a new square onto Pearse Street would be very positive for the City Quay / Westland Row area, and would provide pedestrian links from the docklands to the Georgian city.

↑ Grand Canal Dock
– with Hanover Quay in the distance

← Hanover Quay from Forbes Street – showing the grain established by own-door duplex units

ENDNOTE

The issue of metrics is very important in comparing residential densities. In the UK, there are no minimum requirements for residential room sizes or storage space, so the market tends to deliver much smaller units than are required in Ireland. A lot of recent British urban developments have high percentages of studios and one-bedroom apartments. These produce much higher numbers of units/ha than larger apartments, though they may not, in fact, yield any more bed spaces/ha than the larger units. This approach generally does not generate social capital, as people tend to move on to larger units and leave the developments. Fortunately in Ireland we have the DoEHLG minimum sizes, so there has not been the same problems as have been experienced in the UK. See the UK Institute for Public Policy Research report by Max Nathan and Chris Urwin, *City People: City Centre Living in the UK* (2006).

———

JOHN McLAUGHLIN is a graduate of UCD School of Architecture. He worked in Paris and London on major civic and cultural projects, before returning to Dublin, where he is Director of Architecture & Urban Design with the Dublin Docklands Development Authority. He is an occasional studio lecturer at UCD

↗ Alto Vetro residential tower by Shay Cleary Architects – seen from Grand Canal Square

→ Royal Canal Linear Park (2008-2010)

Strategic Planning Issues in the Cork Region

RODDY HOGAN

Strategic planning in the Cork city region is founded on a single clause in the first Cork County Development Plan in 1967, which laid down that 'the Council's policy will be to induce new development away from the environs of the City into the villages and towns capable of growth in their own right...' Written by the County Architect without any town-planning input, this initiative became known as the Satellite Towns Strategy, and the intervening rural hinterland became the Cork Green Belt. Whilst a popular concept at the time ('Cork, the Compact City'), and in tune with planning fashion then dominated by the British post-war New Towns policies, the Council's strategy carried with it the major latent defect of spreading growth over a wide area of difficult terrain, a problem exacerbated over the years by a lack of political will to control one-off housing in the spaces between the towns.

These problems have long been evident, but the Satellite Towns Strategy has nevertheless been consistently maintained as the guiding policy for planning in the region. The consequence has been the present widely dispersed car-dependant population, and a rural hinterland rather more grey than green. It is an interesting example of the sometimes unintended influence of planning policy in Ireland, and a type of planning that is, perhaps, unique.

CITY / COUNTY BALANCE

In 1967 the population of the city stood at 122,000, and in the county part of the Greater Cork Area (the city plus the contiguous area of the county, including the nearest towns and villages) there lived an additional 48,000 people. Thus, the city dominated its hinterland with a population ratio of 2.5:1, and it had ample space within its boundaries for future development. Today, with the exception of its docklands, the city is virtually fully built up but with a population reduced to only 119,500 due to the steady decline in the number of persons per household from 4.0 to the current 2.64. In contrast, the population of the county part of the Greater Cork Area, now called Metropolitan Cork, has expanded threefold to 153,000.

Thus, the city, which is the heart of the region, with the University Hospital, the university and the Institute of Technology, the School of Music and the Opera House, theatres, major public and private galleries and high-street shopping, is now very seriously constricted within its 40km² confines. In contrast, the County Council has under its management some 800km² of Metropolitan Cork, and, accordingly, has effective control of all strategic options, including transportation, settlement pattern, port development and major industry.

← Proposed towers by Foster Associates at the approach to Cork Docklands
(Howard Holdings plc / photomontage by Pederson Focus)

It is true that the two bodies have, over the years, jointly commissioned strategic planning studies, as well as housing and retail strategies, but the fact is that the city now depends on the goodwill of the county for the sustainability of its internal planning policies. In these circumstances, it cannot participate in a properly robust manner in the formulation of planning strategies which will have a profound impact on the future of the city proper.

CORK AREA STRATEGIC PLAN (CASP)

The legendary Cork Landuse & Transportation Strategy of 1978 (LUTS) basically overlaid a road network on the given Satellite Towns Strategy settlement pattern. It acquired its exalted reputation when the new roads were built, the expected cars didn't arrive due to the recession of the 1980s, and Cork became free of its hitherto crippling traffic congestion.

Its replacement, the Cork Area Strategic Plan (CASP), was adopted in 2002 with the objective of carrying the city region through to 2020 (fig. 1). CASP's principal concern was the perceived imbalance between the prosperous areas south and west of the city and the disadvantaged northern and eastern sectors – parts of which were. indeed. close to dereliction. It proposed to redress this by redirecting development into a corridor along the existing north-west to south-east rail line from Mallow, through the city, to Cobh, and along the abandoned east-going line to Midleton, which it proposed to reopen. The investment in this upgraded service was to be made viable by four major new neighbourhoods along the corridor at Blarney, Monard-Rathpeacon, Carrigtwohill and Midleton. To ensure that the necessary population-shift occurred, the traditional growth areas south and west of the city were to be consolidated and rounded off.

A second major strategy, designed to reverse the population decline in the city, was the redevelopment of Cork's docklands to accommodate a population of some 12,000 by 2020.

At the time, concerns were expressed that the redirection of population growth to remote and unfashionable areas would result in very low-density development, since higher densities can only be achieved in areas of market demand, and that insufficient development land was being allowed to accommodate the appropriate proportion of the national housing need, as forecast by the Bacon reports. It was argued that it was unrealistic to expect the new neighbourhoods along the Mallow-Midleton railway line to achieve their ambitious targets in the short time span allocated, and overall it seemed that the abrupt disruption of established land-use trends would neither be practicable nor worthwhile for a transportation system projected to carry only 5% of total trips in 2020.

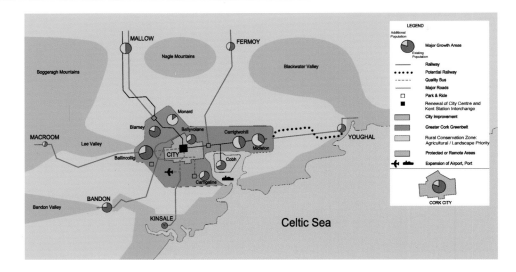

↑ 1 – CASP Strategy for Metropolitan Cork
(*Cork Area Strategic Plan 2002-2020*, courtesy RPS)

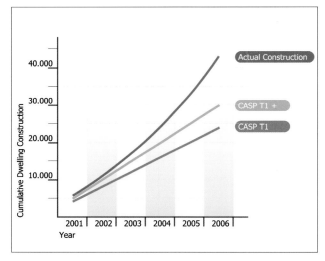

→ 2 – Housing Construction in Cork, 2001-2006
(Cork County Council / DoEHLG Housing Bulletin)

→ 3 – Proposed towers by Foster Associates at the approach to Cork Docklands
(Howard Holdings plc / photomontage by Pederson Focus)

CASP IN PRACTICE

Now, just seven years into the CASP programme, a wholly unexpected landscape has emerged. The booming economy has transformed the previously run-down areas of the city, and speedy Government investment has ensured that the new railway system will be operational by mid-2009. And, whilst the unanticipated house-building surge has overwhelmed not just Tranche 1 of the CASP programme to 2007, but also much of Tranche 2 (intended to stretch to 2013), none of the four new railway neighbourhoods has yet commenced (fig. 2).

The largest of these, at Monard-Rathpeacon, north-west of the city, scheduled to accommodate some 5,000 dwellings by 2020, is indefinitely delayed due to infrastructural deficiencies. The other three, at Blarney, Carrigtwohill and Midleton, have each been the subject of very loose Local Area Plans which require that the landowners come together and jointly prepare and agree a master plan for consideration by the Council. Crucially, it was stipulated that until such a master plan has been agreed and adopted, no individual proposal could be considered for permission.

The only master plan so far agreed is for the 2,500-unit neighbourhood at Blarney, where there are just two landowners, both developers. However, none of these houses is likely to be completed before 2010, as significant planning issues remain to be resolved. Predictably no master plan is even close to emerging for the neighbourhoods at Carrigtwohill or Midleton, which each have some sixteen landowners with inevitably conflicting aspirations.

At the same time, the docklands initiative has been delayed due to infrastructural, financing and public-transportation issues, with the consequence that the population of the city has continued its historic decline. Nevertheless, planning applications are currently being processed for very substantial developments, including three spectacular towers by Norman Foster (fig. 3).

During this period, an unprecedented number of houses were built, but they went largely into unintended places – areas of strong market-demand south and west of the city, which were supposed to be scaled down, into the ring towns outside Metropolitan Cork, and, most worryingly, into the intervening rural areas: 20% of new houses in the Metropolitan Cork Green Belt were built in non-urban locations, whilst in the surrounding rural areas some 64% have been one-offs. In fact, the population shortfall in the city has been almost exactly matched by the excess growth in the rural areas just outside the green belt.

This ready availability of very low-density housing has had a serious impact on the housing market. Apartments, even duplexes, have been generally

unsaleable, except in city locations close to bus routes. Thus, developers of zoned lands in urban locations have been increasingly obliged to provide wide-frontage, semi-detached houses, each with two on-curtilage car spaces. Consequently, the density of new housing has been steadily declining, contrary to sustainability and the urgings of the Government and local authority planners. Overall, the position at the close of the recent housing surge is an escalation of the region's dysfunctional low-density, car-dependant settlement pattern, with a series of voids around the projected new stations in the rail corridor, and in the docklands.

CASP UPDATE

The scale and seriousness of these problems impelled the City and County councils to jointly commission an urgent update of CASP with the objective of informing the already advanced review processes of their respective development plans. The appointed team was headed by international consultants Indecon because of the perceived overriding importance of economic and transportation issues.

This CASP Update, completed in May 2008, recommends an economic development strategy designed to deliver the necessary uplift in economic growth and employment capable of sustaining the projected population, but stresses in very stark terms the implications of the vast low-density conurbation that Cork has become. It calculates that unless there is a significant modal shift from private cars, all roads around the city centre will be at peak-hour capacity by 2010, leaving no scope to handle the additional growth projected to 2020.

For this reason, the update makes vigorous recommendations for the front-loading of major transportation initiatives, including two new rapid-transit corridors. The first of these is proposed to run east-west through the docklands, interfacing with the principal railway interchange at Kent Station, and passing onwards to the university, Institute of Technology and University Hospital in the west of the city. A second, later, route is projected to run north-south, connecting the airport via the centre, with a new development node on the north side of the city (fig. 4).

The update recommends major support for the docklands proposal, and endorses an objective to substantially increase its final population to some 25,000. It stresses the urgency of developing railway-based neighbourhoods, and recognises that the Council will have to take the lead in preparing the master plans.

Paradoxically the delays at these locations may well result in the market being receptive to higher and more sustainable densities as the new rail service will be up and running, congestion on the roads will have increased, and the more peripheral, lower-density developments will have been exhausted.

PORT OF CORK

The CASP Update is a refreshing document, but it remains fundamentally an overlay on the original CASP strategies. This is accepted, not least by its title. There was neither the time nor the resources to undertake a review, and the consequences of this have quickly become apparent. Both CASP and its update accepted uncritically the Port of Cork's Strategic Development Plan of 2002, which proposed the phased relocation of its operations from the docklands to new facilities at Ringaskiddy on the western side of the harbour, south of the city. However, An Bord Pleanála, after a fourteen-day hearing, refused permission for the construction of new container facilities at that location on the fundamental grounds of the quantum of heavy traffic that would be directed through the already stressed road system of the city, and because the proposal ignored the option of locating to the eastern side of the harbour where this problem would not arise and where, moreover, an interface with the national railway system was available.

The validity of this decision is generally accepted, but the strategic implications, whilst as yet unquantified, are clearly significant. Not least, there is concern about the potential impact on the docklands redevelopment programme, which is substantially dependant on the relocation of the existing port facilities.

A NEW VISION

Cork is a proud city, with much to be proud of. It is, by a wide margin, the largest gateway in the State, has an enviable setting on one of the largest harbours of the world, has all the cultural and commercial advantages of a significant university town, has fine sporting traditions and an increasingly cosmopolitan population. It is the centre of some very important industrial complexes, and has at hand the wonderful water-based recreational areas of south and west Cork. On the other hand, it clearly faces an immediate and significant planning crisis, with a dispersed population needing significant upfront investment in public transportation at a time when resources are scarce, and credibility in the Government surely damaged by its default on the population growth promised along the rail corridor.

For many years, the concept of a linear city of employment and residential modules along the floor of the Lee valley has been an obvious option. Bounded

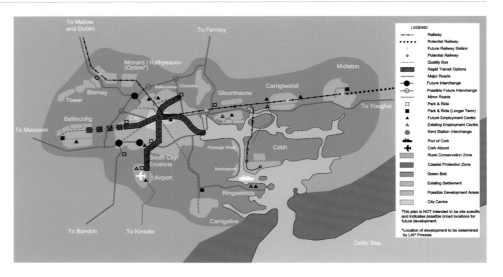

↑ 4 – CASP Update – structural diagram for Metropolitan Cork
(CASP Update 2008)

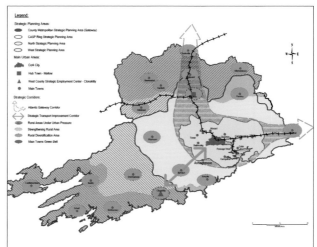

→ 5 – Cork County Draft Development Plan strategy to link into Atlantic Corridor
(Cork County Council)

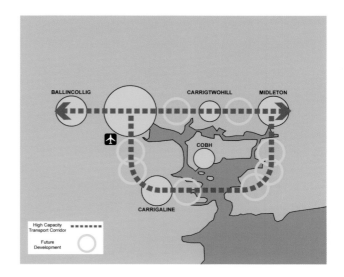

→ 6 – Alternative development strategy proposal to embrace the harbour
(Brady Shipman Martin)

north and south by the high ridges, the modules would be separated by green recreational wedges and traversed by a strong transportation spine, giving easy access to the central facilities of the city. The mix of land-uses along the transportation corridor would promote reverse commuting rather than the present conventional and much less sustainable radial system, and slow modes of transportation (walking and cycling) would be encouraged along the level terrain. Whilst an attractive and practical concept, this option would nevertheless have been rejected as conflicting with the prevailing Satellite Towns Strategy.

But it is now necessary to look much further ahead, preferably without any fixed-time horizon so as to avoid the conventional approach of simply adding incremental blocks to a pre-existing pattern. Instead, such a study should perhaps look towards a certain size for the city region. How, for example, could Metropolitan Cork most advantageously achieve and accommodate a population of over 500,000 people instead of the present 275,000, together with associated centres of employment?

Strategically, the city region must compete for economic investment nationally and internationally, not least with the emerging Dublin-Belfast conurbation. To do so it must aggressively pursue an upward spiral of agglomeration, bringing all its resources into play in an innovative and responsible manner. It has the option of acquiring additional strength by connecting with the smaller gateways of Galway, Limerick and Waterford in the Atlantic Corridor concept – the approach proposed for adoption in the current Draft County Development Plan (fig. 5). But this implies the commitment of resources in a particular direction, perhaps

at the expense of a more desirable and, as yet, unidentified option, and it is to be regretted that the decision appears to have been taken without the extensive public debate it deserves. For example, Brady Shipman Martin's director of strategic planning, Michael Grace, in a recent article, put forward the concept of extending urban development around the harbour, embracing it in the way some other great cities, such as Sydney, have done. A high-level crossing at the mouth of the harbour would be a spectacular and distinctive landmark. This approach may well be a bridge too far, but it is the sort of provocative and visionary thinking that is now needed (figs 6, 7).

The present reviews of the county and city development plans will occupy all planning resources until 2010, but there will then be a two-year interregnum until the processes recommence in 2012. That period could be devoted to the exploration of a new and visionary planning strategy for the city region, for it is clear that there is a pressing need for a root-and-branch review of all options, free of traditional preconceptions. Such a study would help the identification of long-term goals for the city region, and the conventional ten-to-twenty-year planning cycle could then proceed, confident that all options had been evaluated and the most advantageous selected.

RODDY HOGAN is a town planner and architect living and practicing in Cork, and specialising in private-sector development. He has, for many years, been a close observer of strategic planning in the Cork region.

→ 7 – A bridge too far?
(www.sfbayimages.com/golden_gate_bridge)

The New Housing 2

BUILDING BETTER COMMUNITIES

St Joseph's Court Sheltered Housing and Hostel, Gorey, by Paul Keogh Architects

The Irish Town – dying at the crossroads?

PAUL KEOGH

Higher-density residential development in the right locations, well serviced with public transport and community facilities, and built to the best possible standards – that's what lies at the core of Government policy to encourage more sustainable urban development, according to the Department of the Environment's recent guidelines for planning authorities, *Sustainable Residential Development in Urban Areas*.[1] The guidelines are the latest in a decade of policy documents in which Government has sought to encourage more sustainable urban development. The Residential Density Guidelines (1999), the National Spatial Strategy (2002), the NESC housing report (2004), the Sustainable Rural Housing Guidelines (2005) and *Delivering Homes, Sustaining Communities* (2007) all expressed commitments to promote the development, renewal and improvement of towns and villages.

Yet, the vast bulk of housing construction has been in suburban estates and one-off houses in the countryside, with few enough examples of 'new housing development in or at the edges of villages and small towns of a quality of design, character, scale and layout that fits well with the town or village involved and presents a high quality living environment ... supporting public transport and reducing dependency on car-based commuting',[2] or 'attractive and affordable housing options to meet the housing needs of urban communities and persons wishing to live in urban areas'.[3]

On the contrary, weak planning, suburban social values and an uncontrolled market during the boom years conspired to facilitate an overwhelming predominance of low-density greenfield development outside of, and often remote from, existing urban centres. With the exception of tax-driven apartments and social and affordable housing, few family homes have been built in towns and village centres, and essential services, retailing and businesses have relocated to the outskirts. In short, the decline of the inhabited town is in free fall and rural Ireland is becoming overwhelmingly suburban.

If we can learn anything from the current market crisis, it is that the last decade produced not only too many units, but that they were of the wrong type, and they were built in the wrong locations. Yet, notwithstanding the recent collapse of residential construction, commentators continue to forecast that demographic changes in Irish society and medium- to long-term economic growth will create a strong demand for new housing in the decade ahead – up to 45,000 units per annum, according to some projections. Also, the cultural and demographic revolution Ireland is undergoing – more households, smaller families and changing lifestyles – suggests the need for something different to the standard house types offered by the market to date.

Therefore, if we are to manage the projected growth in housing development sustainability, we need to review our uncritical application of the suburban model, and acknowledge that the sprawl it generates has been one of the major contributors to our untenable level of carbon emissions, our unsustainable dependence on private motoring, our inadequate infrastructure provision, our declining levels of social capital, and, not least, the depopulation and decline of our rural towns and villages.

To avoid the mistakes of the past, it is imperative that all stakeholders row in behind the key principles in the DoEHLG's guidelines – i.e. more sustainable urban development, increased densities, and a restriction of excessive suburbanisation. The guidelines provide a timely platform for public debate on the desirability of an alternative 'urban' model, one which focuses on the potential of towns and villages to offer an attractive lifestyle choice, and the type of housing that today's middle class families might aspire to: well-designed homes in attractive surroundings; proximity to high-quality amenities and services; safe, well-maintained streets and landscaped open spaces; facilities for cyclists and pedestrians; availability of public transport; and a sense of place and civic well-being.

The guidelines are timely because the *Suburban Nation* ideal is now in question as never before, not only in Ireland, but also in Europe and even the USA.[4] 'The car and the commute – to work, to school, to shop – are demonstrably bad for community life', according to the influential American sociologist Robert Putnam, sometime mentor to former Taoiseach Bertie Ahern. If what he terms 'social capital' is to be enhanced, planning policies need to ensure that we 'live in more integrated and pedestrian-friendly areas, and that the design of our communities and the availability of pubic space will encourage more casual socialising with friends and neighbours'.[5] Similarly, the Institute of Public Health's 2006 report on the built environment noted the negative impact of urban sprawl on health – increased obesity, pollution, road injuries, stress and isolation. Like Putnam, it also made the case for attractive and accessible urban environments with efficient public transport systems and walkable neighbourhoods.[6]

From an environmental perspective, it would be shortsighted in the extreme to focus on the energy performance of individual homes while ignoring the fact that sprawl, car-dependency and long-distance commuting have been major contributors to the 174% rise in Ireland's transport-related carbon emissions since 1990. In the USA, research by Robert Cervero and Carolyn Radisch has focused on the relationship between settlement and mobility patterns. In different neighbourhoods of the San Francisco bay area, they found that housing design and layout are a crucial influence on car-use: low-density housing estates, built far from shops and services, generate double the car-use of housing in dense, compact layouts. This strongly suggests that people's dependency on their cars varies in direct proportion to whether their neighbourhood is pedestrian-friendly.[7]

There are also compelling economic arguments. Quality local services and amenities – open spaces, shopping, transport, schools, parks and broadband – cannot be provided economically in low-density suburban and rural areas. And, as the American social scientist Richard Florida has pointed out, people in the economically vital 'creative classes' – science, engineering, design, education, finance and law – seek to make homes in places with quality infrastructure, culture and services. Florida's research concludes that social and environmental factors are crucial to attracting inward investment and vibrant economies.[8] This reality has been starkly illustrated by the failure to date of the decentralisation programme to entice middle- to high-ranking public servants to leave Dublin for less well-provided towns in the provinces.

The Government's recent *Framework for Sustainable Economic Renewal* sets out a range of proposed actions to ensure Ireland's prosperity going forward, including, *inter alia*, secure energy supplies, an attractive environment and first-class infrastructure. If the challenges facing the State in these key areas – energy, environment and infrastructure – are to be met, it will require a consensus on the need to reappraise our accepted planning norms. Government, local authorities, developers, planners, architects, engineers and estate agents must use their combined resources and creativity to advance a development template that addresses the fundamental social, environmental and economic shortcomings of the suburban model.

To do this, we need, firstly, to gain popular acceptance of the fact that higher-density urban living can be an attractive alternative to low-density sprawl. This can be achieved, because throughout the developed world there is now an increasing recognition that expanding greenfield development cannot continue indefinitely. Unsustainable volumes of urban-generated housing in rural areas are everywhere

compromising the idyllic country lifestyle that getting out of town promised from the outset; the dream of a house, a garden and an easy drive to work, school and shops is devalued by commuting stresses, traffic congestion, increasing fuel costs, a spoilt rural landscape, the decline of social networks, and the highest car-dependency in Europe.

Secondly, we need to focus on the regeneration of towns and villages as desirable and convenient places to live and work, with homes, businesses and services in close proximity, underpinning the provision of quality amenities, vibrant streets and attractive open spaces. We need housing exemplars which encourage popular taste away from its suburban mentality, and to reconsider the positives of urban, environmentally friendly lifestyles. Otherwise, there is every likelihood that our heritage of vibrant urban environments and attractive rural landscapes will be but a memory for generations to come.

Finally, there is the prejudice that we Irish are not an urban nation. But even those who argue that dispersed rural settlement is integral to Ireland's heritage must acknowledge that towns such as Birr, Kinsale, Kilmallock, Athenry and Westport are an essential part of our cultural inheritance, and that vibrant towns and villages are essential to maintaining dynamic rural communities and strong rural economies. This is highlighted in the National Spatial Strategy, as it is in the British government's white paper *Our Countryside: The Future*. Noting the range of functions which market towns perform – centres for transport, services and amenities – the UK white paper emphasis that if they are to prosper and sustain local shops, pubs, schools, post offices, medical facilities and even farmers' markets, they must also function as sustainable communities, and use urban design 'to make the most of their potential as attractive places to live, work, invest and spend leisure time'.[9]

The DoEHLG guidelines, and the accompanying best practice *Urban Design Manual*,[10] also emphasise urban design and the importance of achieving the highest standards possible. If this is to be achieved, the construction industry needs to be directed away from its default housing typologies. During the boom, developers typically focused on producing the most profitable product with the widest commercial appeal. Compared to the complexities of urban development – site acquisition, protected structures, design restrictions, adjoining stakeholders and access constraints – the two-storey semi-detached house is infinitely easier to build, and less costly. But good planning ought to be about achieving the best, and the most sustainable, long-term goals for society; it is not simply about serving the market on the basis that what has sold before is what's needed today.

This is just as true for retailing. Since the 1960s, the shopping centre has been the market's preferred solution, and the relentless march of the multiples with their agenda to develop more and more out-of-town stores is everywhere draining the vitality from towns and villages, creating retail monopolies and increasing car-generated shopping. Yet, our Competition Authority continues to challenge the

Retail Planning Guidelines for the cause of lower prices. Thankfully, this was addressed by the chairman of An Bord Pleanála's recent warning that 'the long-term price to the community of permitting huge megastores ... outside our towns and cities could be much greater than any short-term gain in terms of grocery prices.'[11] The British experience provides conclusive proof that this is the case: 92% of retail trade is now controlled by the multiples, and 24% of villages are without a shop. Closer to home, the Convenience Stores Newsagents Association recently predicted the closure of 600 newsagents and corner shops this year, with the loss of 7,000 jobs.[12]

The environmental shortsightedness of the Competition Authority's approach is compounded by the fact that the vast majority of supermarket trips – 95% in the UK – are by car, and this generates a further chain of undesirable consequences – major expenditure on non-essential road construction, increased pressure on the existing network, and an accelerating growth in carbon emissions. The filling station has replaced the corner shop as the local convenience store, and the relief road is becoming the new high street. Within towns, the sheer number of cars is generating intolerable demands for parking and unacceptable levels of noise, pollution and congestion, making urban centres increasingly inaccessible and unattractive places for living and working, or to visit for shopping, business and pleasure. English author Lynn Sloman articulates the key issue with graphic simplicity: 'For any town or city, there is in the end a fairly simple choice – do you want to be a car-dependent town or a compact, bustling walking and public transport town? Every single decision about where new buildings should be placed, how people will access them, and how space is shared between different uses, takes us a small step towards one or other of these two choices.'[13]

Do we want to be a car-dependent society or a walking and public-transport-friendly society? Even in the USA, Transport Adjacent Development (TAD) is widely acknowledged as the way to go because of the social and economic a benefits of concentrating development within walking distance of public transport. Yet, in Ireland, comparison of the rail network with the National Spatial Strategy reveals that of the 74 mainline stations outside Dublin, Cork, Limerick, Galway and Waterford, 53 (or 72% of the total) serve towns of less than 7,500 people – i.e. locations with densities and urban populations barely capable of sustaining minimal services and amenities, never mind commuter rail links. For example, the medieval walled town of Athenry, on the Dublin-Galway inter-city rail line, has a population in the order of 3,200 and approximately 480 hectares (1,152 acres) of land zoned for development. Using internationally accepted criteria of sustainable minimum population densities – sixty persons per hectare, gross – this area of zoned land could cater for up to 30,000 inhabitants.[14] Similarly, Portarlington, also an important heritage town with a strategic main-line network location, has a population of 6,000 and zoned land extending to 560 hectares, enough to support almost 35,000 inhabitants. One could go around the State and find numerous other examples of mismatches between population density and zoned development land.

By comparison, development in the hinterland of Copenhagen – a city often compared with and similar in size to Dublin – is concentrated along five corridors radiating from the city towards the towns of Koge, Roskilde, Frederikssund, Hillerod and Helsingor. There is a train line along each finger, and new housing, offices and public buildings are concentrated along these lines, and especially around their stations. I recently saw an excellent mixed-use development in Bagsvaerd comprising supermarket, shops, apartments, car-parking and a civic space, all clustered around a railway station with fast trains to Copenhagen every ten minutes from morning to night. In Ireland, no trains run from Dublin to Arklow after 6.37pm, and the full re-opening of the Dublin-Navan line is still an aspiration.

Meanwhile, elected members continue to rezone swathes of agricultural land remote from schools, shops, services and transport, frequently ignoring the advice of their professional planners and accepted concepts of sustainable development. Recent interventions by Minister Gormley, and the criticisms by the chairman of An Bord Pleanála of 'indiscriminate and excessive land rezoning', are therefore most welcome.[15] In the context of the current over-supply of housing units in particular, there is a strong case to curb further land-rezoning until all rural towns, and particularly those on the rail network, are planned to the density and critical mass required for them to support essential transport and public services economically.

We need to learn from international best practice. Reflecting on visits to Barcelona, Germany and the Netherlands, Lord Rogers, chairman of Britain's Urban Task Force, noted the importance of urban design. The most successful projects analysed in its research were based on implementing a spatial master plan, 'a three-dimensional framework of buildings and public spaces to drive the development process and secure a high-quality product ... a spatial master plan is a vital tool for new development.'[16]

In the Irish context, this suggests that a statutory Local Area Plan should be a prerequisite for major development and a requirement for the zoned area of every town and village. Instead of being merely written statements, they should be prepared by skilled design-led teams, and they should include fully worked-out plans, with layouts of streets and public spaces, recommended densities, mix of uses, heights and massing of buildings, and proposals for the integration of new development into the existing urban structure. Their enactment should be the primary planning function of elected members, redirecting their focus from the simplistic zoning of land to town-planning in the proper sense of the term.

Finally, adoption of the Government guidelines needs to be accompanied by a root-and-branch reappraisal of our development-control standards. When will there be a better time than now – when the industry is in recession and there is time available to reflect on the past and plan for a better future – to revise the lowest-common-denominator suburban models which permeate development plans, as they have since the 1963 Planning Act? Rigidly applied quantitative standards (roads, parking, overlooking, open space, etc) mitigate against the making of

53

places based on qualitative design criteria (character, sense of place, urban structure, permeability, public realm, etc). We must ask what contribution has the 'Celtic Tiger' made to the nation's heritage of quality urban environments for the enjoyment of future generations? Despite its aspirations, the planning system has conspicuously failed to deliver quality or provide for 'proper planning and sustainable development'. On the contrary, current standards restrict designers and curtail the advancement of more sustainable urban models, higher densities and attractive place-making.

The *Urban Design Manual* is therefore most welcome, even if it avoids tackling issues such as our outdated traffic-orientated road standards – promised in a forthcoming manual for streets – or the default 22m 'privacy' separation distance between dwellings, which effectively prohibits conventional residential streets. Notwithstanding, the manual places a welcome and overdue emphasis on design. It will be interesting to see how its recommendations are translated into development plans, and whether its 'best practice' guidance will take precedence over the inflexible application of our current standards. Quality of design should be pre-eminent in planning and development control; urban design is fundamental to the way places look and operate, to the quality of life of those living, working and visiting an area, and to the cohesion of neighbourhoods and communities.

The National Economic and Social Council's 2004 report – *Housing in Ireland: Performance and Policy* – set out a range of key objectives for Irish housing policy. Echoing the findings of authoritative international research, it identified the essential characteristics of sustainable neighbourhoods.[17] In the context of the typical Irish town, this might be interpreted as envisaging the zoned area as a neighbourhood or 'urban village' – i.e. it should be big enough to support a range of services and amenities (at least 6,000 population); small enough to foster a sense of belonging and community (about 100 hectares / 240 acres); and sufficiently dense (gross density of sixty persons per hectare) to enable all of its essential facilities to be within easy walking distance (600-800 metres). In addition, it should be mixed-use, combining work, living and essential services; well designed with attractive pedestrian-orientated streets and open spaces; planned around public transport to minimise car-use for everyday needs; diverse and adaptable to future demands; as well as consolidating the structure and built form of the town or village and separating it from the surrounding landscape.

Can this be achieved and would it be acceptable to the market? The appeal of urban lifestyles – illustrated by the enduring popularity of Dublin's 19th-century inner-city neighbourhoods – is evidence that development at double the density of the typical suburb can be a popular housing choice. Homes in areas such as Portobello and Ranelagh are highly sought after, not only because they are a sound financial investment, but also because they are associated with a sense of urbanity and community, and because the level of density can support essential facilities and public transport within walking distance. The population and density in these neighbourhoods is within the range recommended by the authorities,

cited by the NESC, such as the UK Urban Task Force, the World Health Organisation, the Congress of the New Urbanism, and the Urban Villages Group, proving that the design of a 'high-density' neighbourhood needn't involve over-development or 'urban cramming'. Compare the convenience and quality of life of areas planned at these densities to the 120km daily round-trip that many endure in the Ireland of today.

To bring about this change, we need consensus. Good towns don't happen by accident; they need a spirit of collective possession and a shared vision. Westport, for example, shows the benefits of leadership, co-operation and management in responding to these challenges. Pro-active community, heritage and business sectors, an architect town manager and a town architect, combined with good planning, aesthetic control, public realm and 'Tidy Town' initiatives, have boosted the local economy and enhanced the town's attractiveness as a business and tourist destination, and as a place to live. It proves that architectural and urban quality is good for business and community development. If other towns followed its example by exploiting their distinctiveness and implementing plans with creativity, vision and conviction, they might also capitalise on the economic, environmental and social benefits of quality-driven urban development.

If the housing output projected for the coming years were to be focused on the regeneration of our towns and villages along the sustainable neighbourhood – or 'urban village' – model, it would be a major advance towards the goal of achieving sustainable development for Ireland. The 2004 NESC report concluded that achievement of the new principles of urban development is blocked, more than anything else, by the perception that we are so attached to extensive development and so divided by competing interests that we cannot make sustainable cities and towns. According to the author of the report, Dr Rory O'Donnell, the task of creating high-quality, integrated and sustainable neighbourhoods is one of the greatest challenges facing us today.[18]

It is imperative, therefore, that the Sustainable Residential Development in Urban Areas guidelines are not only adopted, but, more importantly, that they are applied throughout the State. Local authorities must use all the measures available to them to incorporate the Department of the Environment's guidelines and the accompanying *Urban Design Manual* into their development plans. Promoting higher-density residential development in the right locations, well serviced with public transport and community facilities, and built to the best possible standards, would create more attractive environments; provide housing, services and infrastructure more economically; curtail car-dependency; reduce the land take for construction; lower our carbon emissions; and make it possible to adopt renewable-energy systems. It would also reduce the stress and the time spent commuting, release opportunities for leisure, social contacts, civic engagement and the enhancement of social capital.

The realities of peak oil and climate change dictate that there is no longer any choice in this matter. We *must* reconsider the folly of our accepted settlement patterns. It is demonstrably evident that the well-designed mixed-use neighbourhood, or urban village, is the most effective model to lower our carbon footprint and deliver housing of the right type in the right locations – housing which responds to the social, economic and environmental realities of today's Ireland and, not least, contributes to the regeneration of our towns and villages. By any definition, this would be a win-win solution.

———

Endnotes

[1] Department of the Environment, Heritage & Local Government (DoEHLG), *Sustainable Residential Development in Urban Areas*, consultation draft guidelines for planning authorities (Dublin, 2008)
[2] DoEHLG, *National Spatial Strategy for Ireland 2002-2020* (Dublin, 2002) p.106
[3] DoEHLG, *Sustainable Rural Housing: Guidelines for Planning Authorities* (Dublin, 2005) p.10.
[4] Andres Duany, Elizabeth Plater-Zyberk, Jeff Speck, *Suburban Nation: The Rise of Sprawl and the Decline of the American Dream* (North Point Press, New York, 2000)
[5] Robert D Putnam, *Bowling Alone: The Collapse and Revival of American Community* (Simon & Schuster, New York, 2000) pp.205, 408
[6] Institute of Public Health in Ireland, *Health Impacts of the Built Environment: A Review* (Dublin, 2006)
[7] 'Travel Choices in Pedestrian versus Automobile Oriented Neighbourhoods', cited in Lynn Sloman, *Car Sick: Solutions for our Car-addicted Culture* (Green Books, 2006) p.129
[8] Richard Florida, *Cities and the Creative Class* (Routledge, 2005) p.28
[9] Department for Environment, Food and Rural Affairs, *Our Countryside: The Future – A Fair Deal for Rural England* (2000) ch. 7
[10] DoEHLG: *Urban Design Manual – A best practice guide* (Dublin, 2008)
[11] John O'Connor, Chairman, An Bord Pleanála, 'Excessive zonings must be reversed', *Irish Times*, 7 November 2008
[12] Charlie Taylor, 'Over 600 newsagents face closure – group warns, *Irish Times*, 13 February 2009
[13] Lynn Sloman, *Car Sick: Solutions for our Car-addicted Culture* (Green Books, 2006) p.129
[14] Richard Guise, Hugh Barton, Marcus Grant, *Shaping Neighbourhoods – A Guide for Health, Sustainability and Viability* (Taylor & Francis Group, London, 2002) p.99
[15] O'Connor, 'Excessive zonings must be reversed', op. cit.
[16] Urban Task Force, *Towards an Urban Renaissance* (1999) p.49
[17] Guise, Barton, Grant, *Shaping Neighbourhoods*, op. cit., p.202
[18] NESC, *Housing in Ireland: Performance and Policy, Report No. 112 of the National Economic and Social Council* (Dublin, 2004)

Paul Keogh is the founding partner in Paul Keogh Architects, an award-winning Dublin practice.

ADDENDUM

Paul Keogh has set out the dire situation in Irish towns and villages. New planning legislation is promised to halt indiscriminate rezoning and other current errors, but a complete change of approach is needed by most local authorities.

The exemplars in this section are dominated by counties Cork and Mayo, where more enlightened planning policy is in evidence, even though it also needs to develop much further. We have included a number of examples from the urban villages in Dublin to increase the limited number available.

The projects in this section start with urban framework plans for small towns in Co Leitrim, followed by major expansion schemes for towns or villages within the regions of our larger cities, such as Newcastle in Dublin, Mitchelstown in Cork and Newport in Tipperary, close to Limerick. Two competition-winning projects from Tipperary town show further creative ideas for enticing private housing.

Also included are two village expansion schemes in Co Cork, and an approach to the extension of a small crossroads settlement which was frustrated by current planning policies, even in the relatively enlightened environment of Co Cork.

The featured projects then move to examples of infill in small towns, villages and the urban villages of Dublin, from upmarket private housing to social housing and town-centre commercial schemes with a significant housing element.

Many of the social-housing schemes, while well designed, still do not include private or co-operative housing elements, and are possibly too large for the towns or villages, perpetuating the dominance of social housing in our smaller urban settlements.

– JAMES PIKE
January, 2009

Manorhamilton Urban Framework Plan

iCON Architecture & Urban Design

The plan was conceived as a catalyst for action in Manorhamilton. The policy directions reflected those established in our project for Prosperous, Co Kildare, but in a different environment. Manorhamilton is a 17th-century plantation town, with a strong plan character and linear form. It has changed relatively little over the years, and needs investment in order to thrive as the key town in rural north Leitrim.

The aims of the policy framework are:
- to protect and improve the built heritage as a precondition for a dynamic development programme by proposing the designation of an Architectural Conservation Area
- to propose a landscape protection strategy to include green areas within the town as well as on the edge
- to propose and prioritise projects (mainly suggested to us during consultation) within the built area of the town
- to propose a strategy for expansion over a period of about twenty years which would guarantee a harmonious balance between the natural and the built environment and retain the special quality of the town within an outstanding local landscape.

The plan foresees the consolidation of the town centre by completing an urban-block network around the centre to generate new shopping opportunities and define the town's edges, with the dual purpose of strengthening the core and creating a strong edge with the landscape as a measure of protection.

The plan developed, therefore, as a series of projects through the town, which were

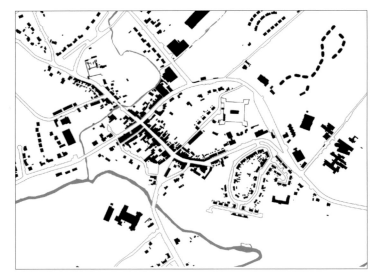

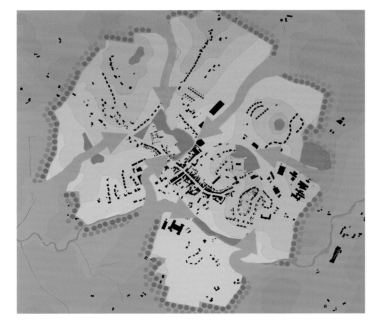

height	mix	percentage	no. of dwellings	site area	density	floor area	bed spaces	site coverage	open space	car spaces	context
2-4 storey	decided at different design phases	mainly residential; mixed uses also proposed	approx 800 over 20 years	approx 60 ha over 20 years	average 35 units/ha	n/a	n/a	n/a	n/a	1.5-2 per dwelling	historic plantation town with a strong landscape context

mapped out as a vision that could be understood, promoted and implemented at local level.

name / address – Manorhamilton:
 A sustainable town for the 21st century – Urban Framework Plan, Manorhamilton, Co Leitrim
design / completion – This is a long-term strategic plan of up to twenty years. Design proposals are also strategic urban-design ideas, not intended as the final design.
client – Leitrim County Council and the local community of Manorhamilton

➔ Projects for consolidation of the town centre superimposed on aerial view. The projects needed to be identified by legend, as it was not immediately apparent which were new projects as they were carefully tuned to the morphology of the town.
↘ The project consolidates the urban form in the town centre by creating a new edge to the block in preference to using backland areas, making a new square with old people's housing, commercial units and central-area parking. The proposed County Council one-stop shop is in the foreground.
↘ Manor Square – The proposal is to create a new block in the town structure by closing the rear areas of the existing Main Street buildings, with a new street fronting onto a new square. The street is typically three storeys, with ground-level shops, offices, businesses and starter units for small enterprises. Upper floors are residential, or, possibly, for business use.

opposite

↖ Map showing footprint of a plantation town with 17th-century castle
↞ Urban/rural-interface plan showing penetration of landscape, proposed urban green areas, and a green edge to define limits to development naturally.
← The diagram represents a synthesis of the plan. Circles show distances of 500m and 750m from the centre – a reasonable walking distance – with most of the growth occurring within the outer circle and all the consolidation projects taking place within the 500m circle. The green strategy is represented by key green spaces, the riverside, country corridor routes, and a green boundary to the town. The capacity of the plan allows for a doubling of the population over a period of more than twenty years.

Drumshanbo Urban Framework Plan

iCON Architecture & Urban Design

Drumshanbo is a small town of about a thousand people, nestled between drumlins in a beautiful and diverse landscape beside Lough Allen. This plan was put together over the course of a year, during which there was substantial consultation and discussion.

The task was to make a coherent whole out of a diversity of ideas, and to formulate a structure to meet the many demands for sustainable and even-handed approaches to development, while conserving both the built and the natural environment.

The traditional 19th-century town is essentially intact and will be robust enough to renew itself for the enjoyment of future citizens. However, the town needs conscious and informed management in order to deliver a revitalised centre. The surrounding landscape is a magical aspect of the town and its hinterland. It is extremely vulnerable to poorly conceived development and lack of judgement about its value. By highlighting this, the plan seeks to ensure that the landscape remains the essence of the town's identity.

A number of projects have been proposed to show a range of possibilities which convey the potential of this town to grow and develop.

address – Drumshanbo, Co Leitrim
design / completion – This is a long-term strategic plan of up to twenty years. Design proposals are also strategic urban-design ideas, not intended as the final design.
client – Leitrim County Council and the local community of Drumshanbo

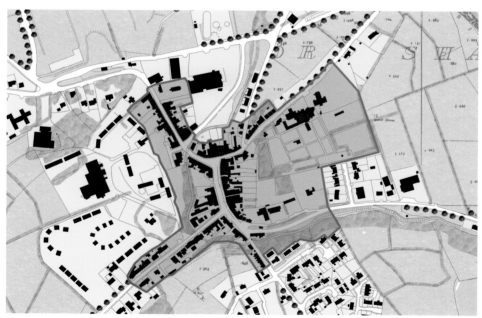

height	mix	percentage	no. of dwellings	site area	density	floor area	bed spaces	site coverage	open space	car spaces	context
2-3 storey	decided at different design phases	mainly residential; mixed uses also proposed	approx 400 over 20 years	approx 30 ha over 20 years	average 30 units/ha	n/a	n/a	n/a	n/a	1.5-2 per dwelling	small lakeside town with a strong landscape context

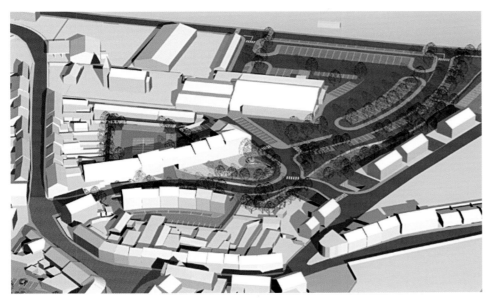

↑ The markets site (top right of picture) is within 150m of Main Street (bottom left).

→ Showing the desirability of developing the centre first, and opportunities for strengthening the urban centre of Drumshanbo.

↗ The market square is rationalised and improved, and the library is reinvented as an info-centre for locals and visitors. Trees which were removed during the construction of housing are reinstated to re-establish the eco-corridor which runs through the town.

opposite

↖ Defining the corridor of river and trees which travels through the town to ensure its future management

↞ Map showing the proposed Architectural Conservation Area superimposed on the built-up area of Drumshanbo

← Protecting the margins of the lake by proposing a walk and management of the edge

← Landscape character assessment superimposed on an aerial view of Drumshanbo showing the vulnerabilities to development of the areas around the town. This analysis helped to offer clear development zones which would have the least impact on the landscape.

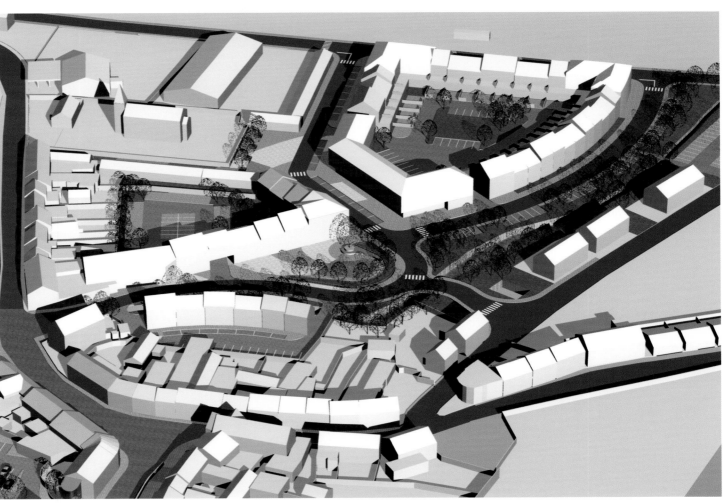

Newcastle Lyons – Residential Development

Anthony Reddy Associates

Newcastle Lyons is a historic village of a thousand people near City West Business Park and Rathcoole. South Dublin County Council adopted a Local Area Plan in November 2003 in order to provide a framework for the future development of lands around Newcastle village.

A master plan was prepared for 28 hectares of zoned lands situated to the south of the village. Several factors influenced the evolution of the master plan in its early development. These factors, which form part of the main aims of the LAP, include:
– the provision of a physical planning framework for the expansion of the existing village
– facilitating development that integrates with the existing village and is consistent with the character of a traditional Irish village settlement
– ensuring that new development is sensitive to the archaeological and historic significance of Newcastle.

The resulting urban grain is made up of a clear and permeable network of spaces. The proposed spine-road takes the form of an urban boulevard, focusing on a major public space at its heart.

Identified at an early stage to preserve and articulate the planimetric layout of the existing burgage plots north of the spine route, these plots have informed the layout and urban grain of this section of the village.

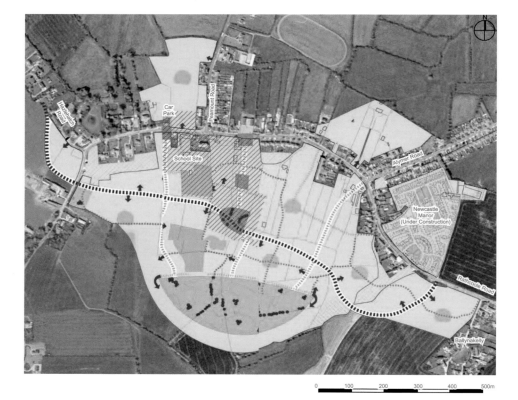

To the south of the burgage plots and the spine route, the density of the urban grain reduces and becomes more free-form. This area will become the future southern edge of Newcastle Lyons, where it is proposed that the open spaces beside the residential area shall become public parkland.

The design takes into account the requirements for higher densities, and accommodation is provided in courtyards, intimate streets and crescents overlooking open space.

The nature of the design intends to give the new village extension a sense of place and identity. The scale of the project has presented an opportunity to create distinct and unique character areas. These areas are as follows:

– Village Boulevard, forming the spine through the new community, composed of three storeys, culminating in the main street
– Burgage Green, with a more urban architecture
– Burgage Lane and New Village Green, comprising mainly two-storey housing arranged to reflect the topography of the existing lands
– Rural edge and Ballynakelly/Park Edge, comprising low-density housing along the edge of the village
– North Oval, Ballynakelly Green, comprising formal three-storey crescents around landscaped open spaces.

address – Newcastle Lyons, near Rathcoole, Co Dublin
design / completion – 2001–2013
client – Tenbury Developments Ltd

↖ Overall strategy map from Local Area Plan, 2003

opposite

↗ Burgage Oval (top) and Burgage Crescent (bottom) comprise formal 3-storey crescents around landscaped open spaces
→ Overall master plan of zoned lands south of existing village

height	mix	percentage	no. of dwellings	site area	density	floor area	bed spaces	site coverage	open space	car spaces	context
2-4 storey	20 x 5-bed houses 51 x 4-bed houses 344 x 3-bed houses 138 x 2-bed houses 225 x 3-bed duplexes 87 x 2-bed duplexes 16 x 3-bed apartments 283 x 2-bed apartments 85 x 1-bed apartments	93.2% residential 2.5% retail 3.2% school 1.1% creche	713 Phase 1 545 Phase 2	38.9 ha	21 units/ha (edge) 42 units/ha (expanded) 53 units/ha (core)	129,950m² (approx)	3,163 (81/ha)	12%	6.2 ha public also private gardens, balconies, terraces	1,090 Phase 1 850 Phase 2	expansion to existing village

← Newcastle boulevard
↙ Plans of typical 3-storey residential block –
   ground, 1st, part 2nd-floor
↓ Completed 3-storey crescent and terrace
   (Ballynakelly Mews)

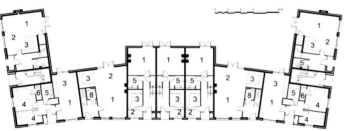

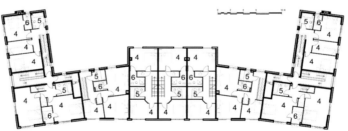

1. Living Room
2. Dining Room
3. Kitchen
4. Bedroom
5. Bathroom
6. Ensuite
7. Store
8. WC

Newcastle Lyons – North Village Centre

O'Mahony Pike Architects

Specific Objective 63 of the South Dublin County Development Plan provides an opportunity to redress the development gap effected by the omission of the subject lands from the 2003 Local Area Plan. This Action Plan views these lands as an opportunity for development that can integrate Main Street into the proposed village core in a manner complementary to the LAP.

As illustrated here, the LAP proposes a new village core located south of Main Street on the new parallel road that runs through the village expansion area. A new link road runs between this new mixed-use village core and a landscaped square on the south side of the existing village centre. Pedestrian routes within the proposed new residential development area intersect with this link road. The LAP boundary is the south side of Main Street, while the north side is omitted from consideration.

The Action Area Plan presents an opportunity to strengthen the links between Main Street, the historical village core of Newcastle, and the proposed centre of the new residential settlements proposed under the Local Area Plan. Providing new routes for existing communities through the old village core and into the new one, Main Street will benefit from added vitality and connectivity.

address – Newcastle Lyons, near
    Rathcoole, Co Dublin
design / completion – 2007
clients – South Dublin County Council /
    Opus Developments Ltd

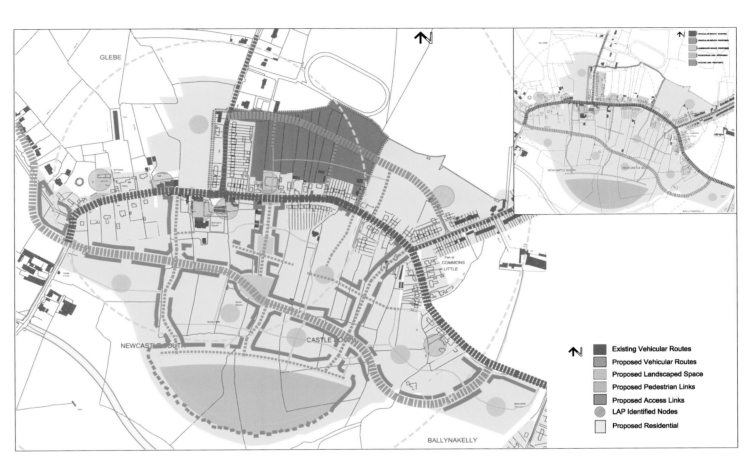

Existing Vehicular Routes
Proposed Vehicular Routes
Proposed Landscaped Space
Proposed Pedestrian Links
Proposed Access Links
LAP Identified Nodes
Proposed Residential

↗ Potential new routes between subject lands and
    extended mixed-use village core
→ Action Area Plan
→→ Corner Park housing plan

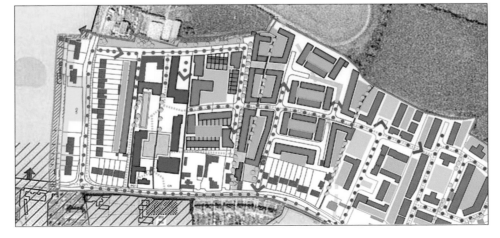

63

Newcastle Lyons – Castle Lyons, phase 1

O'Mahony Pike Architects

The Action Area Plan was approved, and phased development was submitted for planning permission by OPUS Developments. The first phase of this development has subsequently been built and the second phase is in preparation.

The Corner Park development will create a tight residential area near the centre with two- and three-storey terrace houses and three-storey apartment buildings on key corners. A crèche and Montessori school will be included.

A key feature of the housing is that it has been built to achieve an A3 energy rating, and will therefore comply even with the proposed 2010 Part L of the Building Regulations.

Phase 1 of this development is comprised of seventy dwellings (mostly terraced houses with some duplexes/apartments). It achieved SEI 'House of Tomorrow' standard, and received funding in the form a capital grant from SEI under the House of Tomorrow programme. The House of Tomorrow standard identifies a specific airtightness target for developments, and therefore an airtight membrane was fitted internally to the timber frame prior to the first fix, with great care being taken during the subsequent fitting of the services to ensure the membrane wasn't compromised in any way. (Problems occurred on-site with the installation of the airtight membrane and with the integration of the services.)

Having done all that was feasible with the envelope, the building services were examined next. In conjunction with the mechanical and electrical engineers on the

height	mix	percentage	no. of dwellings	site area	density	floor area	bed spaces	site coverage	open space	car spaces	context
2-3 storey	80% housing 20% duplexes / apartments	100% residential	70	1.67 ha (4.13 acres)	42 units/ha (17/acre)	3,015m²	198 (118/ha)	18%	15%	105 (1.5 per dwelling)	village centre

project, the following three items were specified:
- Proair 400 heat-recovery ventilation system
- a high-efficiency Viessmann Vitodens 100 gas combi-boiler
- 5m² of Calpak Solar Collector and 210-litre twin-coiled copper tank solar water-heating system. In addition, the kitchens were all fitted with A-rated appliances.

The overall calculated energy saving for the units was in excess of 40% based on all of the above, with the solar panels accounting for 18% of that energy saving. The units achieve an A3 rating, with an average mid-terrace three-bedroom house using 54 KW/hr/m² per year, and producing 14.5kg of CO_2 per m² per year, based on the BER system and using Sustainable Energy Ireland's DEAP software to calculate these values. The average estimated additional construction costs in achieving this standard were in the region of €20,000 per unit. This project complies with the requirements of the proposed part L regulation.

COST BENEFIT ANALYSIS

Construction Type: Timber Frame Unit: Type M from Newcastle Phase 2		Services Package for Compliance with Part L 2005 (Base case from which 40% improvement in energy efficiency is calculated)	Services Package Needed to Achieve Compliance with Part L 2007	Services Package Needed to Achieve A3 Energy Rating
1. Traditional Timber Frame External wall 140mm stud with 140mm glass fibre batt between studs, internal plasterboard and 40mm cavity and 100 rendered blockwork outer leaf. ***Overall U-value = 0.26 W/m2/K**	Space Heating/DHW Solar Ventilation Any other feature Total Cost (ex VAT)	Normal efficiency gas boiler None Natural – trickle vents in windows 2 zones of control * maximum u-values – wall 0.27 W/m2/K, floor 0.25 W/m2/K, roof 0.15 W/m2/K, windows and doors 2.2 W/m2/K €1,476	Cond. boiler/control €1,726† 2 panels – 300L tank €3,173 None €0 Solar install. €0 * based on €500 per person per day † inc. boiler, controls, sensors, CWS €5,899	Cond. boiler/control €1,726† 2 panels – 300L tank €3,173 WHR180 €2,533 Solar & HRV install. €2,500* * based on €500 per person per day † Inc. boiler, controls, sensors, CWS €9,932
Cost of kit: €17,022.68 (for supply of timber frame only) Cost incl. installation: **€21,025.10**	Energy per year BER	141.13 KWhr/m2/yr **MPEPC = 84.68 KWhr/m2/yr (60%)** B3	100.82 KWhr/m2/yr **doesn't comply** B2	64.43 KWhr/m2/yr **complies** A3
2. Structural Insulated Panel System (SIPS) External wall 142mm SIPS panel ie. 15mm OSB, 112 polyurethane rigid insulation, 15mm OSB, internal plasterboard and 40mm cavity and 100 rendered blockwork outer leaf. U-value = ***Overall U-value = 0.18 W/m2/K**	Space Heating/DHW Solar Ventilation Any other feature Total Cost (ex VAT)	Normal efficiency gas boiler None Natural – trickle vents in windows 2 zones of control * maximum u-values – wall 0.27 W/m2/K, floor 0.25 W/m2/K, roof 0.15 W/m2/K, windows and doors 2.2 W/m2/K €1,476	Cond. boiler/control €1,726† 2 panels – 300L tank €3,173 None €0 Solar install. €1,000* * based on €500 per person per day † Inc. boiler, controls, sensors, CWS €5,899	Cond. boiler/control €1,726† 2 panels – 300L tank €3,173 WHR180 €2,533 Solar & HRV install. €2,500* * based on €500 per person per day † Inc. boiler, controls, sensors, CWS €9,932
Cost of kit: €30,223.00 (for supply of SIPS system only) Cost incl. installation: **€37,360.00**	Energy per year BER	141.13 KWhr/m2/yr **MPEPC = 84.68 KWhr/m2/yr (60%)** B3	80.17 KWhr/m2/yr **complies** B1	61.98 KWhr/m2/yr **complies** A3
3. Kingspan *Optimal Wall* Timber Frame External wall – 9mm OSB on external face, 89mm stud with 100mm of fibre glass insulation between studs factory-fitted, with 50mm of Kooltherm rigid phenolic insulation internally factory-fitted, 25mm battens to create service void, SD2 vapour check ***Overall U-value = 0.14 W/m2/K**	Space Heating/DHW Solar Ventilation Any other feature Total Cost (ex VAT)	Normal efficiency gas boiler None Natural – trickle vents in windows 2 zones of control * maximum u-values – wall 0.27 W/m2/K, floor 0.25 W/m2/K, roof 0.15 W/m2/K, windows and doors 2.2 W/m2/K €1,476	Cond. boiler/control €1,726† 2 panels – 300L tank €3,173 None €0 Solar install. €1,000* * based on €500 per person per day † Inc. boiler, controls, sensors, CWS €5,899	Cond. boiler/control €1,726† 2 panels – 300L tank €3,173 WHR180 €2,533 Solar & HRV install. €2,500* * based on €500 per person per day † Inc. boiler, controls, sensors, CWS €9,932
Cost of kit: €19,072.68 (for supply of *optimal wall* system only) Cost incl. installation: **€24,494.68**	Energy per year BER	141.13 KWhr/m2/yr **MPEPC = 84.68 KWhr/m2/yr (60%)** B3	80.49 KWhr/m2/yr **complies** B1	63.5 KWhr/m2/yr **complies** A3

*u-value for the entire wall build-up incl. air cavity and external leaf of block and render

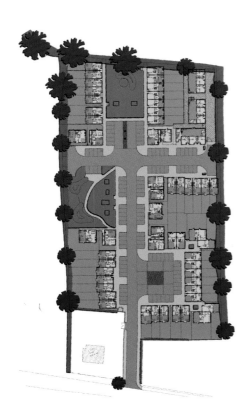

name / address – Castle Lyons, Phase 1, 'House of Tomorrow' Residential Development, Newcastle Lyons, near Rathcoole, Co Dublin
design / completion – 2005–2007
client – Opus Developments Ltd

opposite

← Views of Phase 1, completed in 2007, which mainly comprises 2- and 3-storey houses in terraces and courtyards, with 3-storey apartment buildings on key corner sites.

↑ Cost-benefit analysis
← Site plan of Phase 1
↙ Front and rear elevations, ground and 1st-floor plans
↓ Thermal efficiency

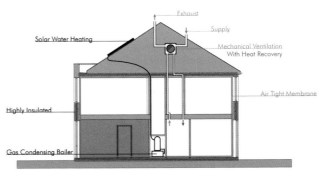

Newport, Co Tipperary – Master Plan

Cox Power Architects

To prevent Newport from becoming a housing dormitory of Limerick city, the Newport Local Area Plan 2004 required a mixed-use master plan for this twenty-hectare site beside the town centre.

The town 'edge' is defined by a linear park (and inner relief road), linking the Cully and Mulcair rivers. New streets and squares are two- and three-storey, with higher buildings on the town square providing enclosure.

A mix of uses and a range of house types is proposed to form an integrated sustainable community. The mix of uses ensures day and evening-time activity.

To improve legibility and orientation, each street and square has a distinct design. Pedestrians locate themselves by reference to the new park and existing town centre. New links are made to the existing town to increase permeability. Streets are short and gently curved to avoid long walking times and to provide interest, as entire street lengths are revealed only gradually. The curve provides passive traffic-calming. Group car-parking is provided in order to avoid excessive circulation.

Following agreement on the master plan, a planning application was made for the town square, with a supermarket forming the 'anchor' and catalyst for other commercial uses.

The building design respects the scale of Newport, but materials and language are contemporary. Residential design is based on *Sustainable Urban Housing: Design*

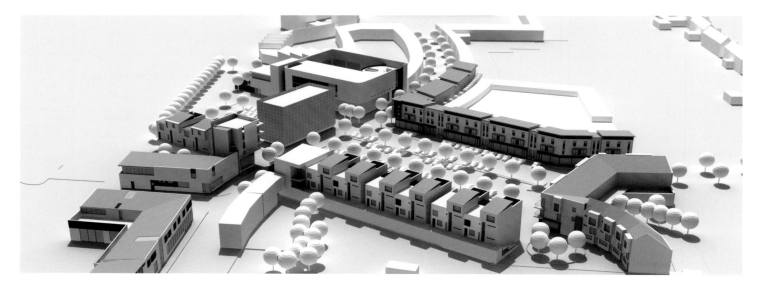

Standards for New Apartments (DoEHLG, 2007), encompassing dual-aspect, generous storage and large balconies. Apartments are generally own-door, with the live/work units having a 'work' courtyard at ground level and a raised terrace at first-floor level.

design / completion – 2004–2010
client – Thomas Croffey

↑ Model of Town Square development
← New tree-lined streets and square

opposite

↗ Site plan of Town Square development
→ Master plan and isometric view (with site plan outlined in red)
→ Detail of Newport Objectives Map

height	mix	percentage	no. of dwellings	site area	density	floor area	bed spaces	site coverage	open space	car spaces	context
2-3 storey MASTER PLAN	482 buildings total 377 houses 52 apartments 9 daycare residents 9 guest houses	mainly residential	447	19.65 ha (48.53 acres)	24.53 units/ha (9.93/acre)	74,826m²	2,235 (114/ha)	18.94%	159,180m²	n/a (will be in accordance with Development Plan)	village housing

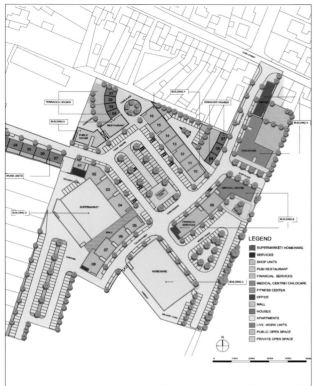

LEGEND

SUPERMARKET / HOMEWARE
SERVICES
SHOP UNITS
PUB/ RESTAURANT
FINANCIAL SERVICES
MEDICAL CENTRE/ CHILDCARE
FITNESS CENTER
OFFICE
MALL
HOUSES
APARTMENTS
LIVE -WORK UNITS
PUBLIC OPEN SPACE
PRIVATE OPEN SPACE

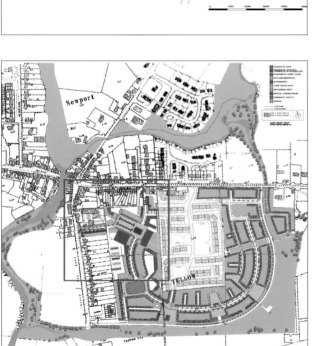

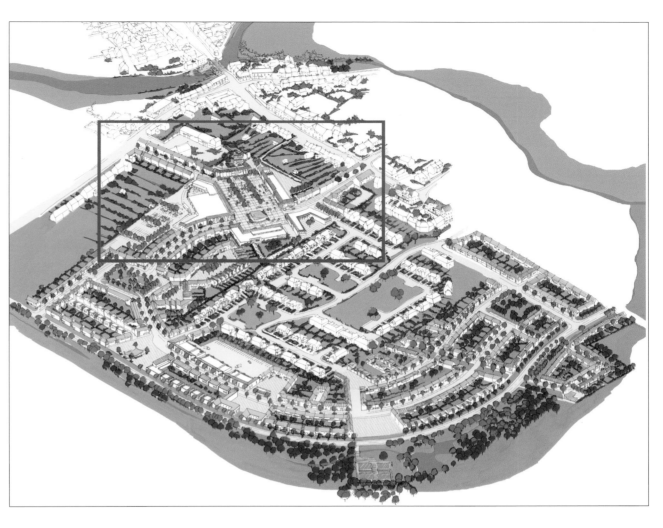

Newport Objectives Map
Key

← →   Transport / Road Access
- - -   Pavement / Pedestrian Improvements
        Opportunity Sites
        Road Junction Improvements
        Settlement Boundary
▲   Protected Structures
🌳   Protected Trees
        Zone of Archaeology
        Conservation Area
A.99   Objective

height	mix	percentage	no. of dwellings	site area	density	floor area	bed spaces	site coverage	open space	car spaces	context
2-3 storey	4 x 4-bed houses 3 x 3-bed houses 43 x 3-bed apartments 11 x 2-bed apartments	mainly residential	63	3.13 ha (7.74 acres)	20 units/ha (8 units/acre)	16,340m²	346 (110/ha)	30%	3,100m²	351	town-centre extension
NEW TOWN SQUARE	2 x 1-bed apartments										

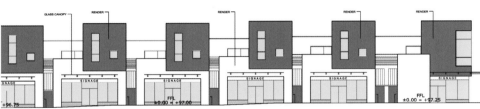

MASTER PLAN, NEWPORT

↑ South elevation to Town Square (type F)
↓ Plans – ground, 1st floors (type F)

↗ North elevation of Custom Gap Street,
with 3-storey live/work units
→ Live/work unit plans – ground, 1st, 2nd floors –
with raised terraces above work areas

Stag Park, Mitchelstown, Co Cork

Wain Morehead Architects / Frapolli Green Chatin

The density aspiration for this 33-acre site was influenced by the existing scale of the town, with 362 rented, affordable and private units (with facilities) proposed.

The lands have been farmed since the early 1700s and the hedgerow pattern remains almost unchanged since then. The overall site fall of 1:20 was maintained, and the opportunity to provide for deficient services (crèches, etc) for the locality was integrated.

The village shop, the crèche and the provision of a large public park, easily accessible by the existing community, will assist with the integration and long-term sustainability of the scheme. The proposed public realm is of a high quality, with references made to existing street patterns. The public realm is as much influenced by the urban landscape as it is by views and vistas.

The development consists of 362 dwelling units, four retail units, a family resource centre, community centre and crèche, all ancillary siteworks and landscaped areas. To address future demographic trends, 'grow houses' have been incorporated. By using traditional design elements such as tall pitched roofs, two-bedroom units are easily extended within the attic space to become three-bedroom units, creating a sustainable new housing stock and preventing stagnation.

The sheltered housing is strategically sited adjacent to community facilities, purposefully laid out on a pedestrian scale. The provision of disabled access in the

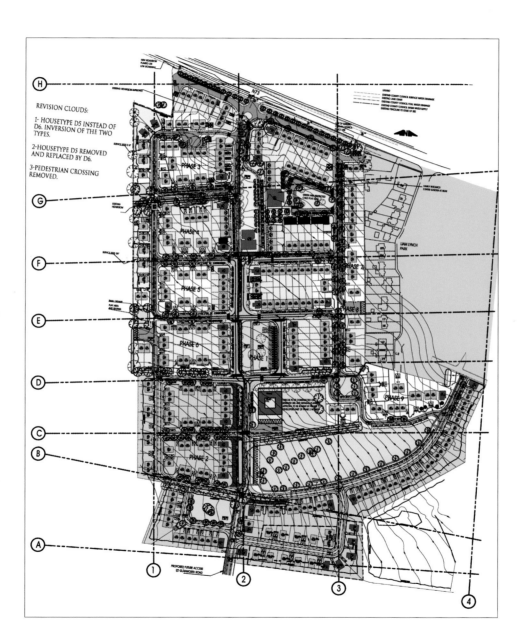

Site Context

↑ Aerial view showing site context
← Site plan

general housing stock at this stage allows for easy adaptation to elderly or disabled use, reducing the need for future extension.

Cycle lanes are fully integrated into the urban layout, protected from vehicular traffic by the footpaths and hedgerows. The hierarchy of streets, secondary roads and distribution lanes is logical and easily understood.

The houses have been sited with consideration to the vistas generated within the scheme and external vistas such as the church spires to the east and the Galtee Mountains to the north. The retention of original hedgerows provides shelter from prevailing winds.

height	mix	percentage	no. of dwellings	site area	density	floor area	bed spaces	site coverage	open space	car spaces	context
2-3 storey	264 x 3-bed houses 34 x 2-bed duplexes/apts 24 x 2-bed grow-houses 40 x 1-bed maisonettes/apts resource centre, crèche, retail	85% residential 12.5% communal 2.5 commercial	362	133,548m² (33 acres)	11 units/acre	31,200m²	1,627 (51/acre)	24%	13% green space	340 on-street 240 off-street	outskirts of small town

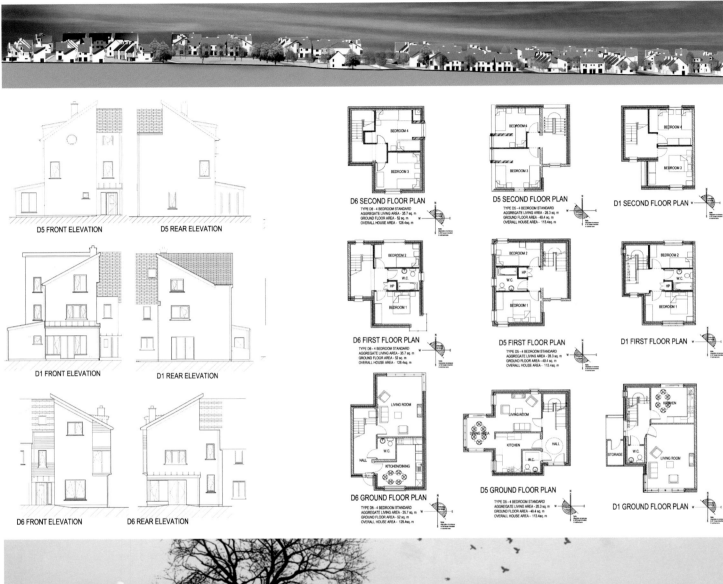

D5 FRONT ELEVATION

D5 REAR ELEVATION

D1 FRONT ELEVATION

D1 REAR ELEVATION

D6 FRONT ELEVATION

D6 REAR ELEVATION

D6 SECOND FLOOR PLAN

TYPE D6 - 4 BEDROOM STANDARD
AGGREGATE LIVING AREA - 35.7 sq. m
GROUND FLOOR AREA - 52 sq. m
OVERALL HOUSE AREA - 128.4sq. m

D5 SECOND FLOOR PLAN

TYPE D5 - 4 BEDROOM STANDARD
AGGREGATE LIVING AREA - 28.3 sq. m
GROUND FLOOR AREA - 49.4 sq. m
OVERALL HOUSE AREA - 113.4sq. m

D1 SECOND FLOOR PLAN

D6 FIRST FLOOR PLAN

TYPE D6 - 4 BEDROOM STANDARD
AGGREGATE LIVING AREA - 35.7 sq. m
GROUND FLOOR AREA - 52 sq. m
OVERALL HOUSE AREA - 128.4sq. m

D5 FIRST FLOOR PLAN

TYPE D5 - 4 BEDROOM STANDARD
AGGREGATE LIVING AREA - 28.3 sq. m
GROUND FLOOR AREA - 49.4 sq. m
OVERALL HOUSE AREA - 113.4sq. m

D1 FIRST FLOOR PLAN

D6 GROUND FLOOR PLAN

TYPE D6 - 4 BEDROOM STANDARD
AGGREGATE LIVING AREA - 35.7 sq. m
GROUND FLOOR AREA - 52 sq. m
OVERALL HOUSE AREA - 128.4sq. m

D5 GROUND FLOOR PLAN

TYPE D5 - 4 BEDROOM STANDARD
AGGREGATE LIVING AREA - 28.3 sq. m
GROUND FLOOR AREA - 49.4 sq. m
OVERALL HOUSE AREA - 113.4sq. m

D1 GROUND FLOOR PLAN

The internal layout of the houses adopts the statuary requirements of parts L and M of the Building Regulations. In addition, single bedrooms are avoided throughout the scheme, encouraging better use of the space provided, enabling home-based enterprise and providing better storage facilities for the future needs of the dwelling. At ground-floor level, the use of full-height or low-level windows maximises the penetration of light, solar-gain and the visual integration of garden spaces.

The house design caters for optimum orientation in order to obtain the full benefits of climatic factors, encouraging energy-efficiency. A number of dwellings are being monitored to analyse the actual performance of the energy-efficient system.

Building materials are simple, traditional, renewable, and easy to maintain, while the retention and management of hedgerows and mature trees, and a general respect for the existing topography, minimises earthworks and provides natural shelter. This has also heavily influenced the public realm.

architects – Wain Morehead Architects (Cork) / Frapolli Green Chatin (Aix en Provence)
design / completion – 2005– (2 years for Phase 1; 9 phases in total)
client – Cork County Council

↖ Section through site
↑ Plans and elevations of type D houses
← Computer-generated view of completed scheme
→ Views of completed scheme and of Phase 1

Scalaheen, Tipperary

Carew Kelly Architects

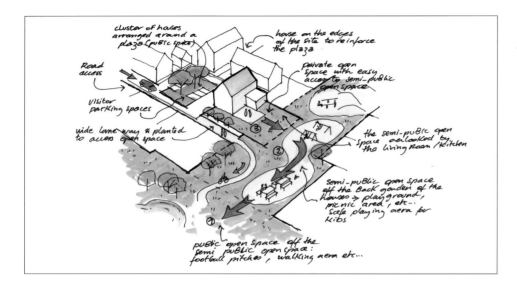

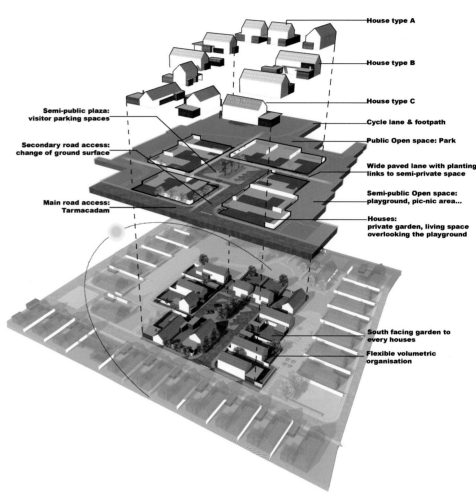

House type A

House type B

House type C

Cycle lane & footpath

Public Open space: Park

Semi-public plaza:
visitor parking spaces

Wide paved lane with planting:
links to semi-private space

Secondary road access:
change of ground surface

Semi-public Open space:
playground, pic-nic area...

Main road access:
Tarmacadam

Houses:
private garden, living space
overlooking the playground

South facing garden to
every houses

Flexible volumetric
organisation

The key design objectives were to provide comfortable, high-quality housing in a sustainable environment, combining the desire for privacy with the need for social interaction and activities. These objectives are achieved by means of public/private progression, the use of courtyards and the overlapping of semi-public and semi-private layers, all wrapped around a central 'heart'. The tradition of simple built forms in the landscape and the grouping of buildings in an informal manner to create communities were central to this.

The key strategy is based on groupings of courtyards and 'fingers' of green space, and the interaction between the two. The main organisational framework is of 'clusters' of courtyards – i.e. a number of houses grouped around a plaza-type central space in a semi-formal

arrangement. A hierarchical route is created from public space (plaza) to private space (house/garden) to semi-private space (fingers) to public space (central 'heart').

The courtyard layout allows for privacy and shelter from the elements for a more comfortable micro-climate. Houses can be orientated to make maximum use of their southerly and westerly orientation. The design of the individual houses is traditional in shape and materials, but modern in layout and expression.

design / completion – 2005–
    (announced as joint-winner 2006;
    no further progress)
client – Tipperary Town Council

opposite

↑ Exploded axonometric view of typical cluster, showing (a) house types, (b) circulation and public open space, (c) context and orientation
↖ Concept sketch

→ Typical plans and elevations
↗ Site plan
↠ Conceptual diagrams showing (a) public open space, (b) circulation, (c) house types and plots

height	mix	percentage	no. of dwellings	site area	density	floor area	bed spaces	site coverage	open space	car spaces	context
1-3 storey	29 x 5-bed houses 58 x 4-bed houses 34 x 3-4-bed houses 51 x 3-bed houses 11 units over shops	98% residential 1.5% communal 0.5% commercial	183	30.7 acres	6 units/acre	31,211m²	1,050 (934/acre)	20.4%	24% park, 4% plaza, 5% semi-private	300	town fringe

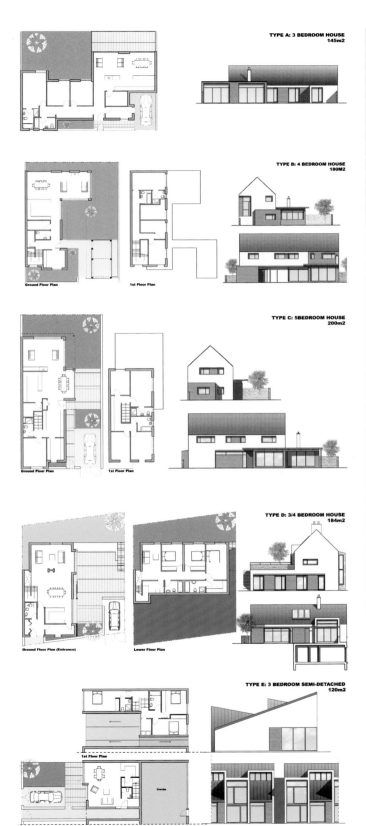

TYPE A: 3 BEDROOM HOUSE
145m2

TYPE B: 4 BEDROOM HOUSE
180M2

Ground Floor Plan   1st Floor Plan

TYPE C: 5BEDROOM HOUSE
200m2

Ground Floor Plan   1st Floor Plan

TYPE D: 3/4 BEDROOM HOUSE
184m2

Ground Floor Plan (Entrance)   Lower Floor Plan

TYPE E: 3 BEDROOM SEMI-DETACHED
120m2

1st Floor Plan

Ground Floor Plan

N

PUBLIC OPEN SPACE
◼ Public Open Space
◼ Semi-Public Open Space

CIRCULATIONS
◻ Roads
◻ Cycle lane-pedestrian

HOUSE TYPES & PLOTS
◻ Type A1 & A2
◻ Type B
◻ Type C
◻ Type D1 & D2
◼ Type E
◻ Creche+ Retails
◼ Community Hall

73

Development at Scalaheen, Tipperary

MCO Projects

The master plan for lands at Scalaheen was developed from MCO Projects' winning RIAI competition entry in 2006 and a subsequent commission by Tipperary Town Council in 2007. The Council's brief was to find a new solution to medium-density housing in a rural, edge-of-town location.

In June 2008 the master plan was adopted within the context of the Tipperary Town and Environs Development Plan 2007. The master plan and development brief will provide the framework for any future planning applications on the Scalaheen lands.

The master plan is for a site of 25.9 hectares located to the south-west of Tipperary town. It aims to:
– provide a framework for an integrated and viable addition to the town's urban, social and economic fabric that respects the existing landscape and the wider environment, creating a positive identity for the area
– address the demand for one-off houses in the countryside by providing an attractive alternative that provides many of the characteristics desired in one-off houses
– provide safe and secure environments for a mix of family types in the middle-income bracket
– to include provision for children and the elderly.

The site layout follows closely the existing contours and hedgerows in order to minimise the impact of the development on the landscape. Clusters of courtyard and terraced houses around home zones will engender a sense of community and a strong sense of place.

design / completion – 2005–
    (announced as joint-winner 2006; MCO subsequently appointed to develop master plan)
client – Tipperary Town Council

———

↑ Diagrams showing
(top) context, site plan, public space
(bottom) private space, home zones, movement and access

height	mix	percentage	no. of dwellings	site area	density	floor area	bed spaces	site coverage	open space	car spaces	context
1-2 storey	188 houses 22 social and affordable	96% residential 4% community	210	64 acres	3.2 units/acre	30,000m² approx	680	11%	170,000m²	52 for community centre	rural edge-of-town location

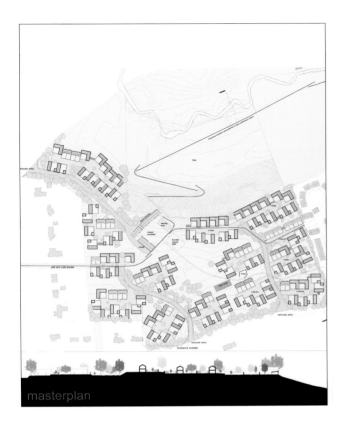

↑ Master plan
↗ View from parkland
↗ Sketch and computer perspectives of housing cluster
↓ Typical cluster-house plans

masterplan

75

Residential Development at Waterfall, Co Cork

O'Mahony Pike Architects

This is envisaged as a low-density, landscape-based and energy-conscious scheme which fully integrates with its rural village context whilst fulfilling a demand for larger detached houses in close proximity to Cork city. The 10.5-hectare site comprises three fields, with a gently sloping topography and triangular geometry. It is located in the village of Waterfall, about 1km from the city boundary and within the metropolitan greenbelt. It is bounded by a public house and farmyard to the south-west, a recent suburban-style development to the north-west, the village to the west, and farmland to the south and east.

The agricultural characteristics of the site, with its hedgerows, drainage channels and adjacent farmyard, suggested the use of traditional Irish field patterns as a model for the subdivision of the lands. This resulted in an organic arrangement of housing clusters around cul-de-sac roads. These generally comprise between three and six dwellings, and are intended to create identifiable community groups. The landscaping in the cul-de-sac is designed so that, while all road engineering requirements are accommodated, planting and surface treatment bring a certain informality to the spaces and allow them to be considered as semi-public courtyards to the surrounding dwellings. Clustering of volumes, which is a significant feature of settlement in the rural landscape, is also used to define space in the individual house plots, thus fragmenting the size of the 42 large dwellings.

There are four main house types in the scheme, ranging from 250m² to 345m², each with a separate garage. The design

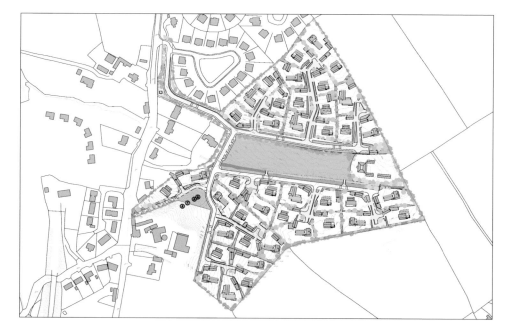

of the buildings draws on the scale, form, language and materials of vernacular rural architecture. The pitched-roof forms and occasional barrel-vaulted roof are familiar in the Cork landscape. Walls are of painted render, and roofs are of natural slate and metal (zinc). Dry stone walling and planted earthen bank boundaries complete the limited palette of materials and complement the existing hedgerows, which have been retained and used to define housing areas and public open space in the scheme.

The development proposes a hierarchy of open spaces – public space, cul-de-sac, parking courts and private gardens. The primary open space is a linear strip of land, defined to the north by an existing hedgerow and to the south by the existing stream, with a large house to the east providing a focal point. Another public open space is located around the cypress trees in the southern field.

Houses have been designed to benefit from passive solar-gain, with living spaces opening onto south-facing gardens. In addition, active measures such as increased insulation and heat-recovery systems have been used in order to achieve a favourable energy-rating for the houses. This project complies with the requirements of the proposed part L regulation.

design / completion – 2006–2008 (Phase 1)
    (future phases on hold)
client – John Fleming Construction Ltd

↖ Aerial view of site
↑ Site model
← Overall site plan

height	mix	percentage	no. of dwellings	site area	density	floor area	bed spaces	site coverage	open space	car spaces	context
2 storey	41 x 5-bed houses 1 x 6-bed houses 3 offices	100% residential	42	10.5 ha (26 acres)	4 units/ha (1.6/acre)	18,106m²	422	10%	1.5 ha (2.84 acres) 10.9% of site	217	village

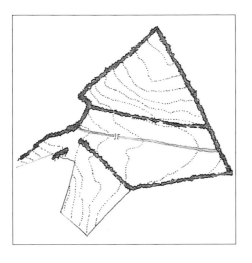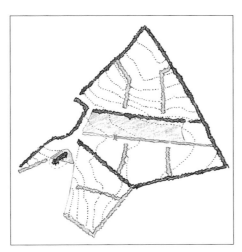

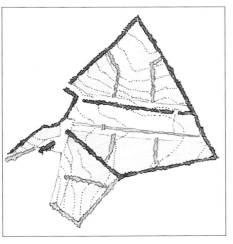

Part L	Building Energy Rating	Carbon Dioxide Emission Rate	
2007	**A3**	**± 17kg** of CO_2 per square metre per annum	
Building Envelope Specification:			
Ground Floor	Concrete suspended groundfloors 90mm screed on 110mm Polyurethane insulation on reinforced concrete slab on blinding, hardcore etc. Underfloor heating requires lower value.		**U-value** **0.15 W/m²K.**
External wall	Fusion steel frame wall, 92mm steel stud filled with fire retarded, EPS insulation fused between and outside the studs, resulting in 162mm Expanded Polystyrene insulation 50mm cavity and 100mm rendered blockwork outer leaf		**U-value** **0.21 W/m²K.**
Main Roof	Natural slate pitched ventilated roof with pre-fab timber trusses. 150mm Polyurethane insulation between joists and 60mm Polyurethane insulated plasterboard under joists		**U-value** **0.13 W/m²K.**
Flat roofs – hallway and porch	Selected roof covering on Warm deck roof with 160mm average polyurethane insulation .		**U-value** **0.15 W/m²K.**
Windows + Doors	High Quality aluminium/timber composite window system in some cases triple glazing. Must have manufacturer's specified ratings certified in accordance with IS EN ISO 10077		**U-value** **1.40W/m²K**
Air tightness	Air tightness to a high standard and tested to 4m³/H/m²		**4m³/H/m²** **(or 0.2Ac)**
Building Services Specification:			
Heating	Condensing boiler oil heating, boiler located externally in garage		**97% efficiency**
Secondary	All chimneys replaced with fully sealed log burning/gas units with balanced flues.		**70% efficiency**
Details	Underfloor heating with radiators upstairs. Control system to be by thermostatic radiator valves, thermostatic zone control on underfloor heating and thermostatic control on hot water system.		
Hot water	Condensing boiler oil		**97% efficiency**
Secondary	Electric Immersion		**electric**
Solar heating – renewable technology	Glazed Flat panel to maximum beneficial size 6 m² aperture area. 62% of required renewables (design calculations)		**6.2 kWh/m²/yr hot water**
Details	Insulated cylinder with thermostatic control and pumped water system.		
Ventilation	Whole house heat recovery mechanical ventilation system installed, with specified manufacturer's data.		**HRMV**
Low energy lighting	Amount of low energy lighting outlets (i.e. all lighting outlets low energy)		**100%**
Additional Renewable technologies	Photo Voltaic panels additional to the solar water heating, as the capacity of hot water required has been met. 37% of required renewables (design calculations)		**1.55 kWh/m²/yr electricity**

BUILDING ENERGY RATING A3

↑ Site plan showing (a) existing site conditions
(b) insertion of open space and new landscape
into existing site
(c) development areas within new and existing
landscape

↑ Phase 1 site plan (5 houses)
↓ Views of Phase 1 nearing completion

↑ A3 building energy rating

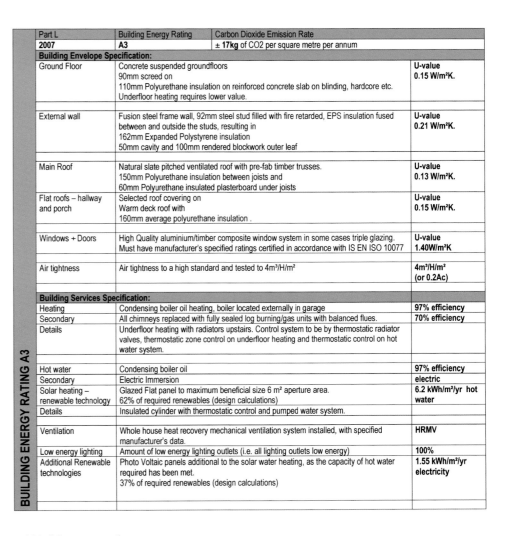

Whitechurch Village Extension, Co Cork

Reddy O'Riordan Staehli Architects

Fundamental to the development of a master plan for Whitechurch village was the decision that the design should evolve from the existing and historical fabric of the village. Roads, cycle ways and footpaths follow the lines of existing laneways and ditches, thus allowing the topography to generate the layout of the master plan. The existing village centre is reinforced and revitalised by the creation of a new village square, whose edges are drawn by the existing traditional farm buildings now to be restored for retail and accommodation uses. House design draws upon traditional and contemporary themes, retaining the character of the village while providing an attractive and modern living environment.

The first phase of this project consisted of developing three sites within the development boundary of the village. The first site lies to the north of the village centre on a south-facing hillside, with panoramic views towards Cork city and accommodates detached, low-density housing. The second site lies to the south, adjoining the main approach road from Cork, and consists of a mix of detached, semi-detached and terraced houses. The third site lies between the two – linked via a cyclepath and footpath – and is the location for a childcare facility. Later development in this area will see the provision of flexible retail and office units, community facilities, apartments and higher-density housing arranged around a new village square.

design / completion – 2004–2010
    (Phase 1 completed 2008)
*client*s – DBW Construction Ltd

↑ Phase 1 – views of north (top) and south sites
← Master plan

opposite

↗ Views of courtyard and open space
→ Plans and elevations (type A)
⇥ Plans and elevations (type G)
↓ South site – view to north-west and street view

height	mix	percentage	no. of dwellings	site area	density	floor area	bed spaces	site coverage	open space	car spaces	context
1.5-2 storey	7 x 5-bed houses 53 x 4-bed houses 51 x 3-bed houses 14 x 2-bed houses 6 x 3-bed apartments	94% residential 6% crèche	131	7.4 ha (18.3 acres)	17.7 units/ha (7.16/acre)	16,315m² (+ crèche 569m²)	460 (62.1/ha; 25.13/acre)	7%	14%	328 (2-3 per dwelling + visitor spaces)	rural village setting

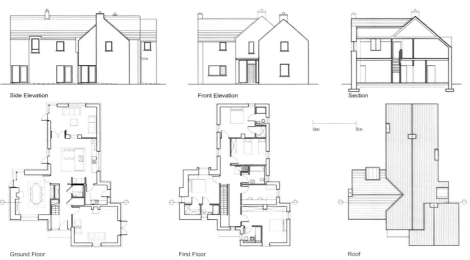

Side Elevation

Front Elevation

Section

0m   5m

Ground Floor

First Floor

Roof

Front Elevation

0m   5m

Side Elevation

Section B-B

Ground Floor

First Floor

Roof

Mixed-use Development at Dunshaughlin, Co Meath

Collins Maher Martin

The site is on the eastern side of Main Street, Dunshaughlin, on the heavily trafficked N3. The brief was to provide a mixed-use town-centre development comprising shops, offices and apartments, while retaining the existing 18th-century house. Urban-design considerations included:
– the formation and continuation of a defined street edge
– opening up the back of the site to form a viable public space
– development at an appropriate scale in relation to the existing streetscape.

The project is an arrangement of five elements – the existing house; a two-storey structure to the rear containing four shop units at ground-floor level with four apartments overhead; two buildings containing retail/commercial units at either side of the old house, all joined by a single-storey flat-roofed area to the rear of the house.

The existing house is located in the middle of the site fronting onto Main Street. As a result, the new development wraps around the old building and bookends it with two structures. These two structures are set apart from the old house, which allows its original stand-alone form to be read, resulting in two external corridors – one forming a separate entrance to offices at first-floor level, the other offering a glimpse straight through to the apartment entrances behind.

address – Supple House, Main Street, Dunshaughlin, Co Meath
design / completion – 2003–2006
client – Pat Delaney

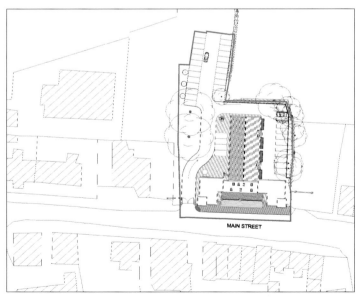

MAIN STREET

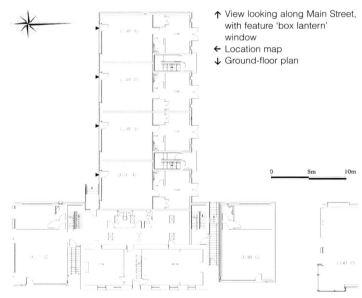

↑ View looking along Main Street, with feature 'box lantern' window
← Location map
↓ Ground-floor plan

height	mix	percentage	no. of dwellings	site area	density	floor area	bed spaces	site coverage	open space	car spaces	context
2 storey	4 x 2-bed apartments 6 shops 3 offices	20% residential 80% commercial	4	2,561m² (0.63 acres)	6.3 units/acre (residential) 20.6 units/acre (total)	1,279m²	12 (19/acre)	25%	390m² at ground level 4 x 5m² private balconies	36 (1.5 per dwelling; remainder for commercial)	main street in town centre

Detached Housing at Inchinattin Cross, Clonakilty

Mike Shanahan + Associates

New draft Local Area Plans for most small unsewered villages and settlement nuclei have been published by local authorities. These typically state that 'All new development should be low density subject to proper planning and sustainable development, connected to the existing water supply and provide individual sewerage treatment facilities to the satisfaction of the area engineer.'

Local authorities do not have the resources to plan and construct small treatment systems for the many hundreds of small settlements across this country. Individual one-offs are currently seen as the affordable way forward. The challenge therefore is to devise and develop more attractive ways of arranging our buildings within that framework.

DEVELOPMENT PATTERN 'A'

This is an example of the type of development pattern of the past. It assumes substantial growth, which is unlikely to happen in reality because of current fairly relaxed planning policies for scattered one-off houses in the surrounding countryside. Its purpose is to contrast with Development Pattern 'B'.

It highlights how and why our former ways of developing settlements were so successful in creating places with a very strong sense of place and, in the process, a strong sense of community. By placing buildings in a manner so that they relate to the road, to approaching vistas, and to each other, space is enclosed and small streets and a square are made, all of which enhance the visual amenity and living

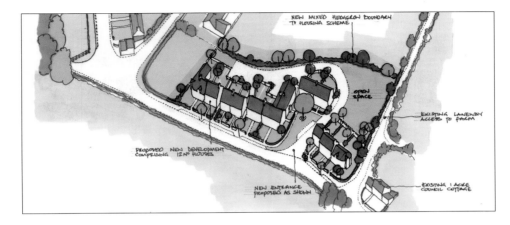

environment for residents and visitors alike. Cars and traffic are secondary, but could, with imagination and a village traffic-management strategy, be accommodated in most instances.

DEVELOPMENT PATTERN 'B'

This is the type of development pattern we are currently seeing and that, in some respects, our planning system is actively promoting.

Engineering issues and the individual now predominate. Each house has its own treatment system. The supremacy of the car rules uncontested. Roads are widened, rural ditches destroyed. Prescribed turning circles and sightlines are achieved. Numbers of new vehicular entrances are minimised. Large car-parking and turning areas are located out front for the convenience of the drivers.

New buildings are deeply set back from the road and isolated from their

neighbours. Each has its own cocooned environment. Cul-de-sac developments, preferably with security-access controls, prevail. The new residents aspire to live in gated communities. Older, existing buildings of former diverse uses are demolished to facilitate replacement houses. Most buildings are for residential use only.

The physical environment does not lend itself to encouraging the incidental day-to-day contacts essential to making strong communities. There is little or no sense of place here anymore. It could be anywhere. This is the future.

AMENDED PLANNING PROPOSAL

This amended scheme for housing at Inchinattin Cross strives to retain the objectives of the first scheme whilst seeking to find a way to meet the prescribed requirements of lower-density housing with individually sewered treatment facilities to each house.

The solution in this instance is to maintain the layout, using detached houses to make an 'edge' extension to the settlement. Sewerage treatment is placed at a remove from the houses in separate gardens. Remote gardens are not an uncommon solution in housing of the past or allotment garden models prevalent elsewhere. If the settlement grows substantially, a mains treatment system can be installed and densities increased.

The revised proposal is for seven houses, in four house types, all different but given similar treatment in order to provide cohesiveness to the scheme. Roof spans are narrow and similar in all houses to make some economies. House sizes range from small to medium size, with options to add single-storey sunrooms and first-floor bedrooms.

CONCLUSION

We contend that current planning policies are making it extremely difficult to create physically rich living environments in these areas. Engineering requirements compound matters enormously and make it even more difficult to gather buildings in an attractive fashion.

if we are to value and enhance our smaller villages and crossroads, questions need to be asked as to whether there are alternatives, and how we can achieve them.

address – Clonakilty, Co Cork
design / completion – 2004–2007
client – private

height	mix	percentage	no. of dwellings	site area	density	floor area	bed spaces	site coverage	open space	car spaces	context
2 storey	12 x 3-bed houses 2 x 2-bed houses	100% residential	14	6,300m² (1.55 acres)	9 units/acre	1,278m²	40 (26/acre)	12%	1,749m² public	2.7 per dwelling	rural site adjacent to existing crossroads development

THE PROBLEM

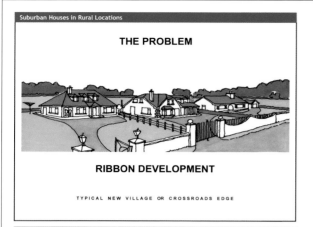

RIBBON DEVELOPMENT

TYPICAL NEW VILLAGE OR CROSSROADS EDGE

PLANNING PROPOSAL LIKELY TO SUCCEED

DETACHED HOUSES ON OWN SITES WITH INDIVIDUAL TREATMENT SYSTEMS
PER PLANNING POLICIES

PLANNING PROPOSAL LIKELY TO SUCCEED

LOW DENSITY INDIVIDUAL ONE-OFF'S WITH OWN TREATMENT SYSTEMS
PER PLANNING POLICIES

INCHINATTIN CROSS, CLONAKILTY
– unsuccessful planning proposal

UNSUCCESSFUL PLANNING PROPOSAL

HOUSING SCHEME AT INCHINATTIN, CLONAKILTY
SCALE 1:1000

DIRECT RELATIONSHIP WITH ROAD EXTENDS CROSSROADS EDGE

UNSUCCESSFUL PLANNING PROPOSAL

DIRECT RELATIONSHIP WITH ROAD EXTENDS CROSSROADS EDGE

DEVELOPMENT PATTERN 'A'
AS CROSSROADS MAY HAVE DEVELOPED IN THE PAST

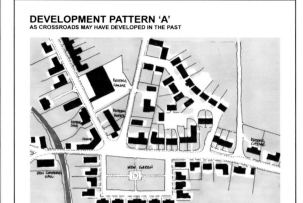

GOOD PLACE MAKING

- BUILDINGS ARRANGED IN A COHERENT FASHION, CONTAIN SPACE, RELATE WITH ROAD, CREATE VISTAS ETC.
- MAXIMISES COMMUNITY AMENITY

DEVELOPMENT PATTERN 'B'
AS CROSSROADS LIKELY TO DEVELOP TODAY

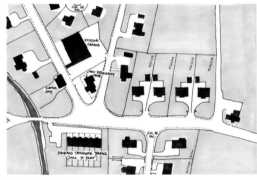

POOR PLACE MAKING

- LOW DENSITY, CAR DOMINATED, INDIVIDUALLY SEWERAGED 'ANYWHERE' HOUSES
- MAXIMISES INDIVIDUAL PRIVATE AMENITY

INCHINATTIN CROSS, CLONAKILTY
– amended planning proposal

AMENDED PLANNING PROPOSAL

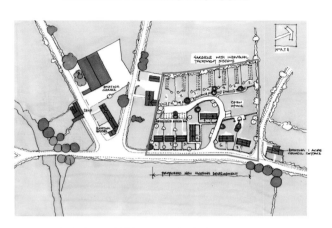

HOUSING SCHEME AT INCHINATTIN, CLONAKILTY
SCALE 1:1000

REVISED SCHEME OF DETACHED HOUSES ARRANGED TO EXTEND EDGE

REAR

FIRST FLOOR PLAN

WEST

FRONT

GROUND FLOOR PLAN

EAST

HOUSES 4 & 5 - TYPE C

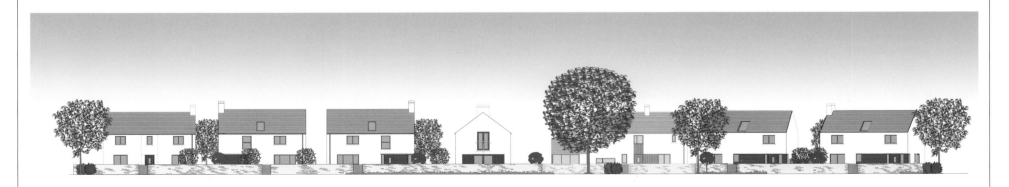

Residential Development at Cunningham Road, Dalkey Denis Byrne Architects

The development site is located to the rear of 'Santa Maria', a large Victorian house on Cunningham Road, listed as a protected structure in the County Development Plan. The site itself is accessed via a new entrance from Cunningham Drive at the rear of 13 Cunningham Road.

The sloping site has a certain romantic *rus in urbe* quality, like a 'lost' garden. Encompassing the former gardens of Santa Maria, it is over 150m long and is situated over 30m from the house. The architectural strategy proposed accepts the nature of the place as a landscaped garden, and seeks to integrate the new buildings into the garden to form a synthesis of building and landscape, with the landscape predominant. The buildings become pavilions in a new garden of terraces, steps, planting, trees and levels.

A line of terraced mews dwellings, whose form and materials are intended to complement the house, spatially demarcates the limit of Santa Maria's large rear garden (formerly a lawn tennis court) from the remainder of the landholding. In addition to these mews houses, ten detached houses and nine apartments are proposed, arranged as a dispersed cluster of buildings. These have been designed to maximise exposure to the south and the sun whilst providing discrete and carefully chosen views to the north and the sea.

A height limit has been imposed on the site in order to ensure a good 'fit' of the various new buildings into the surrounding context. An upper datum level of 7.5 m above the natural slope of the land fixes the roof

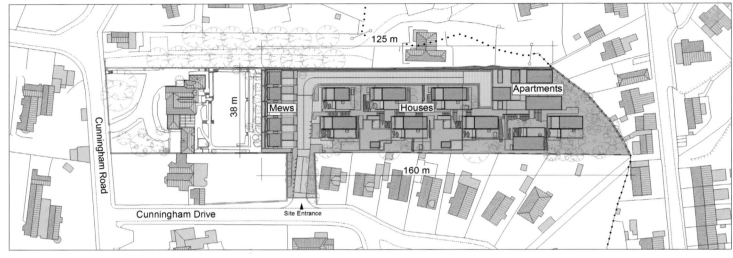

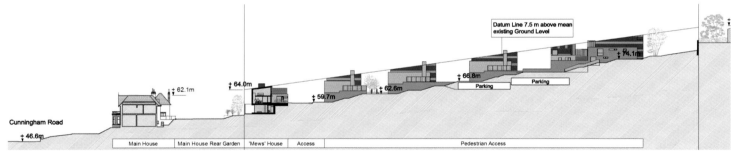

levels of all the new buildings as they step down the hill. This datum line is in keeping with the average height of dwellings in the surrounding area.

Advantage is also taken of the natural slope of the land. The slope is 1:7, or a storey height every 20m, to allow the buildings to nestle into the hill, using efficient semi-basement areas to accommodate bedrooms and the smaller

service rooms. This allows the visible above-ground built forms to emerge from the landscape as relatively small pavilion-like volumes. These volumes contain the main living areas and are designed as large light-filled, airy spaces with good access to the adjoining external private terraces.

The materials proposed for the interior of the houses will also be used externally in

order to blur the distinction between inside and outside.

address – Dalkey, Co Dublin
design / completion – 2006–
    (project suspended)
client – Otranto Properties Ltd

↑ Location map and section through site
→ Plans, section and elevation of typical house
⇒ Views of (top) single- and 2-storey houses

height	mix	percentage	no. of dwellings	site area	density	floor area	bed spaces	site coverage	open space	car spaces	context
1-3 storeys	8 x 3-bed houses 7 x 2-bed houses 1 x 3-bed duplex 6 x 2-bed apartments 2 x 1-bed apartments	100% residential	24	5,904m² (0.59ha)	40 units/ha	2,942m²	55	28%	1,350m² public 1,043m² private	45 (1.75/unit)	suburban infill in elevated coastal location, with views of Dublin Bay

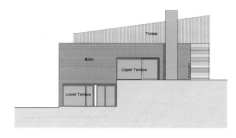

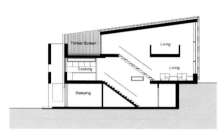

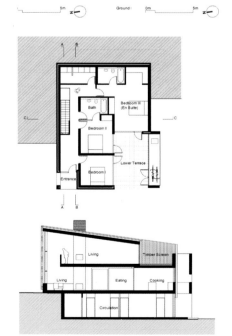

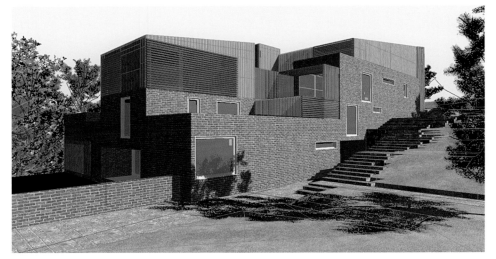

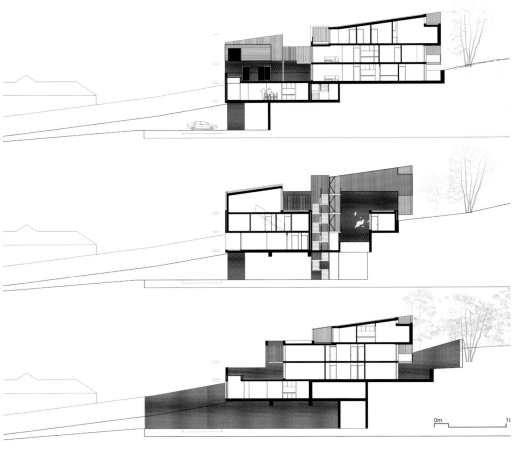

CUNNINGHAM ROAD, DALKEY

↖ from top: Mews houses, apartments, standard house

↑ Sections through apartments

Apartment plans
→ – 2nd floor
↘ – 1st floor
↓ – ground floor

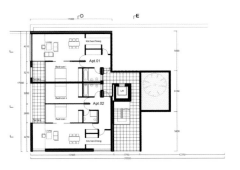

St Gerald's Court, Urban Infill Scheme, Ballyhaunis

MV Cullinan Architects

St Gerald's Court is located on the former Fair Green site near the town centre. The scheme is organised as a perimeter block to an existing telephone exchange building established on the site earlier. This site strategy allowed the edges of the site to be freed up to provide a series of public and semi-private spaces which connect to the urban plan of the town.

An existing building on Main Street was retained and refurbished as duplex apartments over a community resource centre. The adjacent street was closed to traffic to create a small paved plaza, laid out facing the church.

The existing line of mature trees along the western boundary provides a strong, well-defined edge to the courtyard located at the upper section of the site. The slope in the site suggested split-level family houses with living areas rooms above, overlooking the courtyard and bedrooms located below at garden level.

A new street of townhouses leads from this courtyard down to the plaza opposite the church. These houses face south towards the church. The rear of the buildings along Main Street are screened by a rubble stone wall, which forms the backdrop to the new plaza. A terrace of single-storey dwellings is located south of the telephone exchange to knit in with the estate alongside. The external walls are lime-dash with slate roofs and timber windows.

address – Ballyhaunis, Co Mayo
design / completion – 2002–2005
client – Mayo County Council

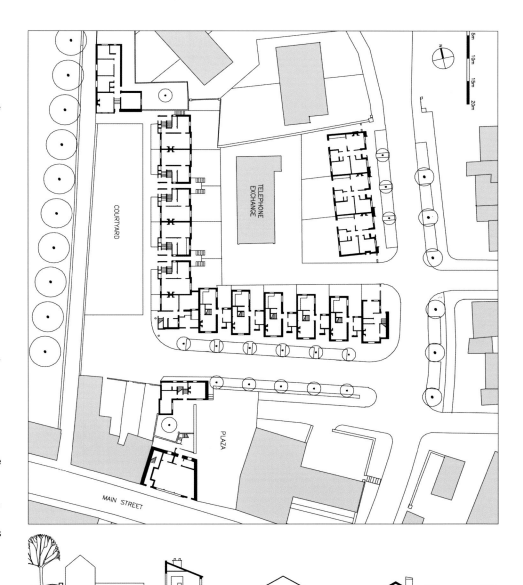

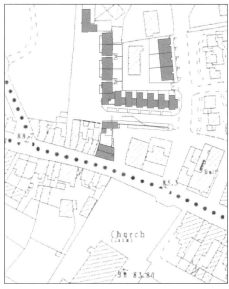

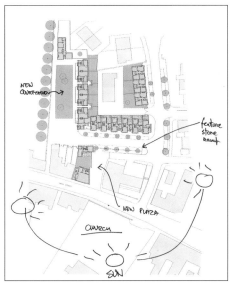

height	mix	percentage	no. of dwellings	site area	density	floor area	bed spaces	site coverage	open space	car spaces	context
1-2 storey	4 x 3-bed houses 8 x 2-bed houses 4 x 2/3-bed bungalows 2 x 3-bed duplexes	95% residential 5% communal	18	0.85 acres (0.35 ha)	22 units/acre (48 units/ha)	1,456m²	70	28%	17% in plaza and courtyard	15	backland site in centre of town

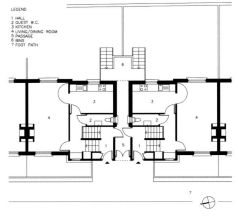

LEGEND

1 HALL
2 GUEST W.C.
3 KITCHEN
4 LIVING/DINING ROOM
5 PASSAGE
6 BINS
7 FOOT PATH

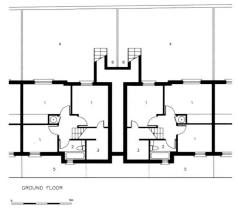

GROUND FLOOR

ST GERALD'S COURT, BALLYHAUNIS

↑ Courtyard housing
⇇ from top:
  Route via plaza to church
  Single-storey terrace of special needs housing
  Courtyard houses
← Ground and 1st-floor plans of duplex units
↙ Axonometric of entrance hall
↓ Town houses

opposite

→ Views of new street (top), plaza and townhouses
→ Elevations of single-storey special needs housing and 2-storey townhouses

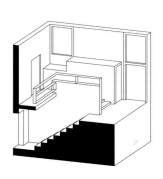

AXONOMETRIC OF ENTRANCE HALL

Hunter's Court, Ashbourne, Co Meath

Cooney Architects

Ashbourne has developed as a linear village along the N2, to become the second largest town in Co Meath. Bachelors Walk leads from the junction of the recently developed urban square, south of Frederick Street, and the new high street (Killegland Street).

This development forms the south-eastern corner of a new transitional urban / suburban block at the junction of Bachelors Walk and Hunters Lane. Our brief was to integrate a commercial and residential development into this context, and to create a block relating to both the urban street and the suburban road.

Block A contains ground-floor commercial units addressing the urban context, and three-bedroom duplex apartments accessed from the rear courtyard. These apartments are dual-aspect, with full-width kitchen / dining / living rooms at first floor, north-facing bay windows, and large, shaded south-facing balconies.

The architectural expression of Block B reflects the urban block transition. One-bedroom apartments at ground floor and three-bedroom duplex apartments above are accessed from ground-floor level. Kitchen / dining / living areas are located at top-floor level to provide large balconies to the front and rear.

Block C contains gallery-access duplex apartments with car-parking at courtyard level. The block creates a sense of enclosure to courtyard, and is single-aspect to screen further development.

On north-facing elevations, glazed areas

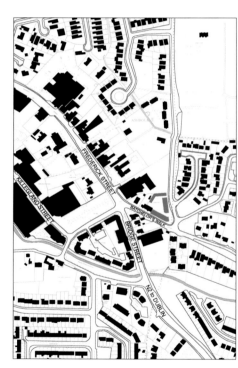

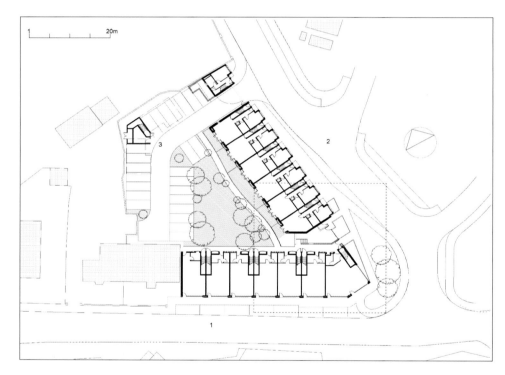

are reduced and bay windows are used to catch morning and late evening light. The east elevation aspires to achieve a generous secure threshold space at ground floor. The overall two storey with a set-back form respects the built scale on the opposite side of Hunters Lane.

The overall architectural expression reflects function and environmental intent by utilising deep overhanging eaves, recessed usable balconies, reflective and solid elevations, alternation of materials, tactile surfaces, and accessible shop fronts. The enclosed courtyard forms a

communal open space, expressing and reflecting the vibrancy of urban living.

design / completion – 2004–2006
client – C&M Holdings

→ Part-plans – ground, 1st, 2nd-floor

height	mix	percentage	no. of dwellings	site area	density	floor area	bed spaces	site coverage	open space	car spaces	context
3-4 storey	11 x 3-bed duplexes 4 x 2-bed apartments 8 x 1-bed apartments 7 retail units	84% residential 16% commercial	23	2,513m² (0.6 acres)	c.50 units/acre	2,396m²	49	39%	350m² (c.0.08 acres)	24	urban corner site on Bachelor's Walk and Hunter's Lane

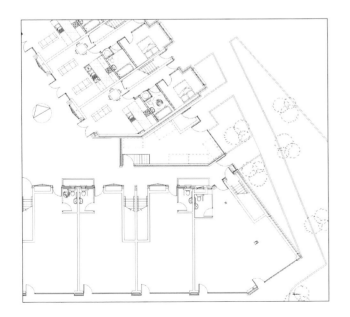
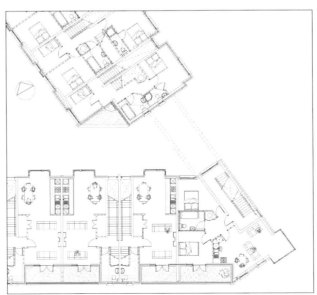

Market Lane Development, Westport

Cox Power & Associates

In order to provide for the expansion of the town into the new millennium, Westport UDC commissioned an Integrated Action Area Plan in 2000, which detailed the physical nature of the expansion as opposed to the traditional zoning. The proposal suggested that the interior of large blocks within the town should be opened up for development and connect to the existing streets. Living accommodation should be provided as part of this strategy.

Market Lane is the first phase of a new street running from the town's main street down to the river. The laneway consists of shops on the ground floor and apartments overhead. The individual elements of the building are expressed to reflect the traditional scale of Westport's streetscapes, thus eschewing a 'big building' in the town centre. Living rooms have been placed on the top floor to take advantage of the large volume of roof space and to maximise natural light. All apartments are provided with private open space in the form of balconies, large enough to accommodate tables and chairs. Semi-public open space is also provided in the form of a shared landscaped roof terrace over the shops. Linkage to the newly formed Brewery Lane and final landscaping works were completed in 2008.

address – Bridge Street, Westport, Co Mayo
design / completion – 1997–2004
client – Thomas S Joyce & Sons Ltd

↗ Aerial photo showing pedestrian permeability and urban sub-spaces
↗ Bird's-eye perspective, with Market Lane outlined
→ Master plan with Market Lane outlined

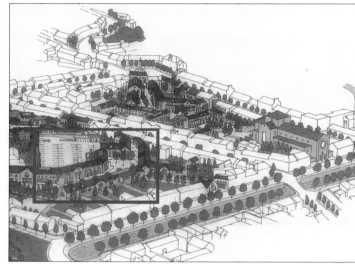

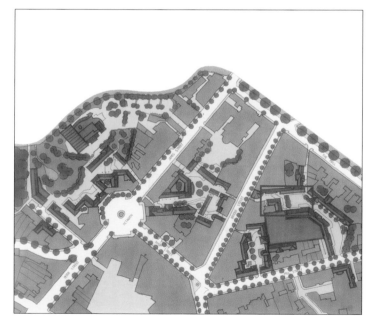

height	mix	percentage	no. of dwellings	site area	density	floor area	bed spaces	site coverage	open space	car spaces	context
3 storey	9 duplex apartments 9 retail units	56% residential 44% commercial	9	0.32 acres	28 units/acre	1,342m²	27	45.5%	13% in roof terrace 4m² private balconies	41	town centre urban infill

↑ Street corner on Market Lane
→ Evening view of Market Lane
↘ Apartment levels – 1st-floor plan (with raised terrace) and 2nd-floor plan
↘ Rear elevation
↓ Retail level – ground-floor plan with retail units opening off pedestrian areas

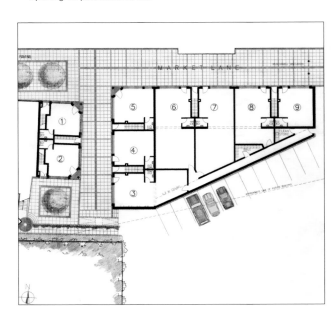

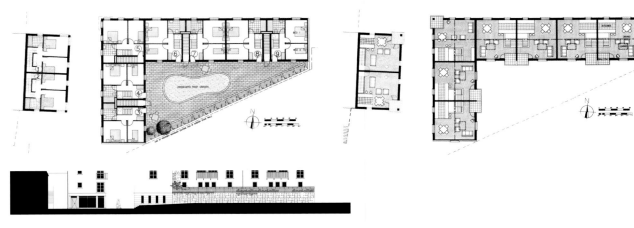

Kilmeena Village, Co Mayo

Cox Power Architects

A new village centre is proposed for Kilmeena, a townland with a dispersed population. Instead of the typical mono-use housing estate, there is a mix of house types, a crèche and community centre, forming a vibrant village centre. The layout is based on the traditional cluster of grouped farm buildings or *clochán*. The informality of the *clochán* is considered more appropriate than the formal street planning of a typical town or village. It allows the integration of buildings with the surrounding landscape, and the informal set-backs create organic sheltered communal spaces and neighbourhood meeting points.

Phase 1 consists of affordable housing and a community centre. House design is traditional in form but contemporary in detail. Roofspaces are inhabited to reduce built volumes. Downstairs bedrooms can accommodate elderly residents. Southern elevations have large glazed areas to increase passive solar-gain, and living spaces are triple-aspect to maximise light. The hall of the community centre is screened by a two-storey edge to the street. Visible elevations are fully fenestrated to avoid blank street elevations. Landscape elements such as stone walls, screens and garden buildings provide screening and visual interest.

address – Kilmeena, Westport, Co Mayo
design / completion – 2006–2009
client – Mayo County Council

↗ Bird's-eye perspective of development
  (with community centre at top right)
→ Aerial view of location
↠ Elevations of community centre

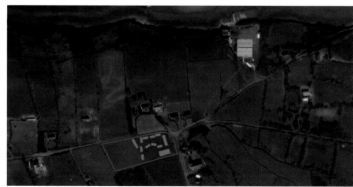

NORTHWEST

height	mix	percentage	no. of dwellings	site area	density	floor area	bed spaces	site coverage	open space	car spaces	context
1-2 storey	1 x 4-bed house 8 x 3-bed houses 5 x 2-bed houses	76% residential	14	2.78 acres (gross) 1.08 acres (net, after proprietary treatment unit)	5 units/acre	1,552m²	67	6%	4,659m²	24	village location

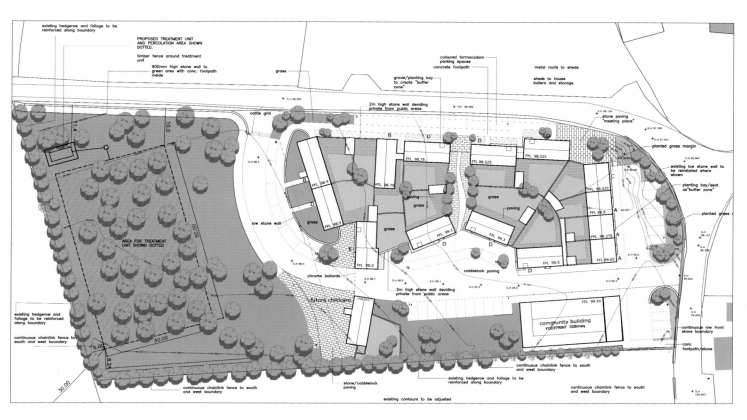

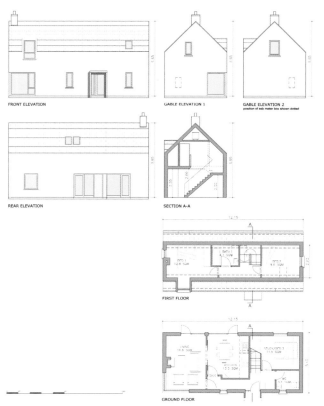

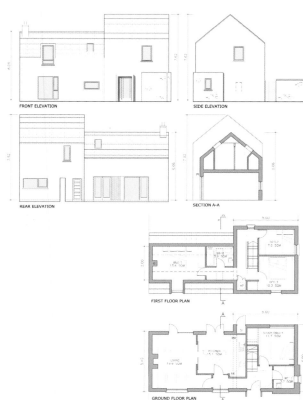

↑ Aerial view of site
↗ Site plan
→ Plans and elevations (house types B, D, E)

95

Old Tramyard Site, Castle Street, Dalkey, Co Dublin

HKR Architects

The Old Tramyard Site redevelopment has been designed to integrate with Dalkey village centre, with the courtyard/tramyard becoming an extension of the public domain of Castle Street and permanently accessible from it.

The development, providing for a mix of uses in line with the area development plan, will include 23 apartments and a commercial/retail space in three three-storey blocks, arranged around an open courtyard, all over a basement car park. The design includes new hard and soft landscaping works. The existing tramlines, along with gate piers, gates and cobble stones within the yard, are deemed protected structures and will be retained.

The general building forms and height are designed to be in character and sympathetic to the location in a conservation area. The building forms are based on pitched slate roofs with gable ends: on the site perimeter, the elevations are pitched roofs with straightforward window treatment; on the courtyard side, the elevations are contemporary in nature.

A small palette of materials – including rendered walls, timber cladding and slate roofs – is used in a contemporary manner.

design / completion – 2005–2010
*client*s – J & P Monaghan / R Sheils

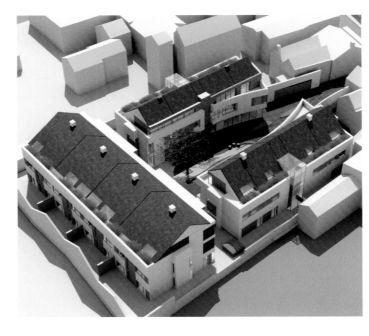

↗ Location map and model
➤➤ Elevations and sections through the development

height	mix	percentage	no. of dwellings	site area	density	floor area	bed spaces	site coverage	open space	car spaces	context
3 storey	19 x 2-bed apartments 4 x 1-bed apartments commercial + retail units	94% residential 6% commercial	23	0.57 acres (0.23 ha)	40 units/acre	2,525m² (+1,235m² basement carpark)	84 (147/acre)	38%	787m² at ground level; also private balconies and terraces	29 (1.25 per dwelling)	courtyard housing on a compact site in a conservation area

SECOND FLOOR

0 1   5   10 METER

FIRST FLOOR

↑ 1st and 2nd-floor plans
↗ View towards Castle Street (top), and of courtyard
↓ Ground-floor plan

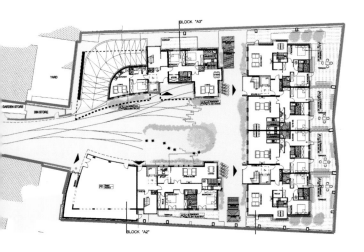

Social Housing, Loughrea, Co Galway

Paul Keogh Architects

This 28-unit housing development is located on a greenfield site at the western edge of Loughrea. The one-hectare site slopes by almost six meters to the public road at its southern boundary. The brief was to design a medium density (24 units per hectare) social-housing development, including two special-needs units for members of the travelling community. The design aspires to establish a strong sense of place, which would be conducive to the creation of an attractive, secure and well-landscaped residential enclave.

From a range of preliminary studies, the selected option consists of two courtyards enclosed by two-storey housing terraces, therefore maximising passive surveillance and contributing to safety and security for residents, especially children. The wide-frontage unit types, with special corner dwellings, ensure that each house has dual-aspect rooms with well-lit, sunny living spaces, irrespective of the orientation.

All houses have a generous private garden to the rear, which is accessed by a shared pen from the front. On-street car-parking is provided to the standards set out in the Galway County Development Plan.

design / completion – 2004–2007
client – Galway County Council

↗ Typical elevation
→ Site plan and section-elevation

opposite

→ Views of completed development, and typical floor plans

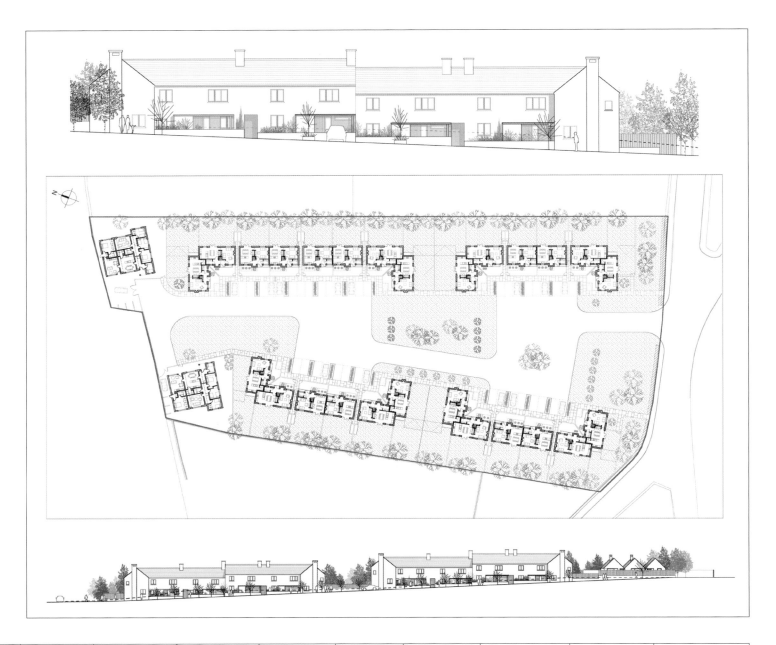

1-2 storey	2 x 5-bed houses 26 x 3-bed houses	100% residential	28	2.87 acres (1.16 ha)	10 units/acre (24 units/ha)	3,200m²	116 (40/acre)	13%	2.5 acres	40	greenfield site on the outskirts of a small town
height	mix	percentage	no. of dwellings	site area	density	floor area	bed spaces	site coverage	open space	car spaces	context

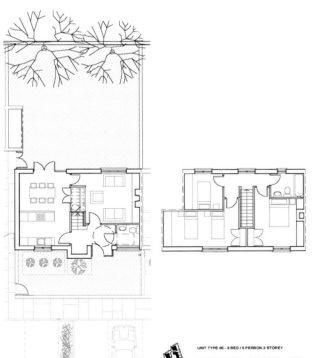

UNIT TYPE 06 - 3 BED / 5 PERSON 2 STOREY

SCHEDULE OF AREAS:	D.O.E. TARGET	ACTUAL
KITCHEN / DINING	14 SQ.M.	20 SQ.M.
LIVING ROOM	15 SQ.M.	15 SQ.M.
AGGREG. BEDROOM	29.2 SQ.M.	35.4 SQ.M.
GROSS FLOOR AREA	86 SQ.M.	91.2 SQ.M.

Ardrahan Housing, Ardrahan, Co Galway

Simon J Kelly & Partners

The project is the proposed development of fourteen housing units on the edge of Ardrahan village, located about 25km south-west of Galway city. The long teardrop-shaped site resulted from the construction of a new road from Galway to Ennis. The aim of the project is to integrate the scheme into the village of Ardrahan in a coherent manner rather than taking the usual approach of building a suburban development in open countryside.

The houses are grouped in two clusters of seven each. Such clustered arrangements are frequently seen in countryside farming environments. As such, they are designed to have façades of equal importance rather than the traditional arrangements of 'front' and 'back'. A streetscape is created onto the main road, giving access to a new pathway which runs back into the village centre.

The houses are a mixed arrangement of single, double and three to a terrace. They use traditional rural Irish forms, colours and materials, interpreted in a modern way. The development is within walking distance of the proposed western rail corridor, which will hopefully provide quick and easy access for commuters to nearby urban areas.

design / completion – 2005–
        (awaiting planning permission)
client – Luke McNamara

↗ Perspective view of scheme from village
→ Location map
↠ Ground and 1st-floor plans

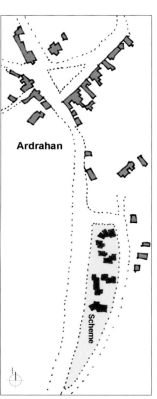

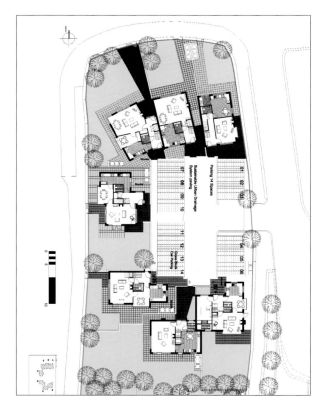

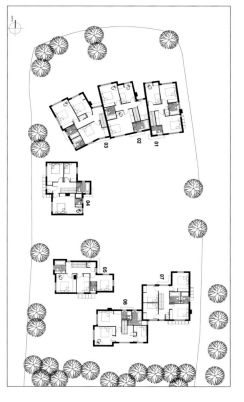

height	mix	percentage	no. of dwellings	site area	density	floor area	bed spaces	site coverage	open space	car spaces	context
2 storey	1 x 5-bed house 12 x 3-bed houses 1 x 2-bed house	100% residential	14	0.49 ha	28.4 units/ha	1,611m²	43	19%	2,525m² in private gardens and shared public spaces	28 (2 per dwelling)	edge of historic village 25km from Galway city; close to future western rail corridor

St Joseph's Court Sheltered Housing and Hostel, Gorey   Paul Keogh Architects

This project, commissioned by the Society of St Vincent de Paul, consists of two elements – the renovation and extension of a former Christian Brothers' monastery as a hostel for the elderly, and the development of the grounds to the rear to provide thirteen sheltered housing units.

The design focused on the making of a sheltered courtyard to provide a communal open space for the residents. The hostel and the houses look onto the courtyard, which has an existing mature tree as its centrepiece.

The housing consists of two terraces along the perimeter of the site. The single-storey terrace on the north side contains eight two-bedroom and one single-bedroom elderly people's housing units, while the two-storey terrace on the south side consists of four two-bedroom emergency housing units for the County Council. The hostel has eight bedrooms, plus social and ancillary facilities for the entire development.

Each house has a private open space, either to the rear of the terrace block or between the detached two-storey units. The hostel and houses are fully accessible, and meet all the relevant standards for disabled access and visitable housing.

The project received three national housing awards in 2005: the Irish Council for Social

---

↗ Section-elevation through courtyard
→ Site plan

height	mix	percentage	no. of dwellings	site area	density	floor area	bed spaces	site coverage	open space	car spaces	context
1-2 storey	4 x 2-bed houses 8 x 2-bed bungalows 2 x 1-bed bungalows 6 x 1-bed hostel units communal facilities building	63% residential 37% community units	20	2,370m² (0.675 acres)	30 units/acre (73 units/ha)	1,383m²	50 (74/acre)	42%	1,587m²	10 (0.5 per unit)	vacant urban backland site in the centre of an expanding town

Housing Community Housing Award;
Best Housing Project in the RIAI Regional
Awards, and winner of the OPUS
Architecture and Construction Awards.

address – St Michael's Road, Gorey,
    Co Wexford
design / completion – 2000–2005
client – Society of St Vincent de Paul

_____

opposite

← top:
  – 2-storey houses
  – Single-storey housing, with covered seating
    areas
  – Residents gather to chat
↙ bottom:
  – View of the courtyard between 2-storey houses
  – Looking north, with hostel on right
  – Looking south, with view of hostel

→ Courtyard, looking west
↘ Section-elevation to courtyard
↘ Plans of 2-storey house type
↓ Plan of single-storey house type

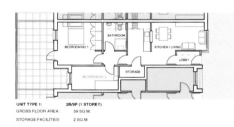

UNIT TYPE 1:   2B/3P (1 STOREY)
GROSS FLOOR AREA: 59 SQ.M.
STORAGE FACILITIES: 2 SQ.M.

FIRST FLOOR PLAN

Housing at Dunbo Hill, Howth, Dublin

Robin Mandal Architects

The brief was to intensify the use of the site while respecting its sensitivities and its importance to the landscape and the urban form of Howth. The two-acre site, located at the interface between the town and the Howth Estate, contained two houses – one from the 1930s and one from the 1970s.

The combined effect of the strategy used was to quadruple the density while minimising the spatial and visual impact. It involved
– extending the existing street into the site
– continuing the fragmentation at the edge of the town
– retaining the existing houses (considered a sustainability issue), making each into two houses, thus doubling the density
– constructing a further three houses, set into the landscape as pavilions.

The project was completed in three phases: i.e. making two houses out of the 1930s house; the construction of three new houses; and making two houses out of the 1970s house.

The design of the new houses arranges the dual-aspect living accommodation and master suites over two floors, taking advantage of the views northwards and the sun to the south and west. A single-storey wing to the south houses the remainder of the accommodation, facing west. For the existing buildings, the basic principles were the same, but the southern wings end in two-storey elements.

Materials are self-finished white lime render, elements of russet brickwork in a Flemish bond, dark-stained timber windows framing large areas of glass, anthracite

coloured pre-patinated zinc roofs, and light sandstone and gravel paving.

Each house responds differently to the site conditions, but the scheme is unified by a consistency of materials and approach.

name / address – Housing at Evora/Thulla, Dunbo Hill, Howth, Dublin 13
design / completion – 2003–2007
*client*s – Ballybrown Investments and Keverville Ltd

↑ Photomontage from Howth Harbour
↑ Site plan and conceptual sketch from the south

opposite

↗ Courtyard of house 1; house 2; Phase 1 from west
→ Plans of houses 1-2, houses 3-4-7, houses 5-6

height	mix	percentage	no. of dwellings	site area	density	floor area	bed spaces	site coverage	open space	car spaces	context
1-2 storey	3 x 5-bed houses 1 x 4-bed house 3 x 3-bed houses	100% residential	7	2.1 acres (0.85 ha)	3.3 units/acre (8 units/ha)	1,980m2	56 (28/acre)	23%	3,900m² private 1,400m² public	14 (2 per unit)	edge of town on a prominent, sensitive site overlooking harbour

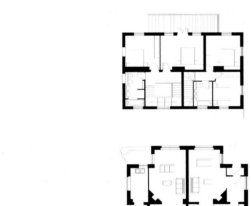

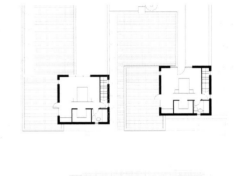
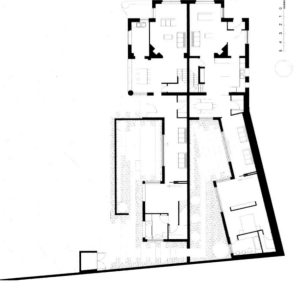
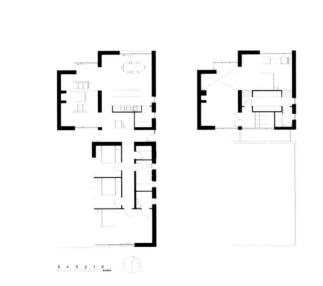

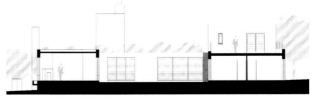

Bolton Green, Callan, Co Kilkenny

Fionnuala Rogerson Architects

Callan in Co Kilkenny, reputedly named after one of the High Kings of Ireland, was founded in the 13th century. It became the second largest fortified medieval town in the country before being captured by Cromwellian forces in 1650.

The site for this voluntary social housing scheme adjoins the southern medieval town boundary, and archaeological excavations during the course of construction revealed some significant remains of a possible medieval rampart and fosse along its boundary with Fair Green Lane. This impacted on vehicular access to some of the houses and on a proposed line of trees.

The scheme was designed with simple terraced houses around a communal village green and children's play area. The formal layout was reinforced with limestone walls and trees defining small open-plan front gardens. The approach to the landscaping of the front gardens was carefully considered and has proved successful. The majority of houses have traditional plan forms and all have south-facing rear gardens. Special house types were designed to deal with internal and external corners and to address the ends of terraces.

Feedback from the client and tenants has been very positive. The main problem has been insufficient car-parking due to unexpectedly high levels of car-ownership.

address – Fair Green Lane, Callan, Co Kilkenny
design / completion – 2000–2003
client – Cluid Housing Association

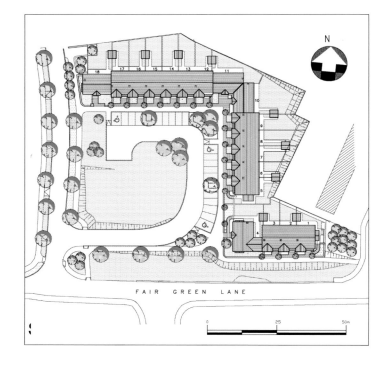

FAIR GREEN LANE

↑ Site plan
→ Plans of some of the different house types

opposite

→ Views of the completed scheme

ELEVATIONS (Nos. 1 TO 4)

GROUND FLOOR PLAN (Nos.10 & 11)

GROUND FLOOR PLAN (Nos. 5 & 6)   FIRST FLOOR PLAN (Nos. 5 & 6)

FIRST FLOOR

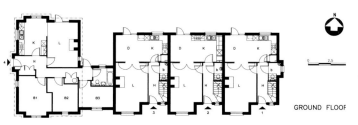

GROUND FLOOR

height	mix	percentage	no. of dwellings	site area	density	floor area	bed spaces	site coverage	open space	car spaces	context
1-2 storey	1 x 4-bed house 14 x 3-bed houses 3 x 2-bed houses	100% residential	18	7,332m² (1.8 acres)	10 units/acre	1,540m²	85 (48/acre)	n/a	3,137m² public (43%) 2,083m² private (116m²/unit)	1 per dwelling 3 wheelchair-accessible	edge of historic town

Riverside Development, Clonee, Co Meath

Sheridan Woods Architects

The Clonee Framework Plan was prepared for Meath County Council as the village had lost its identity as a gateway to Meath through the development of the N3 traversing the northern backlands of the village. The village's character was threatened by potential development on a substantial area of newly zoned residential land. The plan promoted the retention of the existing low scale of the main street, increased building height to the north facing the N3, and medium-scale development to the south. Precincts, character areas with suggested densities, building forms and materials were proposed for each area.

The Riverside development is located to the north-east of the village. It is defined by the N3 to the north, the river to the south, and a connection to the main street to the south and west. The proposal includes a network of streets that connect to the existing streets and permeate the site. The proposal opens up a riverside walk and a newly defined village space. Perimeter blocks provide open-sided, south-facing courtyards and dual-orientated residential units, and establish a strong and positive building form to the N3. The form, organisation and mix of uses, including residential, retail and office uses, create a potential vibrant living and working quarter in the village.

name / address – Riverside Residential and
    Mixed-Use Development, Clonee,
    Co Meath
design / completion – 2003; development
    not expected to commence due to
    infrastructure constraints
client – Maurice Regan

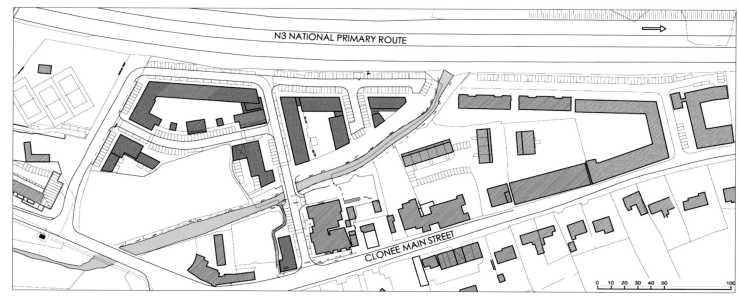

height	mix	percentage	no. of dwellings	site area	density	floor area	bed spaces	site coverage	open space	car spaces	context
1-4 storey	18 x 3-bed apts / duplexes 82 x 2-bed apts / duplexes 24 x 1-bed apartments retail units, office + crèche	93% residential 7% commercial	124	4.7 acres (1.9 ha)	26 units/acre	8,756m²	438	23%	6,352m² public	155 (1.25 per dwelling)	infill town centre backland site

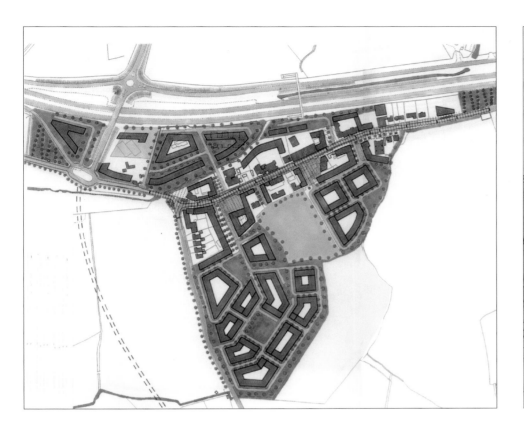

↑ Clonee Framework Plan
↑ Courtyard section and north elevation of eastern block

← Bird's-eye sketch of urban strategy, and location plan of development

↗ View of development on the road from Clonee Main Street
→ Ground-floor plan
↓ Southern elevation to riverside

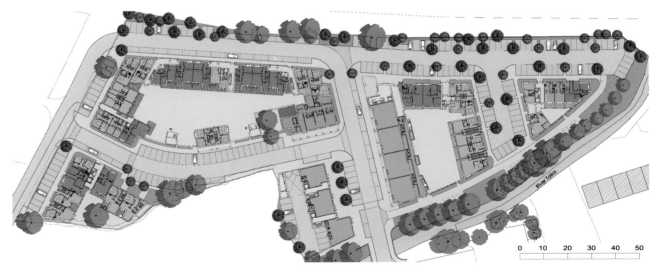

0 10 20 30 40 50

St Waleran's Development, Gorey, Co Wexford

Sheridan Woods Architects

Wexford County Council required the preparation of an Action Area Plan for lands at St Waleran's comprising over 28 hectares. The plan included an overall street network – including a link road designed to open up and create greater accessibility to the north of Gorey from the N11 – a railway station, and residential, commercial and community uses. An urban structure and phasing was suggested, an open-space strategy, and the location of an appropriate range of mixed uses.

Phase 1 comprised the first beginning of the link road development and the first residential phase on a 3.12-hectare site. The proposal suggests a new model for development in greenfield areas adjacent to town, combining traditional detached and semi-detached dwellings with higher-density residential dwelling forms, consisting of courtyard housing clusters and duplex/apartment blocks. The courtyard dwellings are arranged to create home zones between the clusters facing the local road, mediating the scale of the duplexes with existing one-off two-storey dwellings. The duplex/apartment blocks facing the proposed new link road conform with the Area Plan objective to define the edge of the new road. The dwelling design, roof profiles and choice of materials create unity and a strong sense of identity within the overall scheme.

name / address – St Waleran's Residential Development, Gorey, Co Wexford
design / completion – 2003; planning application withdrawn due to infrastructure constraints; alternative model currently being considered
client – D+G Commercial Design Ltd

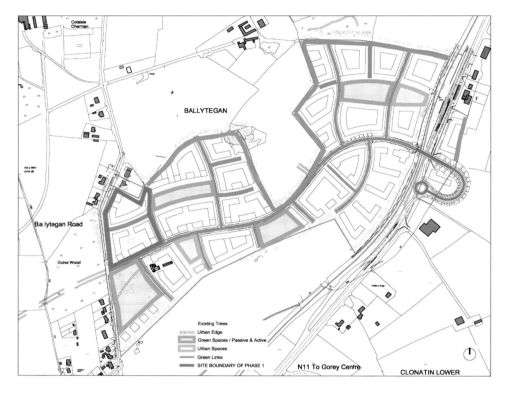

↑ Master plan
← Location map
← Sketch of typical duplex blocks

opposite

↗ Sketch perspective of duplex blocks and courtyard gardens from link road
→ Site plan
→ Typical duplex block plans – ground, 1st, 2nd floors
→ Typical courtyard block plans – ground, 1st floors
↘ Elevation of duplex blocks and courtyard gardens from link road at southern end of site

height	mix	percentage	no. of dwellings	site area	density	floor area	bed spaces	site coverage	open space	car spaces	context
1-3 storey	10 x 4-bed houses 34 x 3-bed houses 32 x 2-bed duplexes / apts 18 x courtyard dwellings	100% residential	94	7.7 acres (3.12 ha)	12.2 units/acre	14,158m²	393	22%	2,986m² public 1,114m² private balconies	107 (1.1 per dwelling)	town extension

Site Plan

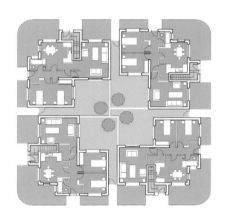

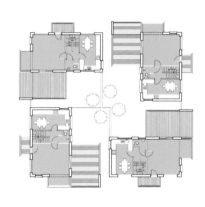

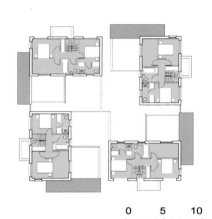

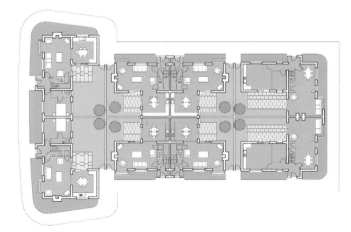

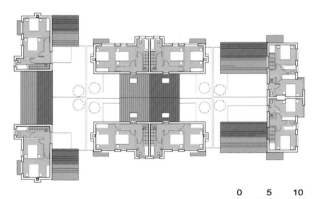

Railwalk, Westport, Co Mayo

Taylor Architects (in collaboration with Richard Murphy Architects)

Railwalk is a high-density, mixed residential scheme. The client brief was to maximise the private housing potential of the site, providing an opportunity to break the mould for housing design in the area.

The design for this scheme evolved from an understanding of its context. The northern boundary of the site is formed by the old railway line that once linked Westport to its harbour. The curve of the scheme originates from this railway line, with the two blocks framing a view of the distant mountain and bay, giving the scheme a sense of place and fixing it to its location. The opposing curves of the two blocks sets up a dynamic that takes the participant from the high point of the site entrance, through the funnel of the new street, into the open space with dramatic views over the landscape.

A density of sixteen units per acre was achieved on this 1.4 acre site. Floor areas are generous and vary from ground-floor two-bedroom apartments at 70m², first-floor three-bedroom apartments at 124m², and four-bedroom houses at 156m². All units have private access, with each first-floor apartment served by a generous external stair. All the usual boundaries, such as driveways, front gardens, fences, etc, have been replaced by a communal paved area which unites the two blocks.

design / completion – 2004–2005
client – Thomas Joyce

→ Conceptual site plan and perspective views

FOCUS TOWARDS THE LANDSCAPE

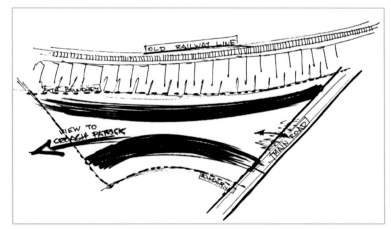

CONCEPTUAL SITE PLAN

OPPOSING CURVES TO DEFINE COURTYARD

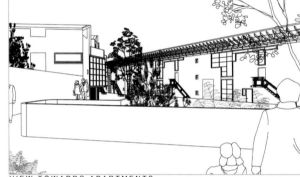

VIEW TOWARDS APARTMENTS

REDEFINING THE STREET

height	mix	percentage	no. of dwellings	site area	density	floor area	bed spaces	site coverage	open space	car spaces	context
3-3.5 storey	9 x 4-bed townhouses 7 x 3-bed duplexes 7 x 2-bed apartments	100% residential	23	5,660m² (1.4 acres)	16 units/acre	2,950m²	113 (81/acre)	23%	1,610m² public 806m² private + balconies	23 (1 per dwelling)	derelict industrial site at edge of town, next to public walkway

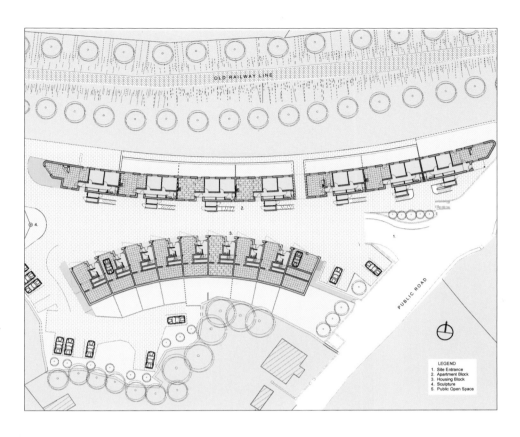

↑ Site plan
↑ Cross-section / elevation looking east through the two oppositely curved blocks
↓ 1st-floor plan

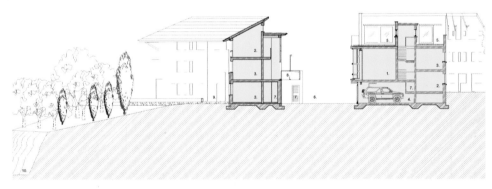

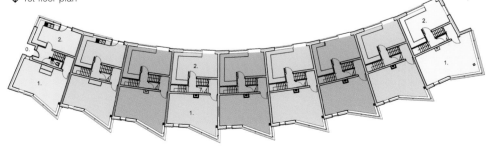

LEGEND
1. Site Entrance
2. Apartment Block
3. Housing Block
4. Sculpture
5. Public Open Space

Cluain Padraig, Westport, Co Mayo

Simon J Kelly & Partners

The site is located between existing two-storey housing estates between Westport's town and quay area. There are mature, seven-metre hawthorn trees along site boundaries. The site itself slopes generally upwards to its eastern boundary.

The scheme is designed to encourage and support community interaction and children's play, and to provide a mix of dwelling types to suit a variety of home owners, in accordance with Westport Town Council Development Plan 2003.

The design response has emerged from a variety of factors, including
– a considered examination of the context
– a study of the topography and orientation of the site
– a desire to offer a unified visual impression
– an appropriate response in building-design terms, creating a synthesis of site analysis and contemporary design.

This proposal for modern living responds to its proximity to the town, its views to the landscape, and its connection to public and private open space. The layout of the scheme maximises the benefits for each unit, with southerly and westerly orientations and views onto the shared landscaped play area. Each unit also has either a private terrace garden, balcony or roof terrace.

address – Springfield Drive, Westport
design / completion – 2004–2006
client – Joyce Contractors Developers

↗ Detail of Local Area Plan (site on left)
➜ Location map and axonometric view

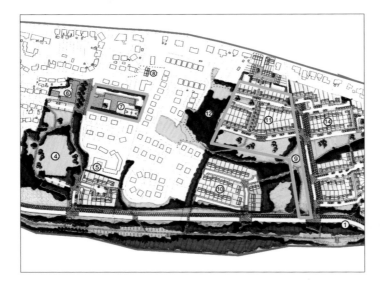

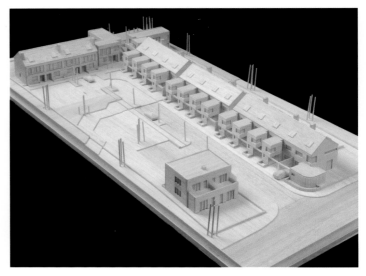

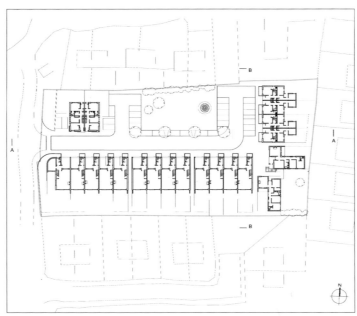

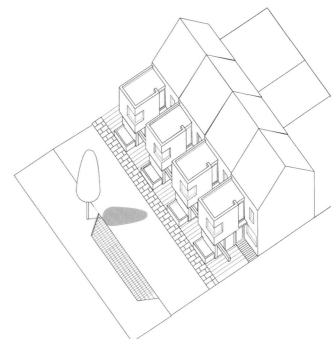

height	mix	percentage	no. of dwellings	site area	density	floor area	bed spaces	site coverage	open space	car spaces	context
2 storey with convertible attics	19 x 3-bed houses 4 x 2-bed apartments	100% residential	23	6,346m² (1.57 acres)	15 units/acre	2,490m²	103 (66/acre)	30%	661m² in communal garden and play area 61m² in courtyard (11.4%)	35	located between existing housing estates at town edge

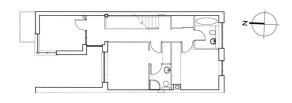

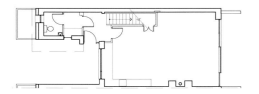

↑ Ground and 1st-floor plans (type A)
↓ Site plan

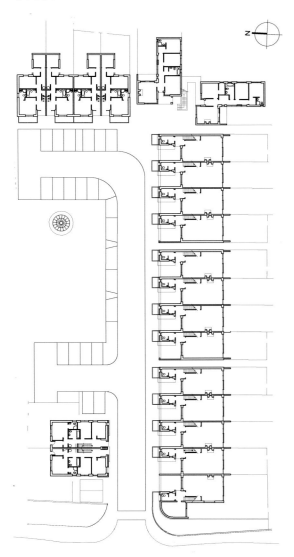

Courtyard Housing, Westport, Co Mayo

Simon J Kelly & Partners

The thirteen-unit Courtyard Housing project forms the heart of a larger master plan for a 112-dwelling and crèche development. The plan proposes a mix of dwelling-unit types to support a sustainable residential community of people of differing profiles and stages in life. Whilst at the same time complying with Development Plan guidelines, the concerns architecturally are

– to propose an appropriate response to the site
– to create useable open public space
– to separate trafficked and pedestrian space
– to provide quality dwellings with a sense of community and place in a series of low-rise, high-density proposals

The site slopes generally downwards from its northern boundary. The upper portion of the site has views to Croagh Patrick and Clew Bay. The master plan proposes development in rows parallel with the general slope of the site, with the higher apartment buildings on the lower contours so that the roofline throughout forms a consistent horizontal canopy. The plan avoids, insofar as possible, the situation of back-to-back rear gardens and the resulting visual clutter and inappropriate orientation of houses. Accordingly, two rows of detached courtyard houses are proposed at the heart of the scheme, with their gardens parallel to the houses, arranged facing each other across a central pedestrian pocket park with vehicular access separated from the park.

design / completion – 2004–
  (planning permission granted 2008; construction pending)
client – Joyce Contractors Developers

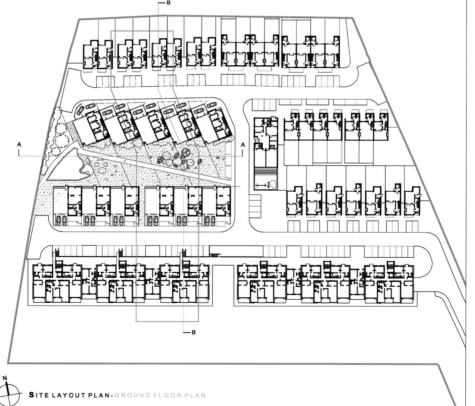

SITE LAYOUT PLAN-GROUND FLOOR PLAN

0 5 10 15 20 metres

↑ Section-elevation AA showing elevation to pocket park (see site plan), and section-elevation BB
← Site plan
↓ Detail of Local Area Plan (by Mitchell & Associates) showing location of site

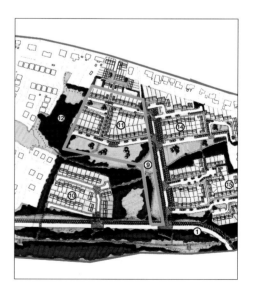

height	mix	percentage	no. of dwellings	site area	density	floor area	bed spaces	site coverage	open space	car spaces	context
2-4 storey	42 x 3/4-bed houses 4 x 3-bed duplexes 66 x 2-bed apartments crèche	100% residential	112	6.81 acres (2.75 ha)	16.5 units/acre (40.6 dwellings/ha)	12.650m²	534	19%	6.654m² in parks play area (24%)	170	outskirts of town

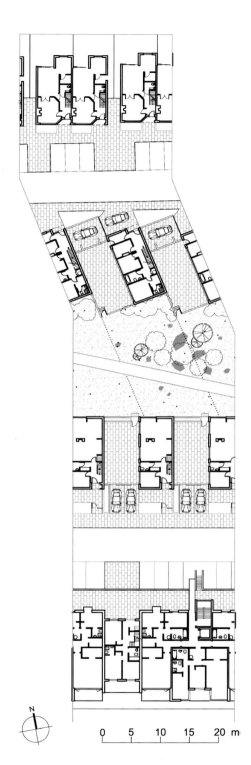

↑ Extract from site plan showing different house types at ground-floor level

↗ Pocket park, looking south

→ Pocket park, looking north, with Croagh Patrick in the background

Alderford, Ballyfarnon, Co Roscommon

Haslette Sweeney Architects

The site is located close to the centre of Ballyfarnon village on high ground overlooking the surrounding countryside to the south, west and north. The top of the site is level and falls steeply to the public road and church to the west. The north and south boundaries are well defined with mature hedgerow and trees.

The layout comprises a terrace-type element of two-storey, three-bedroom houses, which backs onto the site boundary to the east and fronts onto the public common green area. The dwellings in the terrace element are provided with rear-garden access 'ginnells' (covered passages) shared between two houses. The second element of the site layout comprises terraced single-storey, two-bedroom houses with a two-storey, three-bedroom house to the end. These units are arranged perpendicular to the main terrace, thus maintaining through-views to the landscape, while also presenting a row of stand-alone gables to complement the linear element of the main terrace and reflect the traditional gables in the village.

The main materials were selected from existing materials used in the village. Façades generally have a dash finish, with projecting entrance areas in brick. Environmental issues are addressed through the use of increased insulation, low-flush toilets, on-site water attenuation, and the use of recycled fill material. All units have lobbies to reduce heat loss. Provision has been made for future extension of the three-bedroom houses.

design / completion – 2004–2007 (Phase 1)
client – Roscommon County Council

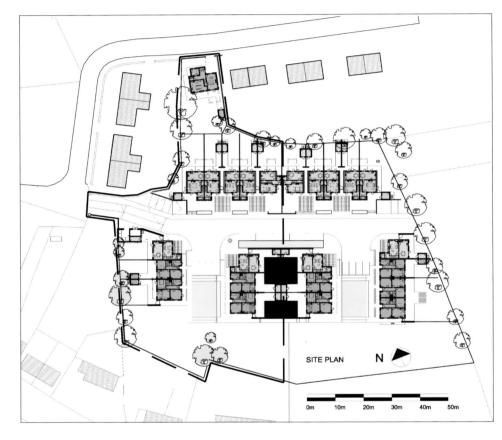

SITE PLAN N

0m 10m 20m 30m 40m 50m

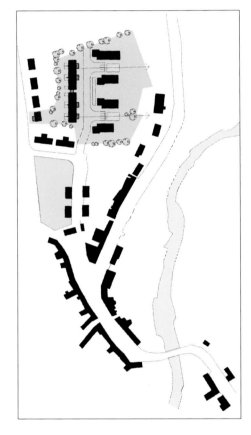

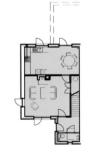

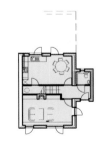

height	mix	percentage	no. of dwellings	site area	density	floor area	bed spaces	site coverage	open space	car spaces	context
1-2 storey	1 x 4-bed house 14 x 3-bed houses 9 x 2-bed houses	100% residential	24	9,150m² (2.26 acres)	10.5 units/acre	1,845m²	64 (28/acre)	20%	15% also private gardens and landscaped areas	36	elevated site in village adjacent to former village green

↑ Views of the completed Phase 1
↘ Sections through site

opposite

← Site plan and location map
↙ Plans of different house types

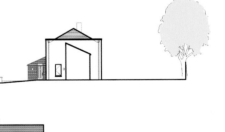

↓ Views of the completed Phase 1

Residential Development, Borrisoleigh, Co Tipperary

Paul Keogh Architects

Borrisoleigh is an attractive linear town on the R498 between Nenagh and Thurles. The 2.7-hectare site is within the town boundaries, between the main street and the River Cromogue. The North Tipperary County Council Development Plan sets down key development criteria for the site, including consolidation of the town centre, creation of a riverside park, and the development of the urban neighbourhood concept.

This proposal seeks to establish a village-type environment, creating attractive streets and a series of public spaces which reflect the character of the town. The scheme will provide a mix of private, affordable and social housing units in a phased implementation programme. The first stage of development will provide 26 social housing units on that part of the site adjacent to the village.

Planning of the development has been based on the home zone or *woonerf* concept, providing streets and open spaces which reflect the needs of pedestrians as well as cars, and enabling residents to enjoy the lifestyle and amenities offered by the town, such as walking to shops, schools, churches and pubs.

design / completion – 2006–2010
client – North Tipperary County Council

↗ Site plan
→ Typical elevation, cross-section, ground and 1st-floor plans

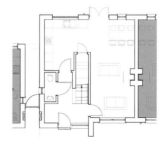
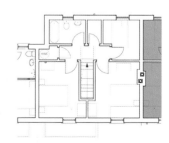

height	mix	percentage	no. of dwellings	site area	density	floor area	bed spaces	site coverage	open space	car spaces	context
2 storey	53 x 3-bed houses 14 x 2-bed houses crèche	100% residential	67	2.15 ha (5.3 acres)	30.73 units/ha (12.4 /acre)	3,130m²	357	15%	4,645m²	134	rural village

↑ Plan of home zone
↗ Bird's-eye view of housing cluster at river's edge
→ Bird's-eye view of riverside housing development
↓ Section-elevation through river and site

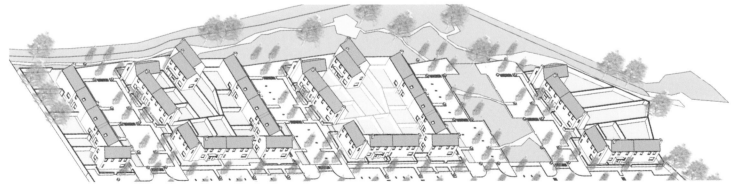

121

Iveragh Road, Killorglin, Co Kerry – Town Renewal

Murray Ó Laoire Architects

The site lies at the northern edge of Killorglin town centre, which, like many other town centres of its kind, has been eroded by traffic. The scale of the new scheme relative to the size of Killorglin offered the opportunity to create a development of civic importance, one which focuses on the public domain and has a discernable sense of place.

A new town square is created by setting two of the new buildings back from the road. The square is furnished with bespoke, over-scaled street furniture and lights. New planters, trees and water features animate the space, introducing noise, seasonal interest and, more importantly, opportunities for people of all ages to gather.

The mixed-use building and the Local Area Centre flank the western and northern edges of the square. The Local Area Centre's transparent ground floor (accommodating the community library) and double-volume atrium offer glimpses of the new park and playground on the north side of the building. This quiet green space, fired with hot colours, bold graphics and playground equipment, stands in strong contrast to the more austere formality of the town square.

The new square has quickly shifted the town centre. Many new cafés and retail outlets have opened around the square, reinforcing its public role in the town.

address – Iveragh Road, Killorglin, Co Kerry
design / completion – 2003–2006
clients – Laune Properties /
   Eamon Costello Ltd

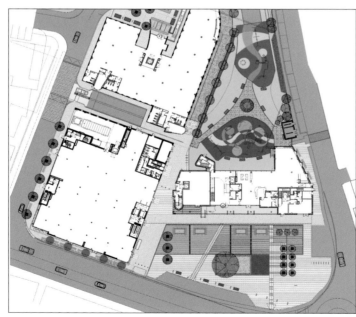

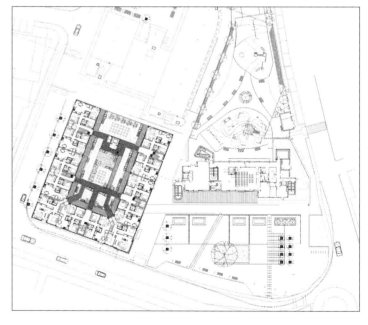

height	mix	percentage	no. of dwellings	site area	density	floor area	bed spaces	site coverage	open space	car spaces	context
3-4 storey	22 x 2-bed apartments 2 x 1-bed apartments council offices, library retail units and offices	41% administrative 35% retail 20.5% residential 0.5% library	24	2.92 acres (1.18 ha)	n/a	10,220m²	46	33%	2,000m² town square 1,825m² playground 700m² courtyard 90m² private balconies	underground car park 13 surface spaces	fringe of small agricultural town

Urban Infill

EDDIE CONROY

Twenty years ago, writing an introduction to the Urban Infill section of a book like this would have been an easier task. In that quieter time, urban infill was an optimistic act, polite and well intentioned. A harbinger of a potentially reparable urban world, its principal pledge was to stave off decay and suggest the value of growth in the future. Smug with the lessons of Rationalism and the Georgian tradition, we imagined the successful rebuilding and growth of towns could be achieved in a sensible and likable way. The Urban Renewal Act and tax designation released a trickle of urban growth, which had since turned into a tide of expansion with the economic and population surge. This tide has, in turn, now withdrawn too.

Urban infill at both the scale of the individual site and the larger brownfield renewal of entire districts, such as Dublin Docklands, has clearly benefited the capital. It and its citizens have enjoyed an economic and urban renaissance. Some towns, such as Westport, have, through careful channelling of physical and economic growth, reinforced their cores with a varied and lively mixture of public realm and diverse uses, encouraging investment and adding value to their economies. Up until recently they were the exceptions, however, as the suburban model became the paradigm for growth in both town and country.

The typical county development plan, until recently, limited to use-zoning as its principal instrument, accepted no responsibility for place-making; process replaces product. Zoning promotes separation and single-use enclaves: retail parks, industrial and residential estates all separated, all developed randomly and incrementally on edge-of-town greenfield sites. All require car journeys for the simplest of tasks. Restricted by outdated and simplistic planning codes (open-space sizes, building separation), with a dwindling resource of building type and with road layouts subverted by their closed cellular nature and over-designed geometries, these uniform and numbing environments cling to the ringroads of most Irish towns. The end-effects are already clear – congestion and pollution, social isolation, declining health and community fragmentation. The decline of many town centres is an unexpected side effect: 80% of residential growth in the last ten years has been in the counties of Kildare, Meath, Louth and Wicklow. This suggests not just suburban growth, but an ex-urban boom, damaging to the whole country.

Even higher-density models seem resistant to urban manners. Driven by industry growth, market changes and statutory objectives, the four- and five-storey apartment blocks which have appeared both in and on the edges of towns and cities are large enough to promise a sense of place and life, but few have delivered it. Their panellised elevations are hamstrung by the demands of construction speed, prefabrication (its source the elimination of the suicidal craft of bricklaying) and the unavoidable rhythm of balcony and toilet window. Clad in timber, render, aluminium, and now copper, the limited number of elevational strategies, combined with the wallpapering of diverse materials, has a strangely deadening effect. Visually clamorous and yet mute in the language of urban affairs – inside/outside, public/private, important/ordinary – they are resistant to meshing with existing fabric or even new adjoining projects in scale and atmosphere. It should be possible for different architects to cohere and create consistent and replicable pieces of town, but recent examples in Ballymun and Dublin show how far away that agreement is.

Urban infill is clearly not as straightforward as we used to think, and yet... The value of master-planning (how to make places, how to connect them) is clear in investment, phasing, environmental and social infrastructure terms. Its clearest advantage is its ability to foretell (and explain) the end product – the place itself. O'Mahony Pike's design for Kilkenny's western environs clearly describes a sane urban neighbourhood of connected streets, public spaces and gardens, the sensible positioning of community facilities, schools and shopping. This is the achievable three- to four-storey medium-density world proven over time to work. Murray Ó Laoire's scheme for Athlone has different ambitions. Here, underused backlands are brought into play in a coherent but intensive intervention in the very centre of the town. The clarity of the strategy secures investment and guarantees a constant intensity of activity and public realm. The diversity of usage will re-animate the town centre with its balance of civic, community and commercial functions, a clear counterweight to the big-box service and retail centres so prevalent on its outer edges.

A master plan is made up of districts, the district is composed of blocks, and blocks are, in turn, divided into lots. The size, form and disposition of the block determines the atmosphere of the neighbourhood, its sense of enclosure, permeability, openness and efficiency. Some of the blocks shown in these projects are large bravura projects, such as Laughton Tyler's Steelworks project in Dublin's north-east inner city – a classic perimeter condition with a central garden. There are alternatives to the perimeter block, but they must be used warily to ensure urban continuity, enclosure and clear definition of public and private space. Derek Tynan's long, cranked apartment blocks are artfully disposed at Victoria Cross in Cork to create a viable urban block with a different reading at ground level than at its airy upper floors. On a tight site in Dun Laoghaire, Denis Byrne Architects form a taut block with a dynamic slot-view of sky and sea, carved at the scale of the block itself – a poetic urban gesture. The most modest urban block, Dublin City Council's 66 senior-citizen units at Islandbridge in Dublin, is one of the most assured. Its robust address to the public park and adjoining sites, its reticent but flawless detailing, and the felicity of proportion of both building and contained garden is a model of urban politesse. Some of the projects fall foul of developers' ambitions and are overscaled, crunching noisily into existing environments.

Some of the smaller schemes act in a grown-up way, creating integrated and believable environments with a language and aspiration to invoke, or even demand, a more considered urban response from the sites around them. In this category, Mitchell & Associates in Artane and Gerry Cahill Architects in Donabate provide calm, well-considered internal and external responses. O'Donnell + Tuomey's restrained scheme at the Timberyard rescues stillness from the visual cacophony of Cork Street. The ingenuity of Murray Ó Laoire's Timber Mill manages to wrench a rhythmic and balanced urban place from an almost impossibly long and narrow site. It is intriguing to imagine an urban neighbourhood composed with these levels of care and consistency.

The block, then, can resolve the balance of building and landscape, sunlight-penetration, and, most importantly, negotiate the relationship between the neighbourhood and the larger demands of the town. If the master plan addresses distribution and connection, the morphology of the block proposes the built priorities of the scheme – interaction with the street, levels of enclosure, boundary of public and private, sunlight and degree of landscape, the balance of commercial and residential.

These values are tackled architecturally through the manipulation of type – i.e. how the individual building interacts with the underlying logic of the block. Seán Harrington references the Georgian tradition in York Street, combining the strong frontal address of an elegant apartment building with corner tower and the mews-like downscaling three-storey villas on the smaller lane behind. In Noel J Brady's scheme at Tonlegee, this understanding of the demands of front and back is developed into an extruded block, its complex section driven by questions of sunlight, overlooking and overshadowing. These schemes show a mature understanding of the possibilities of type, and also how reductive most newer schemes are in their use of this resource. Type can address the knottiest of problems. Paul Keogh Architects have taken an almost impossible site in Cork, and through skilful disposition of type (and a good deal of architectural know-how), created a likable and livable place not compromised by its robust response to its gritty location.

This use of type to humanise and colonise the more unwieldy demands of the block is surely the direct route to the Holy Grail of urban development – medium-density housing which is attractive to families. If the endless suburban and ex-urban expansion is to be halted, life in the centre of town must be made viable and desirable for families. The sequence by which the private open space of the dwelling expands into the sunny, green space of the block, and then into the vibrant, safe streets of the town, is the secret of successful urban life. High buildings, despite their ability to intensify, can rarely generate this connection and make it replicable from the scale of the neighbourhood to the district.

In this discussion, successful infill has a more onerous task than urban repair alone. It is not a symbol of the future; it is today's guarantee of that saner future containing the language and values of a more complex pattern of urban growth – a diverse, intense and satisfying world. (I hope you enjoyed, as I did, the absence of the word 'sustainability' in the above piece!)

Eddie Conroy is County Architect with South Dublin County Council.

→ left to right:

Kilkenny Western Environs LAP
by O'Mahony Pike Architects

Hazel Grove, Donabate, Co Dublin
by Gerry Cahill Architects

York Street Redevelopment, Dublin 2
by Seán Harrington Architects

Alto Vetro Tower, Grand Canal Quay, Dublin 2

Shay Cleary Architects

This scheme is for a sixteen-storey glazed residential tower at a key Dublin location on the corner of Pearse Street and Grand Canal Quay. It marks a threshold when entering the city centre from the east. The site, measuring 9m x 20m, is directly adjacent to the bridge over Grand Canal Dock. It is adjacent also to the Waterways visitor centre and is on the edge of the area under the control of the Dublin Docklands Development Authority.

The design is seen as a pristine glass-object building, with a stone band expressing the slab at each level. The aesthetic of the building is considered to allow it to read as a singular element in the city.

A series of internal sliding wooden screens provide sun-shading and privacy to the apartments. The combination of screens and crisp glass detailing will lend a complex and sophisticated layering to the façade which will move and change throughout the day.

There are two apartments per floor, arranged around a single core, on the lower levels, and two duplexes on the two uppermost levels. Living rooms are positioned at each end and have panoramic views on three sides. Each apartment has private outdoor space in the form of cantilevered balconies. There is a roof terrace, protected by a two-metre high glass balustrade, and a private gymnasium, both of which are for residents' use.

At ground-floor level, the building is set back on all sides. This floor accommodates

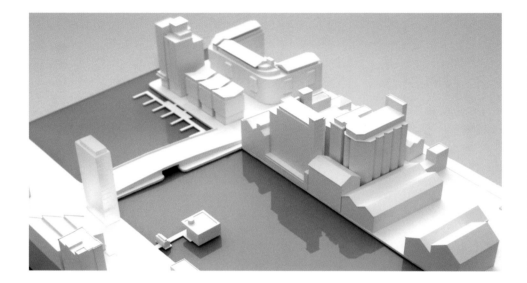

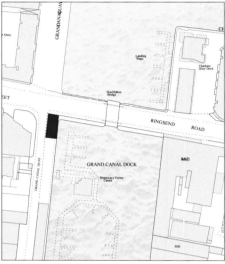

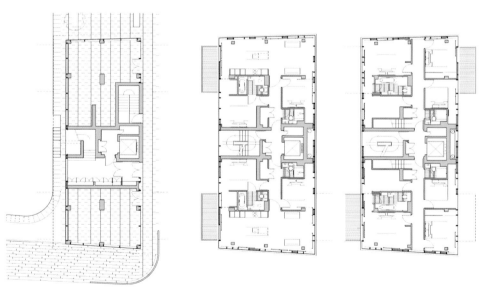

a generous entrance space to the apartments, fully glazed to give views through to the water. There are also two commercial/retail units, which seek to encourage a more intensive inhabitation of the open campshire area to the south.

address – Grand Canal Quay, Dublin 2
design / completion – 2002–2008
client – Treasury Holdings Ltd

↑ Location map
↖ Model of Grand Canal Dock
← Plans – ground, 1st-12th, 13th floors

opposite

→ Views of the residential tower in context

height	mix	percentage	no. of dwellings	site area	density	floor area	bed spaces	site coverage	open space	car spaces	context
16 storey (above ground level)	2 x 3-bed duplexes 24 x 2-bed apartments 2 pavilions + 2 retail units	95% residential 5% commercial	26	169m²	1,420 units/ha	2,616m²	54	100%	130m²	6 (0.23 per dwelling)	inner-city site adjacent to Grand Canal Dock

Hanover Quay, Dublin 2

O'Mahony Pike Architects

The Dublin Docklands Development Authority (DDDA) master plan had a simple objective – to create both a vibrant city area and an integrated, pleasant place to live and work. This project works on two scales: the grand scale of the Grand Canal Basin and River Liffey, and the smaller, more intimate scale of the side streets. Office, retail and restaurant functions are located on Hanover Quay and Sir John Rogerson's Quay to reflect this hierarchy and enliven the water frontage, while a series of own-door family duplexes line Forbes Street and North-South Street, establishing a more domestic environment.

The clear and stated objective of the DDDA was to integrate the social housing seamlessly within an otherwise private scheme. The social housing was to enjoy all the similar benefits of the private housing – own-door access to streets, similar construction standards, access to common gardens and play areas, and provision of a suitable dwelling mix. The integration of the social housing has been most successful, complementing the mostly owner-occupier profile of the remainder of the development.

Family 'own-door' houses are located at ground floor, with street frontages. These units are provided with private patio areas, which give directly onto the shared garden spaces. Duplex-type units each have their own door, retaining the sense of the

→ View of Grand Canal Dock with Hanover Quay under construction in the distance, and OMP's Charlotte Quay in the foreground
↗ Model
⇥ Location map

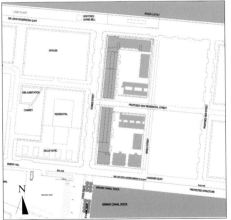

height	mix	percentage	no. of dwellings	site area	density	floor area	bed spaces	site coverage	open space	car spaces	context
5-8 storey	61 x 3-bed units 169 x 2-bed units 60 x 1-bed units	83% residential 12% commercial 5% communal	290	1.255 ha (3.1 acres)	231 units/ha (93.5/acre)	33,000m²	1,101 (877/ha)	45%	1,453m²	229 (0.8 per dwelling)	dockland area in city centre

individual house. Traditional apartments are located at the upper levels of the taller buildings, where they are accessed from a central day-lit hallway. All are provided with balcony areas. Facilities in the scheme include a crèche and dedicated children's play areas in the communal gardens (designed by Diarmuid Gavin). Communal waste and recycling facilities are located at ground level; bicycle and car-parking is located in an accessible basement.

Grand Canal Basin is addressed by three glazed pavilions facing south onto the water and floating over a heavy base. The strong horizontal expression of balconies on Forbes Street is punctuated at the base by the entrance lobbies, and at the top by sunrooms and roof terraces. The punched ope offers a more domestic expression to the courtyards and North-South Street. The buildings are precast concrete structure and cladding, with glazed balconies and winter gardens. Their expression is defined by aspect and orientation.

design / completion – 2001–2006
clients – Dublin Docklands Development
    Authority / Park / Sisk

———

← Views of completed development
→ View from Grand Canal Basin
↙ Views of internal courtyard
↘ Master plan of block stretching from Hanover
    Quay to Sir John Rogerson's Quay
↓ Typical floor plan

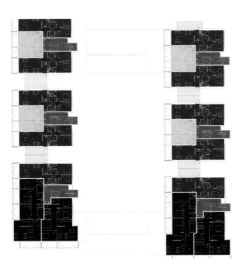

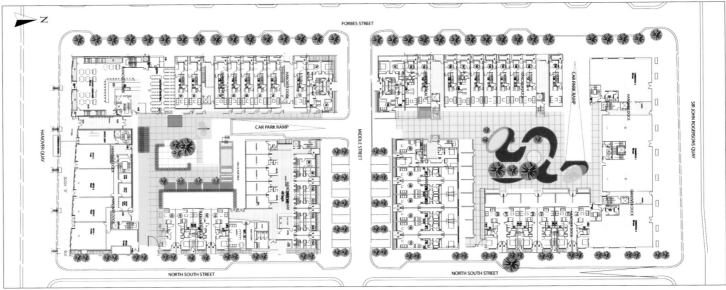

131

The Waterfront, Hanover Quay, Dublin 2

Burke-Kennedy Doyle Architects

The Waterfront forms part of a mixed-use residential, office and retail development. Within the planning remit of the Dublin Docklands Development Authority, the building has been designed to take account of the standards and guidelines set out in the Planning Scheme 2000, which promotes the principles of mixed-use development, active streetscape, design quality, urban scale and quality residential environment.

The development is laid out around a landscaped central courtyard. The office building is six storeys high and forms a C-shape at the eastern end of the site. The residential quarter consists of 68 apartments arranged in two separate blocks, one to the north and one to the south of the courtyard. The south block is predominately eight storeys high and faces Hanover Quay and Grand Canal Dock. The north block is predominately six storeys high and faces the site of the proposed Chocolate Factory Park. Most apartments are dual-aspect, and all have large, south-facing cantilevered balconies with room to accommodate a table and chairs. The western elevation of both blocks are stepped down to three storeys in accordance with the DDDA master-plan requirements, allowing the evening sunlight to penetrate the courtyard. Communal amenity spaces include the landscaped courtyard, roof terraces and a large landscaped terrace on the roof of the north block.

Materials in the residential buildings are manifestly contemporary, with extensive use of full-height glazing creating transparency and interest from the street to

height	mix	percentage	no. of dwellings	site area	density	floor area	bed spaces	site coverage	open space	car spaces	context
3-8 storey	7 x 3-bed apartments 51 x 2-bed apartments 10 x 1-bed apartments	48% residential 49% office 3% retail/other	68	4,600m²	147 units/ha	14,565m² (6,950m² residential)	n/a	49%	1,030m² communal 1,485m² private	103 (64 residential) (0.94 per dwelling)	brownfield site in DDDA master plan area

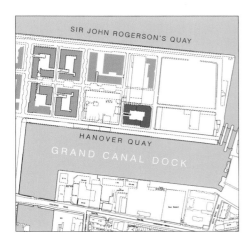

the private domain. Street-level commercial spaces have uninterrupted glazed façades to maximise and enhance their connection with the street.

design / completion – 2005–2008
client – Ellier (Hanover Quay) Ltd

↑ Location map
→ View from The Waterfront roof terrace, with Charlotte Quay (OMP) on left and Grand Canal Square on right
↘ Hanover Quay, with Grand Canal Square on left (showing landscaping feature by Martha Schwartz), and The Waterfront on extreme right

opposite

← View from Grand Canal Dock
↙ South elevation to Grand Canal Dock

Heuston South Quarter, Kilmainham, Dublin 8

Anthony Reddy Associates

Heuston South Quarter (HSQ) is a new mixed-use living quarter adjacent to Heuston Station and the Royal Hospital Kilmainham (home to the the Irish Museum of Modern Art). The master plan for HSQ has its origins in the Heuston Area Action Plan and the Heuston Gateway Regeneration Strategy Development Framework Plan, commissioned in 2003 by Dublin City Council. Planning permission for the current master-plan scheme was granted by An Bórd Pleanála in 2005.

A team of architectural practices worked together to bring a particular vibrancy and architectural quality to this urban scheme. The development is home to a new headquarters building for Eircom, 345 residential units, a 274-bed Marriott hotel, a crèche, significant retail space, an additional 372 m²for IMMA, and a number of fourth-generation office buildings with an emphasis on sustainable design, all located around a new public plaza. The HSQ achieves eighteen hours of use daily as a result of this mix of uses.

From an urban-design perspective, the creation of a new urban space and the integration of significant open space (private and public) has been one of the driving principles of the scheme, together with high-quality design and finish. Particular attention has been paid to the landscaping, its relationship to the Royal Hospital, and the relationship of the spaces in-between the buildings to one another.

design / completion – 2001–2011
(the scheme obtained planning permission in 2005)
client – Office of Public Works

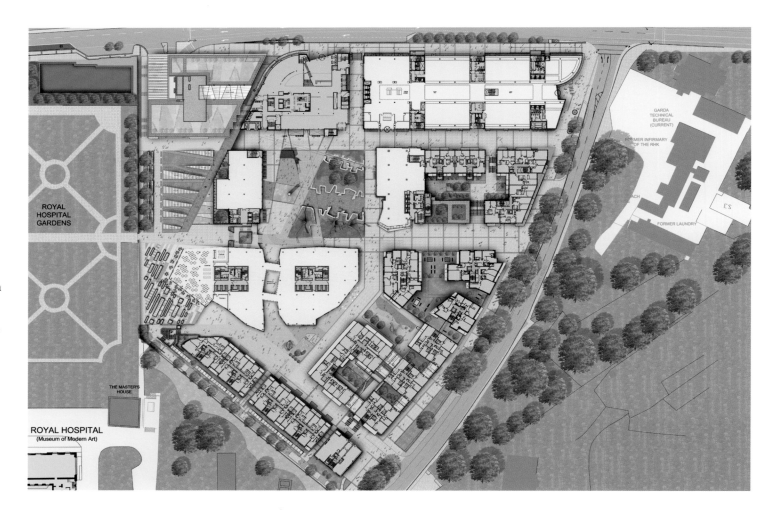

height	mix	percentage	no. of dwellings	site area	density	floor area	bed spaces	site coverage	open space	car spaces	context
generally 6-7 storey, rising to 12 storey	residential, office, cultural, hotel, retail	30% residential 70% other	345	3.24 ha (8 acres)	106 units/ha (43/acre)	110,000m²	n/a	45%	40%	1,100	gateway development near major transportation hub

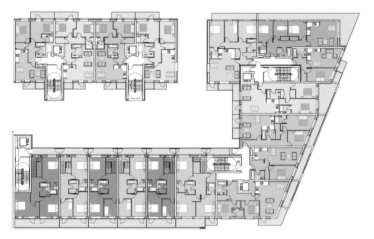

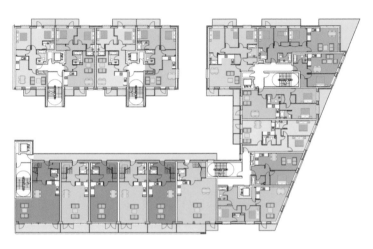

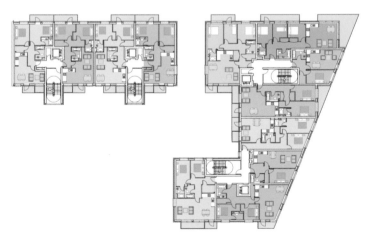

↑ Block 7 – lower-levels, 6th and 7th-floor plans
↖ Site plan (with block 7 at top right, and blocks 8, 10 at bottom left)
← Blocks 8, 10 – 2nd and 3rd-floor part-plans

Heuston Gate, Kilmainham, Dublin 8

Paul Keogh Architects

This major urban-renewal project in Kilmainham contains proposals for Dublin's tallest structure to date – a 32-storey residential tower. The development is to form a new quarter around the Royal Hospital Kilmainham, and create a pedestrian link between Kilmainham Goal, Collins Barracks, the Irish Museum of Modern Art (at the RHK) and Heuston Station.

The proposal is to create a new mixed-use neighbourhood with a vibrant streetscape, promoting active ground-level activities which encourage street life and a pedestrian-friendly public realm. The project will be developed around an established set of key design principles, with particular regard to the strategic location of the site within the city and respect for its historic context. The development includes a total of fourteen buildings, combining work, living, leisure and commercial activities, in addition to the restoration of existing protected structures and national monuments.

The scheme aspires to be a model of environmental sustainability, using energy-saving technologies such as solar power, district heating and heat-recovery systems combined with high insulation levels. The design was audited using the BREAM energy-rating method. Full planning was granted in 2003, and construction is scheduled to be phased over ten years from the granting of permission.

design / completion – 2002–2015
client – Office of Public Works

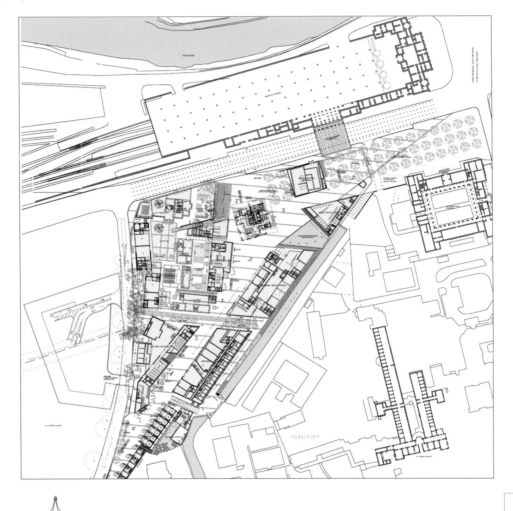

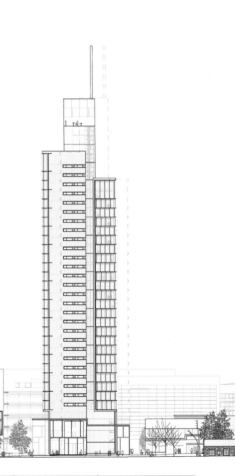

← Location map
→ Photomontages from IMMA Avenue and Heuston Station
↓ North-west elevation to St John's Road (with Dr Steeven's Hospital on left)

height	mix	percentage	no. of dwellings	site area	density	floor area	bed spaces	site coverage	open space	car spaces	context
2-32 storey	1 x 5-bed apartment 3 x 4-bed apartments 15 x 3-bed apartments 162 x 2-bed apartments 16 x 1-bed apartments also commercial + cultural	39% residential	197	7.05 acres (2.85 ha)	28 units/acre (69 units.ha)	52,111m²	789 (112/acre)	40%	3,444m² in courtyards and balconies	365 (1.8 per dwelling)	under-used site at edge of city centre

Mixed-Use Development at Mill Street, Dublin 8

Anthony Reddy Associates

The site comprises privately owned lands. The area forms part of the city council's Regeneration Strategy to provide state-of-the-art development to regenerate the built environment and address the economic and social problems identified in the area. The development provides desperately needed public space, permeability to a large urban block, and a sense of spaciousness to the area. The overall urban design provides a re-introduction of a new axis in its historic location as a main north-south connection. On the west side of the street alternating 3 and 4 storey elements keep a domestic scale to avoid overlooking onto the houses at Sweeney`s Terrace. In total the blocks E, F and G follow this design idea.

Block A, B and C represent buildings which follow a more defined urban form. Two feature towers of 8 storeys at the corner of Mill Street and Clarence Mangan Road and at the south end of the new street act as punctuation marks in the skyline. The southern area of the site is characterised by less density and more open green space including a pond. High quality landscaping with a formal arrangement of trees and paved surfaces, give live street frontage to the new development blocks. The commercial uses at ground floor introduce day and night activity into this area, while the residential units above will provide passive surveillance of the public domain after hours. Permeability of the site is provided by two pedestrian accesses from Warrenmount Lane to the new street and from the new street to Sweeney's Terrace. Visual links are maintained between the public realm and the private open spaces

to the rear of the blocks. The evolution of the urban plan naturally resulted in distinct building blocks, each designed as a separate entity, to enhance the architectural quality of the new public realm.

The overall architectural treatment makes reference to the materials and urban grain of the city, while introducing more modern elements. There will be a good mix of different apartment types and sizes with features that will make them attractive to all types of people. The residential units will be mostly dual-aspect with large balconies or winter-gardens, as well as individual storage units in the basement. The inclusion of private open spaces and secure play areas, as well as a variety of commercial/retail uses will contribute to the long-term sustainability of the development.

address – Mill Street / Sweeney's Lane / Warrenmount Lane, Dublin 8
design / completion – 2005–2009
client – Osprey Properties

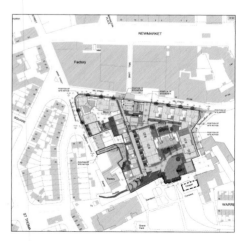

height	mix	percentage	no. of dwellings	site area	density	floor area	bed spaces	site coverage	open space	car spaces	context
3-8 storey	47 x 3-bed apartments 99 x 2-bed apartments 43 x 1-bed live/work apts	70% residential 30% commercial	189	10,399m² (2.57 acres)	73.5 units/acre	23,749m²	571 (222/acre)	49%	26% public space also courtyards, terraces and balconies	230 (1.2 per dwelling)	inner-city site; urban-regeneration area

↑ View of No.10 Mill Street (restored by Shaffrey Associates), and looking east along Mill Street

↑ View of new public park showing route through arch of block C to Warrenmount Lane

↗ View of block B tower and south end of New Street

→ Rear view of No.10 Mill Street complex

⇢ View looking south-west down Warrenmount Lane

opposite

↖ Aerial view of model of proposed development looking south

← Location map

⇇ Typical floor plan

Herberton, Rialto, Dublin 8 – Phase 2

Anthony Reddy Associates / Metropolitan Workshop

Located just one mile from Christ Church in the heart of Dublin, this scheme represented an opportunity to reinvigorate a neglected area of the city. Building on an initial master plan prepared by Dublin City Council and in consultation with the existing community, the redevelopment at Herberton creates a new community within the existing locality.

This project is being financed through the mechanism of a Public Private Partnership (PPP), the first of its kind in urban regeneration and renewal in Ireland. This mechanism has ensured the integration of residential, leisure, community and retail facilities within the development, in addition to the significant provision of high-quality public open space.

The site layout has addressed and embraced the key issues associated with a site of this nature. A key consideration has been the reconnection of Herberton to the locality and the re-establishment of major routes through the site to ensure that the scheme will be an integral part of the surrounding urban fabric. The detail design of the buildings ensures that there is a direct visual relationship between the residential elements of the scheme and the street in order to provide passive surveillance and visual interest.

design / completion – 2004–2009
clients – Dublin City Council / Moritz-Elliot

___

↗ Location map and site plan
→ Proposed contiguous elevations
➵ Views of Reuben Street, blocks A-D and B-E

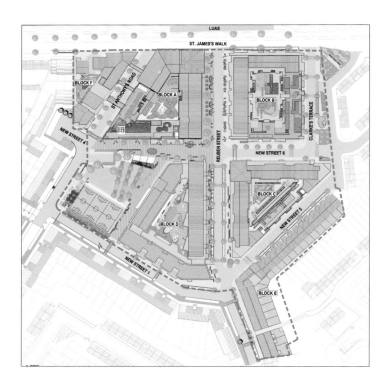

height	mix	percentage	no. of dwellings	site area	density	floor area	bed spaces	site coverage	open space	car spaces	context
2-7 storey	68 x 3-bed apartments 334 x 2-bed apartments 103 x 3-bed apartments	83% residential 14% commercial 3% communal	505	30,773m² (7.6 acres)	66 units/acre	60,064m²	1,548 (204/acre)	45%	10,633m² in courtyard also private balconies	390 (0.8 per dwelling)	inner-city site adjacent to light-rail network

Player's Square Development, SCR, Dublin 8

GCA / Gerry Cahill Architects

The redevelopment of the John Player factory and the neighbouring Bailey Gibson site was originally a joined project to stimulate intensification of use and repopulation of what had become an underused brownfield site.

The brief for the development was to provide a quality and variety of urban residential units within an employment, leisure and cultural environment that would re-establish this overlooked section of the city. The aim was that people could live, learn, work and relax within walking distance of a home which is generous in size and amenity.

In developing both sites as distinct areas, the overall joined scheme has retained this aim but without the explicit colonisation of the existing football pitches and open spaces which separate them. The scheme succeeds in providing a residential development where 96% of the units can

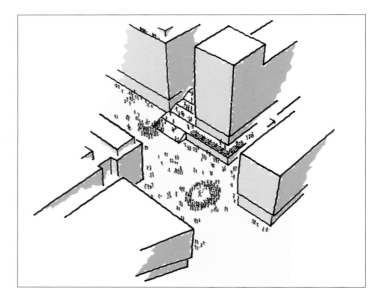

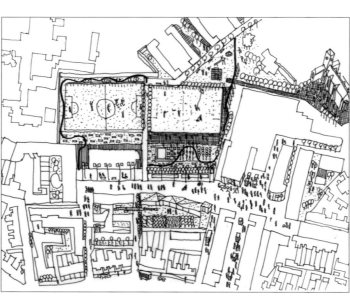

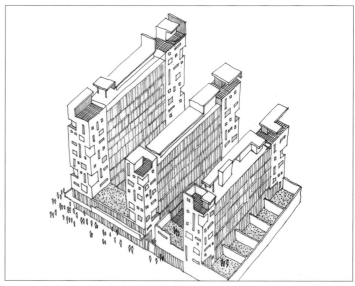

↑ Earlier site development with climbing centre, redevelopment of football pitches and public open spaces
↗ Sketch of people-movement on Player's Square
→ Early sketch of neighbourhood redevelopment
⇉ Sketch of stepped building profile to knit in with area context

opposite

↑ Bailey Gibson site layout plan showing ground surfaces
↗ Aerial view of city quarter showing block density and neighbourhood grain (with Bailey Gibson site on left; John Player's site on right)
→ Aerial view of city quarter showing meeting and movement, and place-based nodes
⇉ Bird's-eye view of joined sites

height	mix	percentage	no. of dwellings	site area	density	floor area	bed spaces	site coverage	open space	car spaces	context
1-14 storey over basement	7 town houses 187 x 3-bed duplex + apts 438 x 2-bed duplex + apts 123 x 1-bed apartments commercial + community	75% residential 13% commercial 12% other	755	43,217m² (10.7 acres)	70.5 units/acre	98,766m²	2,954 (276/acre)	46%	16,148m² public space 14,044 m2 in balconies terraces, gardens	956 (1.26 per dwelling) 946 bicycle spaces	adjacent inner-city sites forming a city quarter around existing open pace, adjacent to Grand Grand Canal + Coombe

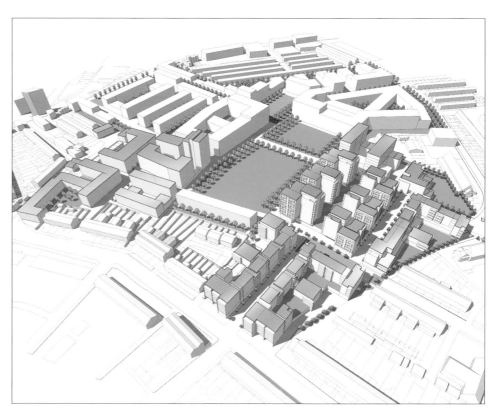

143

receive daylight from two or more aspects, where the overall average size of apartments is over 80m², and where a significant percentage of the development is given over to education, leisure and employment-generating uses.

The project has responded in its architectural forms and layout to the context of a Dublin City Council-commissioned master plan for the area, and recognises the impact and potential of the regeneration of St Teresa's Gardens. It is the intention of the development team that the combination of all of these projects can result in viable and sustainable neighbourhood regeneration.

design / completion – 2003–
    (positive An Bord Pleanála decision
    given in 2008 for revised scheme)
client – Players Square Ltd

↖ Bailey Gibson – view of leisure building and
    adjacent pedestrian streets
↑ John Player's – elevations to South Circular Road
↞ John Player's – site layout with new streets,
    squares and routes
← Bailey Gibson – apartment variety with emphasis
    on aspect, orientation and threshold. The scheme
    has 57 apartment types; 96% are dual-aspect.

Memorial Court, SCR, Dublin 8

City Architects' Division, Dublin City Council

Memorial Court is situated within the Heuston Development Framework Plan area, which sets out a master plan for 3,000 to 5,000 new homes, and 200,000m² of commercial and knowledge-economy space in the area. This senior citizens' scheme is one of the largest such developments undertaken by Dublin City Council to date, and the first older persons' complex built with more than two storeys. It complements the major development underway at Clancy Barracks opposite, which will also provide local retail and community facilities, and contributes to the rejuvenation of this section of the South Circular Road down to the Liffey. Dublin Bus operates a stop just outside the development, allowing easy access to the city centre.

Units are planned in blocks of varying height around a south-facing landscaped courtyard. Many residents enjoy gardening and appreciate the large planted courtyard. The positioning of windows and rooflights allows an abundance of natural light to flood rooms and stairwells. Where appropriate, living spaces have full-height glazed screens onto generous balconies, with views towards Phoenix Park and the Memorial Gardens.

name / address – Memorial Court,
    717-727 South Circular Road, Dublin 8
design / completion – 2004–2007
client – Dublin City Council

↗ Location plan
↗ View from the South Circular Road
→ Ground-floor and typical floor plans

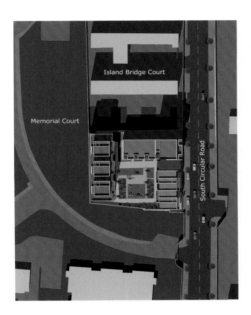

height	mix	percentage	no. of dwellings	site area	density	floor area	bed spaces	site coverage	open space	car spaces	context
3-6 storey	8 x 2-bed apartments 58 x 1-bed apartments	97.8% residential 1.7% retail 0.5% communal	66	2,406m² (0.6 acres)	110 units/acre	4,374m²	139 (232/acre)	44%	1,115m² public courtyard 326m² private balconies	43 (0.65 per dwelling)	former warehouse site adjacent to Memorial Gardens

Mixed-use Development at Marrowbone Lane, Dublin Anthony Reddy Associates

The area forms part of Dublin City Council's Cork Street Regeneration Strategy to rejuvenate the built environment and address the economic and social problems identified in the area. The site consists of privately owned lands to the south and Council-owned lands to the north. The development provides the area with badly needed public space and also contributes to the 'greening' of the area.

The overall design includes a new urban square with a café and crèche, and a new road to allow access to backland sites for future development. High-quality landscaping with a formal arrangement of trees and paved surfaces give a living street frontage to the new apartment blocks. The commercial uses at ground-floor level introduce day and night activity to this space, while the residential units above will provide passive surveillance of the public domain after hours.

Permeability through the site is provided by pedestrian access to Cork Street via Marion Villas. Visual links are maintained between the public realm and the private open spaces to the rear of the blocks. The evolution of the urban plan naturally resulted in four zones or distinct building blocks – each designed as a separate entity – to enhance the architectural quality of the new public realm.

The overall architectural treatment makes reference to the materials and urban grain of the city, while introducing more modern elements to reflect progress and regeneration. There is a good mix of different apartment types and sizes that will make them attractive to a variety of people.

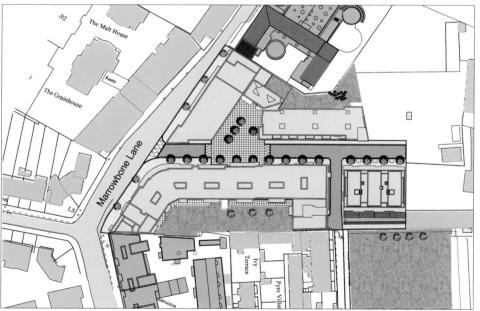

The apartments are mostly dual-aspect units, with generous floor areas, large balconies or winter gardens. They incorporate features such as light wells to provide natural ventilation and light to mid-plan bathrooms, kitchens and corridors, as well as individual storage units in the basement. The inclusion of generous private open spaces and secure play areas, as well as a mix of commercial/retail uses, will contribute to the long-term sustainability of the development.

design / completion – 2004–2010
client – P & G Dormer
collaboration architects for Block D and crèche – Studio M Architects

---

↖ East elevation and location map
→ View of new public square and block D

height	mix	percentage	no. of dwellings	site area	density	floor area	bed spaces	site coverage	open space	car spaces	context
4-7 storey	32 x 3-bed apartments 81 x 2-bed apartments 27 x 3-bed apartments 23 x 1-bed live/work units	75.3% residential 24.7% commercial	163	7,230m² (1.78 acres)	91 units/acre	18,900m²	387 (217/acre)	54%	314m² in public square 1,538m² in semi-private courtyards; 1,331m² in balconies + terraces	202 (basement car park)	inner-city site in urban rejuvenation area

MARROWBONE LANE

↑ 3rd-floor plan
↖ View of Block A from Marrowbone Lane
↙ View of Block B and new street from Marrowbone
   Lane
→ Plan of typical unit
↓ Ground-floor plan

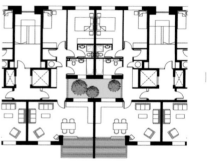

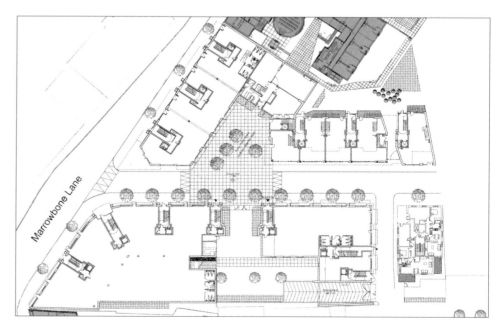

Apartments at Reuben Street / Cork Street, Dublin 12

FKL Architects

This site, on the corner of Dolphins Barn Street and Reuben Street in Dublin's inner city, marks the threshold of the city centre on one of its principal access routes. The project is proposed as two unequal L-shaped blocks, taking its scale from the two adjoining streets and stepping up to twelve floors at the corner. The two blocks, containing seventy apartments, frame a multistorey entrance to the courtyard, with a dramatic light-bridge by the artist Corban Walker at seventh-floor level.

The building draws on two great Dublin architectural traditions – the planar brick of Georgian façades with carefully incised openings, and the more wilful and decorative Victorian tradition. A binary system is used to dis-organise the pattern of the window and balcony opes, producing the maximum variety from a minimum number of window and apartment types. This instills a sense of individuality and ownership in a potentially repetitive commercial development.

The two apartment blocks sit on an articulated podium containing support facilities and retail units, mediating between the semi-public realm of the courtyard and the city. The materials of the podium (granite and mosaic) continue into the shopfront and the footpath surrounding the building, keying into the immediate surroundings. The contrast between the simple brick planar form and the complex base highlights and articulates the concept. The offsetting of window opes on the façades, based on a binary system, addresses the issues of personal identification for residents and the stimulation of variety within a generic

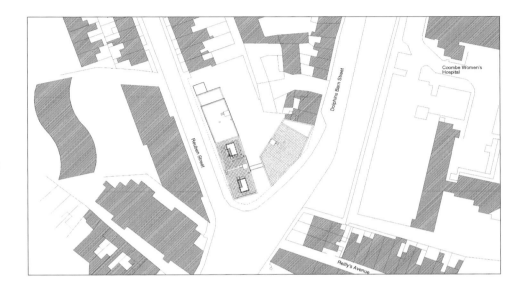

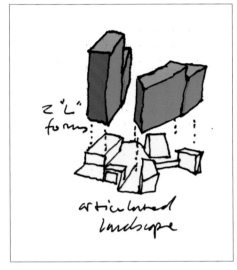

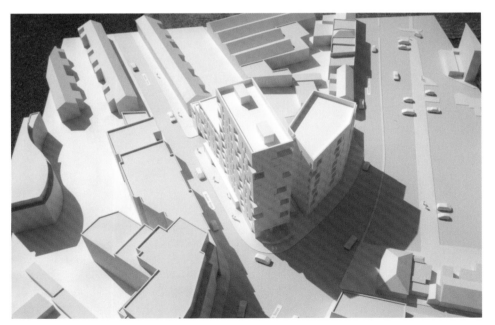

apartment layout. Dual-aspect apartments, where living spaces and recessed balconies are orientated south or west, and where natural light to bathrooms and kitchens is prioritised, ensure that these are apartments that people can live in.

name / address – Apartments at Earl's Court, Reuben Street / Cork Street, Dolphin's Barn, Dublin 12
design / completion – 2003–2006
client – Diamond Leather Ltd

↖ Location map showing site at junction of Reuben Street and Cork Street
↑ Concept sketch showing the two L-shaped forms above an 'articulated landscape' of uses at street and podium level
← Context model

height	mix	percentage	no. of dwellings	site area	density	floor area	bed spaces	site coverage	open space	car spaces	context
12 storey	3 x 3-bed apartments 45 x 2-bed apartments 22 x 1-bed apartments 4 live/work units + retail	93% residential 4% live/work units 3% commercial	74	1,656m² (0.4 acres)	185 units/acre	5,868m²	223 (557/acre)	43%	212m² in courtyard; also private balconies	40 (0.5 per dwelling)	prominent inner-city site at strategic location on major arterial route

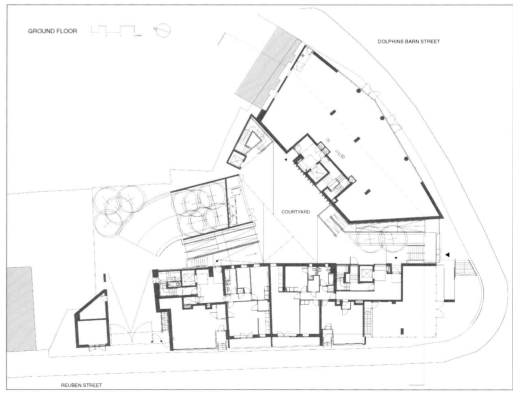

DOLPHINS BARN STREET

REUBEN STREET

GROUND FLOOR

DOLPHINS BARN STREET

COURTYARD

REUBEN STREET

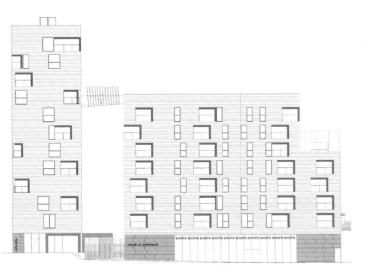

REUBEN STREET

↑ Elevation to Dolphins Barn
↑ Section
↗ View from Cork Street
→ Distant view from South Circular Road

opposite

↖ Typical apartment floor plan (5th)
← Ground-floor plan (retail)
⇐ Views of light-bridge by artist Corban Walker
   linking the blocks at 7th-floor level

151

Timberyard Social Housing, The Coombe, Dublin

O'Donnell + Tuomey Architects

The development consists of a new housing scheme of 47 dwellings and a street-level community facility in the historic Liberties area of Dublin. The project was generated by the construction of the Coombe bypass. A backland site was opened up, and the urban design requirement was for a new street frontage to heal the wounds caused by the road-engineering operation. The design centres on a new public space on the site of a former timberyard, making a residential enclave with a sense of place. The development proposes to provide scale, identity and a piece of living city, connecting new development in the area to its historic context.

The scheme works between the six-storey scale proposed in general along the new Cork Street corridor, and the smaller scale of the existing houses behind the site. The new buildings are in brick, with hardwood windows and screens to terraces and roof gardens. The windows are offset from each other in the walls to work with the complexity of the residential accommodation within, and to emphasise the continuity of the brick surface. The walls are modulated with recessed porches and terraces and projecting bay windows to give a depth and complexity to the building's edge and an interface between the private world of the house and the neighbourhood.

design / completion – 2001–2007
client – Dublin City Council

↗ Concept sketches of courtyard and street frontage
→ Location map and site plan

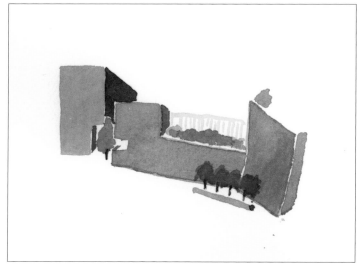

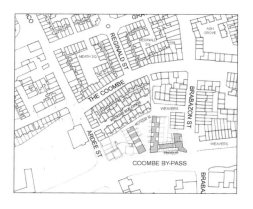

opposite

→ The Timberyard overlaid on maps from 1756 (based on Rocque), 1850, 1939, 2002 (all OS)
↠ View of courtyard; south elevation to bypass

height	mix	percentage	no. of dwellings	site area	density	floor area	bed spaces	site coverage	open space	car spaces	context
3-6 storey	8 x 3-bed duplexes 27 x 2-bed duplexes 11 x 1-bed apartments 1 x live/work unit	96% residential 2% live/work 2% communal	47	2,435m² (0.6 acres)	78 units/acre	3,807m²	169 (282/acre)	48%	625m² public	0.4 per dwelling	major inner-city rejuvenation area

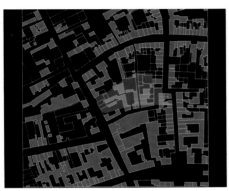

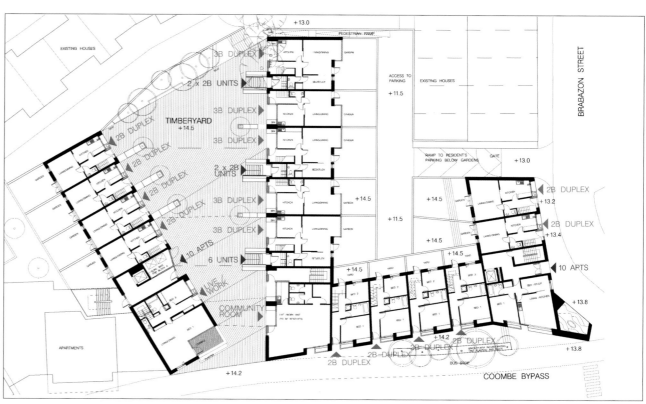

York Street Redevelopment, Dublin 2

Seán Harrington Architects

Working closely with the local community, this scheme near St Stephen's Green in Dublin city centre contains apartments, a community centre, a retail unit and a secure communal garden. The new building will rehouse the tenants of the demolished York Street flats. The building re-establishes the former street line of both York Street and Mercer Street, reintroduces the pattern of mews dwellings, and marks this important city corner with a distinctive and appropriate building.

Based on ecological design principles, the building benefits from controlled passive solar-gain through the use of glazed winter gardens and solar thermal roof panels. It also has an energy-efficient communal heating system, high levels of insulation and Sedum green roofs, increased south-facing glazing and reduced north-facing glazing. (The building has achieved a BER ranging between A3 and B2.) Rainwater from the roofs is collected and stored to irrigate the garden and allotments, and for car-washing. Great emphasis has been placed on communal facilities such as meeting rooms, a shared garden, children's play area and recycling facilities.

There is a large variety of different dwelling types. Most of the apartments are either dual- or corner-aspect. In the building facing onto York Street, the apartments benefit from bay windows on the north façade overlooking the streets below, while

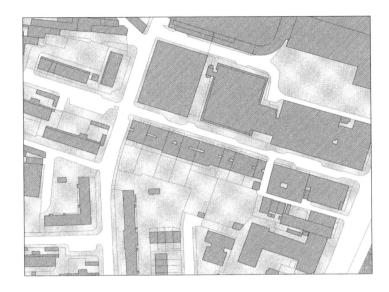
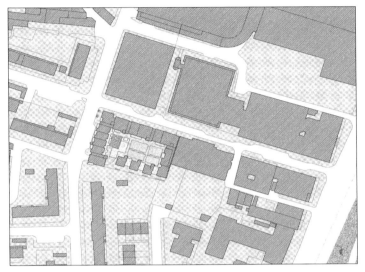

↗ Urban grain – reconstructed terrace, 1940s, and York Street Housing, 2008
→ Bird's-eye views of scheme from Mercer Street and from south-east showing mews and communal garden

height	mix	percentage	no. of dwellings	site area	density	floor area	bed spaces	site coverage	open space	car spaces	context
5, 7 storey	17 x 3-bed apartments 29 x 2-bed apartments 20 x 1-bed apartments	97% residential 3% communal	66	2,263m² (0.6 acres)	113 units/acre	5,619m²	215/acre	56.5%	925m² in communal garden; additional roof terrace and private gardens	21 (0.3 per dwelling)	inner-city site

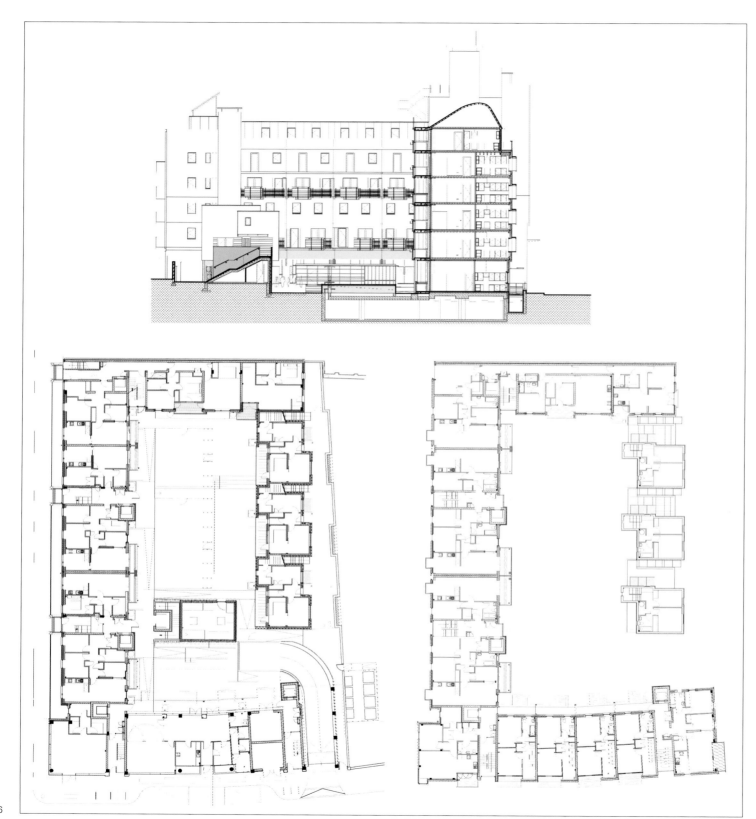

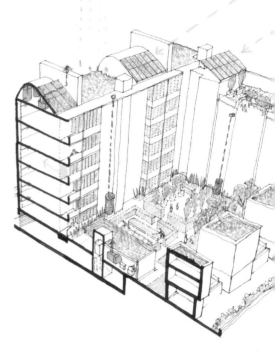

large sunny balconies on the south façade overlook the courtyard. This communal garden and roof terraces were designed in close consultation with the residents.

A shallow-depth block is used where possible, with apartments accessed from single staircase and lift cores. The duplex apartments above the communal facilities on Mercer Street are accessed from an open deck overlooking the communal courtyard to the rear. The mews dwellings along the southern boundary of the site all have own-door access.

The architectural expression of the public face of the building is a reflection of the construction system. The apartment typologies and differentiation between private space and circulation is also clearly expressed. The two main façades of the building are made up of rhythmic elements within a coherent composition which meet at the corner, where they are bookended by an elegant tower.

design / completion – 2002–2008
client – Dublin City Council

↖ Typical cross-section
← Ground-floor plan and typical floor plan

Charlemont Street Regeneration Project, Dublin 2

Paul Keogh Architects

A master plan was prepared for the Dublin City Council-owned lands at Charlemont Street. The Council's objective for the redevelopment project is to maximise the site's potential in an economically, socially and environmentally sustainable manner.

The master plan created a vision for a total regeneration project, replacing the existing council blocks with a mixture of social, affordable and private housing, community facilities and commercial uses. The site will have a total of 181 flats in six blocks.

The scheme is designed around a new street network, which provides a clear urban structure for the area, with pedestrian-accessible connections to local amenities, services and neighbourhood facilities. This plan creates a new identity for the Charlemont Street flats, and seeks to transform the estate into a model sustainable urban community.

Following completion of the master plan (with residents' and elected members' endorsement of the scheme), a detailed design was prepared for the first phase of the development, comprising 62 social housing units on the section of the site bounded by Charlemont Street, Tom Kelly Road and the former St Ultan's Flats site.

design / completion – 2003–
    (Part 8 approval obtained 2008;
    project being advanced in a PPP
    procurement process)
client – Dublin City Council

↑ Elevation to Tom Kelly Road (at rear)
↓ Master plan
↘ Bird's-eye axonometric view from north showing area of master plan stretching back from Charlemont Street

opposite

→ Sketch perspectives of northern corner on Charlemont Street, and Tom Kelly Road
➔ View of Charlemont Street looking north
↘ Charlemont Street elevation

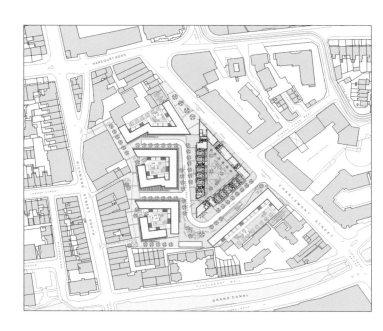

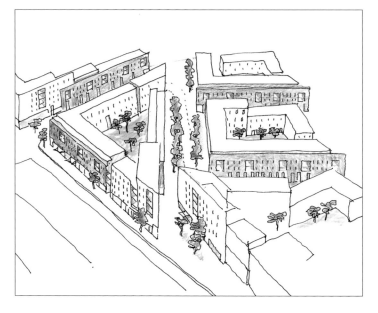

height	mix	percentage	no. of dwellings	site area	density	floor area	bed spaces	site coverage	open space	car spaces	context
5-6 storey PHASE 1	1 x 4-bed unit 28 x 3-bed units 19 x 2-bed units 14 x 1-bed units community / commercial	87% residential 13% community and commercial	62	0.9 ha (2.24 acres)	172 units/ha (27.7/acre)	9,826m²	243 (270/ha)	18.4%	2,220m²	75 (1.2 per dwelling) area	inner-city urban-regeneration area

Seán Treacy House, Buckingham Street, Dublin 1

Paul Keogh Architects

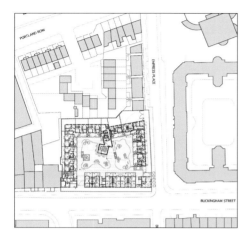

Developed in collaboration with Dublin City Council's City Architect's Department, the North-East Inner-City (NEIC) management team, the city planners and local community groups, this project is part of the NEIC Integrated Area Plan. It involves the demolition of the existing 1960s slab blocks on the site, and their replacement with a new mixed-housing development, accommodating both new and existing residents.

The scheme contains 53 housing units and a community facility. It is organised around a semi-private raised courtyard, enclosed by a perimeter block formed by a six-storey apartment building on Buckingham Street and three- and four-storey duplex units to the rear. The scheme completes the streetscape between Summerhill and Empress Place, and the courtyard provides a shared, semi-private open space. The design of the perimeter block maximises passive surveillance of the courtyard and

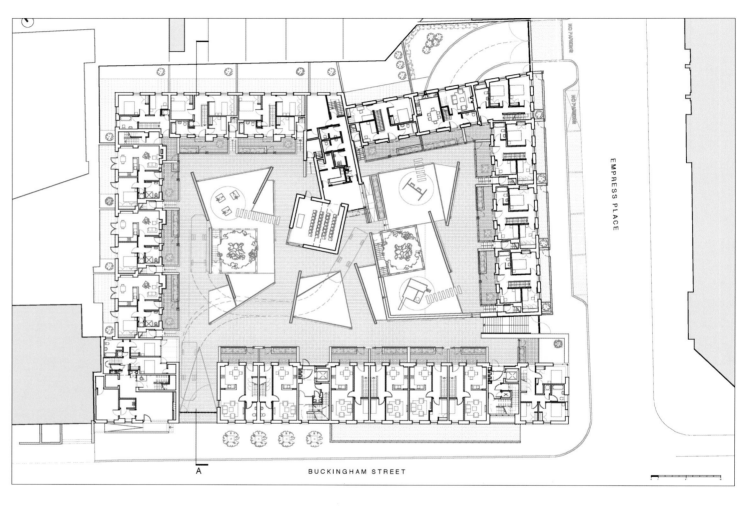

streets, thereby contributing to a secure residential environment.

Prioritised in the scheme is both urban design and residential amenity. All the street-level housing units have own-door

access and their own private outdoor space.

address – Buckingham Street, Dublin 1
design / completion – 2001–2010
client – Dublin City Council

↖ Location map
↑ Site plan

height	mix	percentage	no. of dwellings	site area	density	floor area	bed spaces	site coverage	open space	car spaces	context
4-6 storey	2 x 4-bed units 13 x 3-bed units 25 x 2-bed units 12 x 1-bed units 1 retail unit	98% residential 2% commercial	53	3,982m² (0.98 acres)	54 units/acre (133/ha)	5,220m²	201 (205/acre)	29%	1,170m² in courtyard (2,260m² in total, including private balconies)	60 (1.13 per dwelling)	inner-city urban-regeneration area

↖ Concept sketches of communal courtyard
↗ Corner of Buckingham Street and Empress Place
→ Section through main entrance and courtyard, looking northwards
→ Elevation to Buckingham Street

The Steelworks, Foley Street, Dublin 1

Laughton Tyler Owens Architects

The Steelworks is a new mixed-use development on the extended Ferrum Trading Company site on Foley Street. The sequence of buildings and spaces covers an area from the corner of Beaver Street and Foley Street to the eastern edge of the park. The scheme is part of the North-East Inner-City Integrated Area Plan for the regeneration of the area.

A relatively constrained corner entrance situation helped generate the scheme's arrangement of dynamically curving forms in four mixed-use buildings, varying in height from four to eight storeys. They are grouped around a protected public space with a high amenity value and superior-quality hard and soft landscaping. Also incorporated are numerous generous semi-public and private indoor areas. A five-storey glazed atrium provides a winter garden and indoor communal area for residents, facing onto the park.

Building façades are generally finished in varying combinations of Pertrarch, terracotta, and acrylic-insulated render, with mostly timber-composite glazing systems.

Although the scheme is made up of two distinct areas of accommodation – office and residential – it is the intention that the buildings and spaces relate not only to each other, but also to the neighbouring buildings and open spaces, offering good site permeability and providing a new dynamic image for this central area.

design / completion – 2001–2006
client – Macushla Property Developments

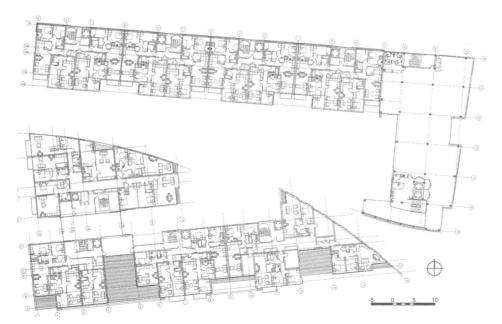

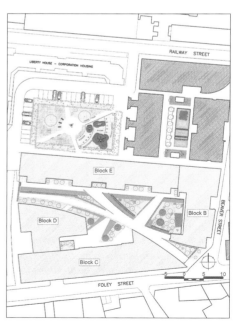

height	mix	percentage	no. of dwellings	site area	density	floor area	bed spaces	site coverage	open space	car spaces	context
4-8 storey	12 x 3-bed duplexes 91 x 2-bed apartments 59 x 1-bed apartments	90% residential	162	6,348m² (1.57 acres)	103 units/acre	18,421m²	368 (234/acre)	43.5%	3,350m² in courtyards, balconies and terraces	0.75 per dwelling	inner-city site, part of NEIC rejuvenation area

↑ Entrance to new Steelworks development on
corner of Foley / Beaver streets
↗ Views of internal courtyard
→ Cross-section

opposite

↖ Views of blocks B and D
← Location map showing site on Foley / Beaver
streets, with Foley Park behind
⇐ First-floor plan of development

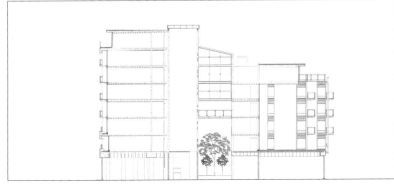

Social Housing, Upr Dominick Street, Dublin 7 City Architects' Division, Dublin City Council

Upper Dominick Street is situated between a number of framework regeneration plan areas – HARP, O'Connell Street IAP and Parnell Square Regeneration Plan. It will be one of the key link routes from the city centre to the proposed Dublin Institute of Technology campus at Grangegorman.

This development is part of a strategy to redevelop the area. It has housed tenants from former demolished flat complexes on Lower Dominick Street, which is due for complete regeneration. Previously comprised of mixed residential and light industrial use, and surface car parks (it was a former newspaper-distribution centre), the site now comprises social housing, DCC offices and an archive store.

Residential units are set back from the street at ground and first-floor level by a continuous raised-level access plinth, which provides privacy from Dominick Street pedestrians and traffic, whilst also providing an active street frontage. The average number of apartments accessed off common stairwells is six, providing for a manageable complex. A courtyard 'street' provides a secure play area for children and access to the mews apartments and basement car park.

All apartments are dual-aspect. The large, usable balconies have excellent south-west orientation and run the full apartment length. Each balcony level steps back to reduce overshadowing below.

address – 65-79 Upper Dominick Street, Dublin 7
design / completion – 1999–2004
client – Dublin City Council

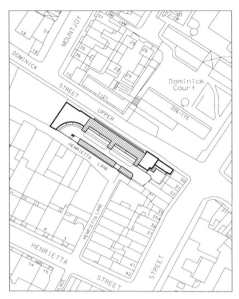

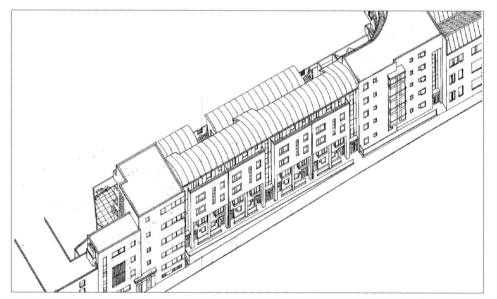

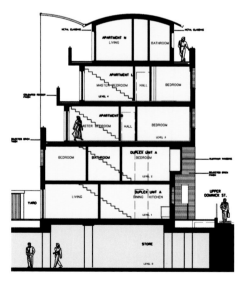

height	mix	percentage	no. of dwellings	site area	density	floor area	bed spaces	site coverage	open space	car spaces	context
2 and 5 storey over basement	32 x 2-bed duplexes/apts 14 x 1-bed apartments DCC facilities + car park communal room	66% residential 23% DCC 9% parking 2% communal	46	0.44 acres (0.18 ha)	105 units/acre (255 units/ha)	3,435m² residential 1,200m² DCC 460m² parking 80m² communal	124 (282/acre)	57% ground level 100% semi-basement level	260m² public 105m² semi-public 505m² private	12 (residential)	inner-city brownfield infill site situated among 3-5 storey buildings

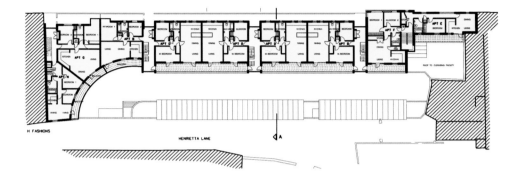

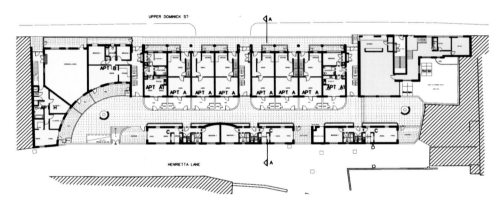

↖ View showing how verticals and horizontals are used to break up the façade
↖ Location map
← Cross-section and axonometric view

↑ Main elevation to Upper Dominick Street
↑ Entry level and typical floor plans
→ Projecting bay to Upper Dominick Street
↓ Semi-basement plan

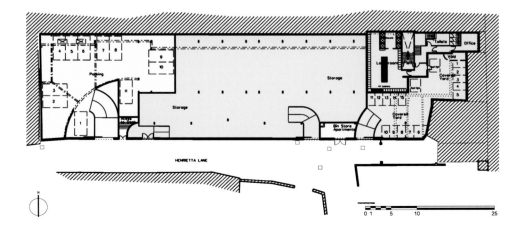

The Cigar Box, Nth Great George's Street, Dublin 1

Denis Byrne Architects

This site on North Great George's Street is within the conservation areas of the north-inner-city Georgian grid. The L-shaped site is situated between a Victorian warehouse and a pastiche Georgian apartment development. The building strategy chosen emphasises the border nature of the site and aims to differentiate between the buildings on the corner and the Georgian terraces. This is achieved by inserting a new space on the site, analogous to a lane or side street.

The building, thus separated from the Georgian discipline, was free to look to the adjoining warehouse building for clues as to how to proceed. The building was intended to be unpretentious and direct – qualities associated with warehouse buildings. The materials used are traditional – brick, stone, timber, glass and metal – all used in a straightforward way.

The main entrance and staircase are found in the new space between the buildings. This space is covered by a glass roof above timber-slatted under-lining, but is otherwise open to the elements. When ascending, views of Georgian Dublin appear, and alternate with the Rotunda's spire. In the afternoon, the sun pours through here.

The large apartments (one per floor) are shaped to maximise available light on a tight site. Each one is entered from the access deck through a private west-facing balcony. The apartments have an oak-lined entrance lobby (the 'cigar-box'), but are otherwise open loft-type spaces, with painted concrete-block walls and concrete ceilings. Oak floors and oak wall-linings

soften this sparse robustness. Bedroom and kitchen balconies and large external double doors in the main living space enrich the restrained interiors. The open spaces allow for flexibility in bedroom sizes and numbers.

name / address – 'The Cigar Box'
– Mixed Development at 26 North
Great George's Street, Dublin 1
design / completion – 2001–2004
client – Brendan Doyle

↖ Photomontage
↑ Elevation to North Great George's Street
↗ Site map – before and after

↗ Views of external stairs, entrance and façade to North Great George's Street
→ Plans – basement, ground, 1st, 2nd, 3rd, 4th

height	mix	percentage	no. of dwellings	site area	density	floor area	bed spaces	site coverage	open space	car spaces	context
5 storey	2 x 3-bed apartments 2 x 2-bed apartments	55% residential 45% commercial	4	192m² (0.0192 acres)	208 units/ha	450m²	18	64%	balconies (min 6.5m²)	none	city-centre infill

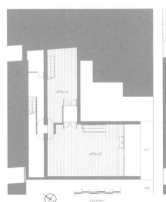
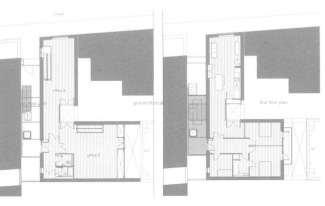
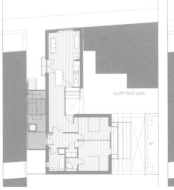
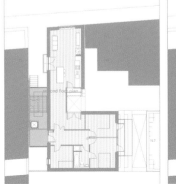
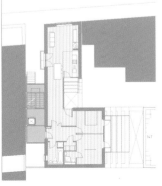

office A

office B

ground floor plan

first floor plan

fourth floor plan

Social Housing, North Frederick Place, Dublin 1

Gilroy McMahon Architects

The site at Frederick Lane and Sheridan Court was formerly a car park. The brief was to create social housing on this limited backlands site, situated behind an existing flat complex and surrounded on the remaining three sides by service lanes. It is Dublin City Council policy to intensify sites such as Frederick Lane.

The challenge was to insert a new apartment block at the rear of the existing 1970s flat complex without diminishing the amenities of the complex. The scheme of 28 apartments is designed to connect the new and existing buildings, enclosing a gated communal courtyard. The courtyard is landscaped to provide small paved gardens for both new and existing ground-floor units, as well as common recreational space, creating a sense of community, ownership and social interaction.

The deliberate graduation of a series of spaces from the semi-public to the private accommodates a varied social interaction amongst the occupants.

The building is broken down in scale into five blocks. Four of these blocks consist of six apartments, two per floor, served by a common stairs. The fifth block consists of four units set around a small courtyard.

The five semi-private common stairs are designed to filter south-east light through to the courtyard space. The new building is sensitively stepped in section to maximise light-passage into the courtyard and to provide private terraces for the upper-level apartments. Car-parking is provided at basement level, accessed from the lower-level laneway.

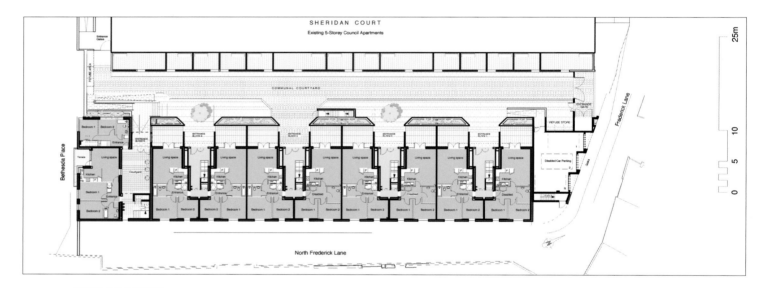

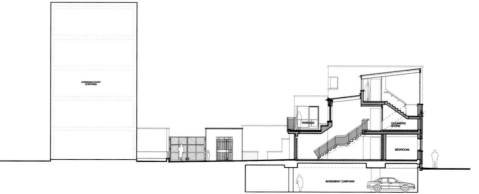

All residential units enjoy dual-aspect rooms along an east-west orientation. The units have open-plan living areas with large windows, looking onto a private terrace area and communal courtyard.

design / completion – 2002–2006
client – Dublin City Council

↑ West elevation to communal courtyard
↖ Ground-floor plan
← Cross-section through development

height	mix	percentage	no. of dwellings	site area	density	floor area	bed spaces	site coverage	open space	car spaces	context
3 storey over basement	20 x 2-bed apartments 8 x 1-bed apartments	100% residential	28	2,375m²	48 units/acre	1,575m² (excl. basement)	48 (83/acre)	41%	880m² in courtyard and balconies	52 (0.3 per dwelling)	inner-city backlands rejuvenation area

Mixed-Use Development, Bridgefoot Street, Dublin 8

Mitchell & Associates

The Bridgefoot Street scheme is a mixed-use proposal in a marginal area of Dublin city urgently in need of regeneration. Contextual analysis of the area established there was the potential for significant height on this corner site, which is jointly owned by Dublin City Council and a developer.

A thirteen-storey tower is proposed to the south of the site, facing up Bridgefoot Street towards St Catherine's church on Thomas Street. A six-storey perimeter block encloses a large residents' garden at first-floor level. The scheme comprises 41 apartments, 1,000m² of retail space and 300m² of commercial space, with a 41-space basement garage, helping to address the lack of retail and commercial space in the immediate area.

The individual apartments are large. They are predominantly dual-aspect and have generous ceiling heights, large balconies and terraces, as well as dedicated utility rooms and storage areas. The scheme also proposes significant environmental improvements, including substantially widened footpaths, tree-planting and street furniture. These improvements to the public realm and the provision of a new urban garden, visible from the street, aim to greatly enhance the area. The main materials used are glass and stone panels.

The conditions attached to the An Bord Pleanála permission have resulted in significant changes to the scheme, which is currently under client review.

address – Bridgefoot / Island St, Dublin 8
design / completion – 2006–2012
client – Dublin City Council

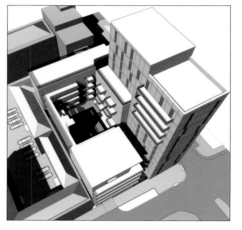

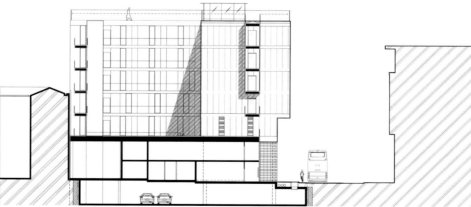

↑ Bird's-eye view of development and model
← Typical floor plan and section through block

↗ Views of raised courtyard
→ Photomontage of development from bridge
→ Top of the 13-storey tower on Bridgefoot / Island Street corner projecting above the roof terrace of 6-storey blocks
→ Main entrance off street

height	mix	percentage	no. of dwellings	site area	density	floor area	bed spaces	site coverage	open space	car spaces	context
13 storey	13 x 3-bed apartments 28 x 2-bed apartments	81% residential 17% retail 2% commercial	41	1,396m² (0.34 acres)	130 units/acre	5,848m²	177 (530/acre)	38%	36m² per apartment in private balconies	41 (1 per dwelling)	underdeveloped urban context, consisting of existing and proposed 6-12 storey housing

Senior Citizens' Residences, Artane, Dublin 5

Mitchell & Associates

This site is typically suburban in nature, on a busy road of low-density, semi-detached and terraced houses. It is situated between semi-detached properties to the south and convent buildings and a primary school to the rear and side.

A total of thirteen one-bedroom (two-person) units are accommodated in the scheme. With a site area of just over a third of an acre, the development represents a density 39 units (78 bed spaces) per acre.

The sense of community and security offered to the residents was the strongest generator of the design concept, which was to provide a central planted courtyard which could be accessed by all the units.

Access to the scheme is through one entrance in the two-storey L-shaped building, which forms a defensive wall to the busy road. This main block wraps around the north and east of the courtyard, which is completed with two one-storey blocks to the south and west.

From the outset, the requirement that all units would be accessible by people with disabilities was factored into the design. The bathrooms are designed to be accessible for disabled users, and wide entrance halls and circulation areas ensure that each unit is comfortably accessible.

A total of six car parking spaces are provided for the thirteen units, located to the front of the building.

design / completion – 2001–2003
client – Linham Ltd
end-user – Dublin City Council

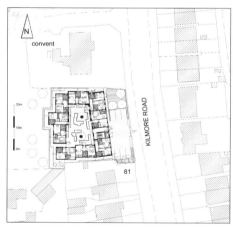

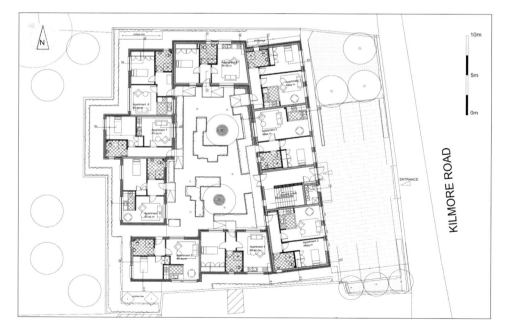

KILMORE ROAD

↖ Views of completed development
← Ground-floor plan
↑ Location map

height	mix	percentage	no. of dwellings	site area	density	floor area	bed spaces	site coverage	open space	car spaces	context
1-2 storey	13 x 1-bed apartments	100% residential	13	1,350m² (0.33 acres)	39 units/acre	605m²	26 (78/acre)	37%	850m² in courtyard; also private balconies	6 (0.46 per dwelling)	suburban site adjacent to convent and school

Timber Mill, Artane, Dublin 5

Murray O'Laoire Architects

Timber Mill is an extensive mixed-use development on a long, linear, sloping site. Organised into six blocks, it ranges from two to four storeys, consisting of 193 apartments, a basement car park, crèche, several live/work units, a pharmacy and a convenience store. Private terraces and gardens are a feature of the development.

In the larger three-storey Block A, ground-floor dwellings are provided with a private courtyard and gardens. The first-floor units have a private rear-terrace space and access to private gardens. The second-floor units are provided with an upper mezzanine level with access to large private terraces.

The three-storey Block B is built entirely over a basement car-park, the roof of which is dedicated to a terrace space for residents with bench seating and raised planters. This block also houses the crèche

A palette of materials, including timber, zinc, stainless steel and opaque glass against a backdrop of off-white render, is used in varying configurations throughout the scheme. In addition, the entrance core of each block type is identified by colour. The balance of materials is subtle, with redwood cedar timber to terraces and balconies, dark-grey window frames and panels, painted steelwork, tinted opaque-glass balustrades to balconies, and zinc cladding to stair cores.

A mixture of high-quality soft and hard landscaping is provided throughout.

design / completion – 2003–2006
client – Werdna Ltd

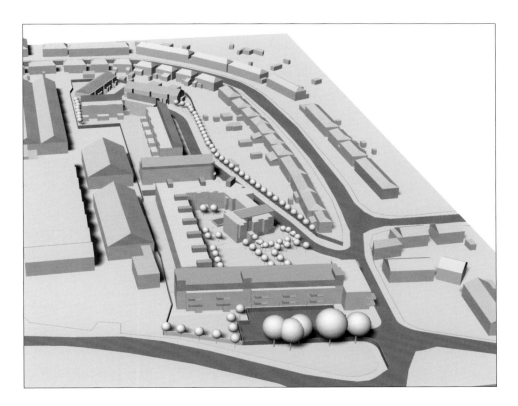

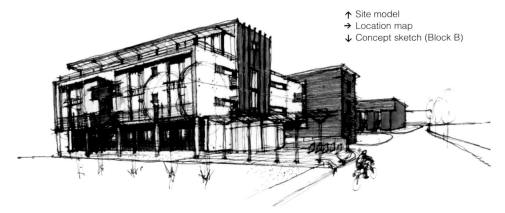

↑ Site model
→ Location map
↓ Concept sketch (Block B)

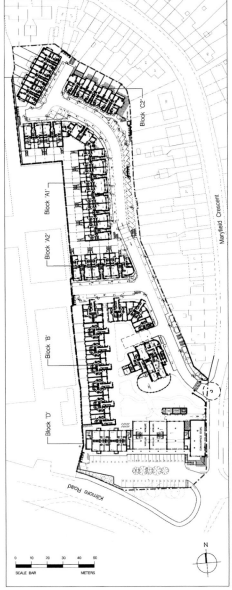

height	mix	percentage	no. of dwellings	site area	density	floor area	bed spaces	site coverage	open space	car spaces	context
2-4 storey	193 x 2-bed apartments 4 live/work units crèche, retail + car park	92% residential 8% commercial	197	4.6 acres (1.85 ha)	43 units/acre	16,362m²	386 (84/acre)	35%	1,800m² public 30m² per unit in rear terraces and gardens	254 (1.3 per dwelling) (133 basement; 121 surface)	suburban site on a former timber yard

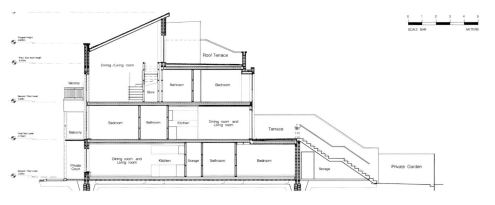

↑ Cross-section through block A

← Views of block A

↓ Ground-floor plans of blocks C (top) and A

opposite

→ Views of block B east elevation and courtyard

↘ View of block C1 from the road

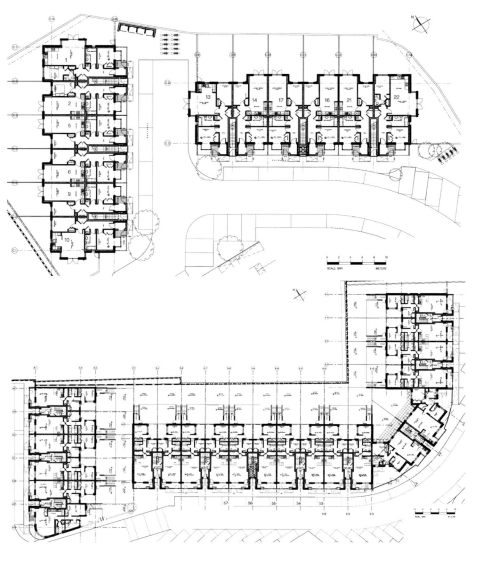

Senior Citizens' Residences, Kylemore Road, Dublin

Paul Keogh Architects

The design of this Dublin City Council senior citizens' residential complex is based around an enclosed courtyard – open on its north and south sides – flanked by two terraces of housing. Both blocks look onto the communal open space (above underground parking), which provides a pleasant space for residents.

Along Kylemore Road, a four-to-five-storey building has staircases and lifts at intervals, leading onto raised access decks. Along the western boundary, a two-storey block contains ground and first-floor units entered directly off a shared staircase from the courtyard. At its southern end, there is a residents' communal building, which also provides recreation, health and social facilities for older people in the wider community. Disabled access has been fully considered, and the design aspiration is to achieve the standards contained in the Joseph Rowntree Trust's Lifetime Adaptable Homes Standard.

The scheme aspires to being a model of sustainability, using energy-saving technologies such as passive solar-gain, communal self-condensing boilers, solar water-heating, heat-recovery systems, a highly insulated building fabric, and compost and waste recycling.

The project was presented to the Council's local area committee in July 2007, and was unanimously approved. It is currently awaiting DoEHLG approval to proceed.

address – Kylemore Road, Ballyfermot, Dublin 10
design / completion – 2006–
client – Dublin City Council

height	mix	percentage	no. of dwellings	site area	density	floor area	bed spaces	site coverage	open space	car spaces	context
2-5 storey	8 x 2-bed units 82 x 1-bed units community centre	91% residential 9% communal	90	0.66 ha (1.64 acres)	136 units/ha (55/acre)	6,950m²	188 (115/acre)	30%	2,482m²	60	suburban

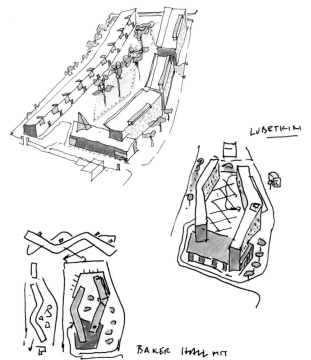

LUBETKIN

BAKER HALL MIT

Addison Lodge, Glasnevin, Dublin 9

Traynor O'Toole Architects

The site is situated in a residential area of Glasnevin, surrounded by traditional brick houses and across the road from the Botanic Gardens. The brief was to create a scheme of apartments and restaurant with a new image, deriving from these contextual elements.

The project is arranged in two blocks. The block along Botanic Road contains one-bedroom duplexes and two-bedroom apartments, with the restaurant alongside. It complements the traditional arrangement of the terraced houses in the area with their brick façades, pitched roofs and vertical windows. The solid appearance of the brick is replaced with steel and terracotta tiles in the new blocks, giving a sense of lightness. Addressing the 19th-century glasshouses in the Botanic Garden, the curved roof allows the fourth floor to be used as a communal terrace, with views of the area. The vertical rhythm of the openings is achieved by a series of louvres in the front façade.

The second block contains two-bedroom duplexes over four stories, and three three-bedroom single-storey houses at the back looking onto a communal garden.

address – Botanic Road, Glasnevin, Dublin 9
design / completion – 2005–
    (still at design stage)
client – Freyne family

↗ Street elevation to Botanic Road
→ Location map
⇢ Elevation to Botanic Road (top), rear elevation and cross-section

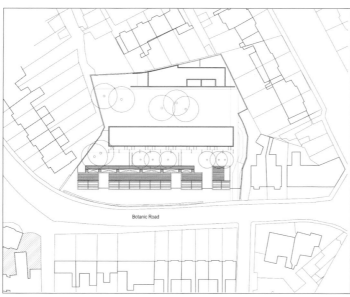

Botanic Road

opposite

→ Plans – ground and 1st-floor, and typical apartment plans
⇢ Views of rear block and landscaped courtyard

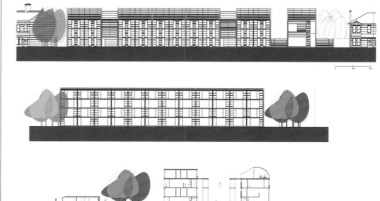

height	mix	percentage	no. of dwellings	site area	density	floor area	bed spaces	site coverage	open space	car spaces	context
3-4 storey	3 x 3-bed houses 24 x 2-bed duplexes 5 x 2-bed apartments 10 x 1-bed apartments restaurant	94% residential 6% commercial	42	4,473m² (1.11 acres)	42 units/acre	3,354m²	77	74%	2,127m² communal garden 346m² communal terrace 158m² balconies	43	traditional inner suburban area

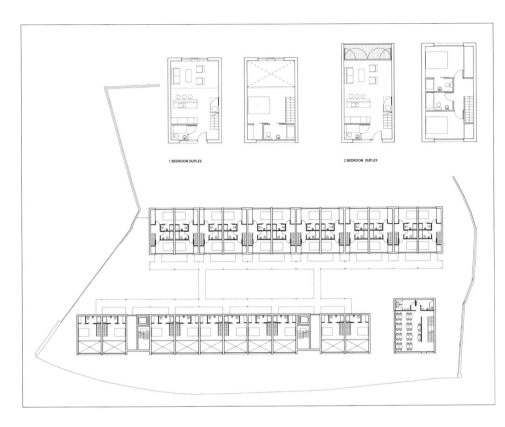

1 BEDROOM DUPLEX   2 BEDROOM DUPLEX

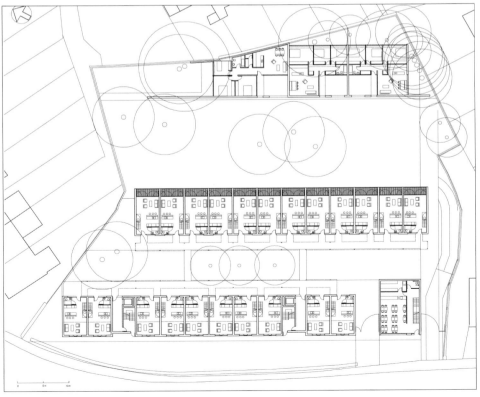

14-17 St Martin's Row, Chapelizod, Dublin 20

Shaffrey Associates Architects

The site comprises a ruined terrace of buildings fronting onto St Martin's Row (acquired through CPO by Dublin City Council) and an open area to the rear in private ownership. The brief was to explore an appropriate design solution and use-mix for the site in a pilot study which could be adapted and applied to similar sites in the village. Consultation with local groups indicated a need for family-type housing to balance the tendency in recent developments for apartment-style accommodation.

The design approach was to reinstate the historic streetfront of 14-17 St Martin's Row while creating family-type units to the rear of the site. The design provides for a three-storey-over-basement block onto the street, with one retail unit, two apartments above, and a three-storey house on the footprint of No. 14. To the rear there are six two-storey-over-semi-basement houses, with west-facing gardens and a communal pathway to the front. This allows the open character of the site to be retained.

Kitchen and dining areas benefit from east morning light and views to the Phoenix Park, while living areas receive early-to-late evening west light, and open onto a large terrace overlooking the gardens. The lower-ground floor can be used as office space, a fourth bedroom or children's play area, building in flexibility and choice. The relationship between houses, gardens and communal pathway will encourage neighbourly interaction and help create a sense of community.

design / completion – 2005–
client – Dublin City Council

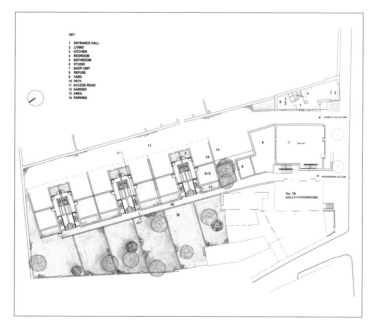

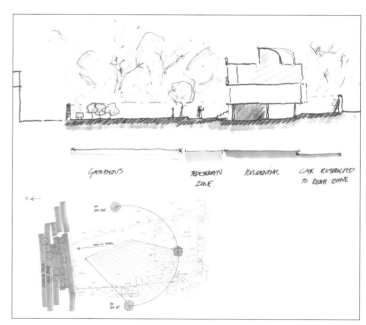

height	mix	percentage	no. of dwellings	site area	density	floor area	bed spaces	site coverage	open space	car spaces	context
3 storey	7 x 3-bed houses 2 x 2-bed apartments 1 retail unit	90% residential 10% commercial	9	2,060m² (0.5 1 acres)	18 units/acre	2,160m²	27 (54/acre)	33%	799m² in private gardens, terraces and balconies	16	inner-suburban site with street frontage in historic village setting

Tonlegee House, Millbrook Avenue, Dublin 5

NJBA Architecture & Urban Design

Originally, the site for this scheme was the centrepiece of a farm that predated Dublin's northward suburban expansion. The existing 20th-century Tonlegee House found itself as an island amongst a mixture of postwar row and semi-detached houses. The solution arrived at was a variant of the popular duplex section, formulated to achieve a sort of double-duplex, which incorporated an undercroft for car-parking.

The design is centred on the split-section of two maisonettes. To accommodate Local Authority standards in relation to privacy, overlooking, parking and public open space, the architecture was carved out of what was left – an asymmetrical section. The site orientation on an east-west axis meant that in order to avail of the sun, the main rooms would be directed towards the south, using the sectional profile to ensure that privacy was maintained throughout and that maximum benefit could be garnered from the available resources. By tailoring the section, it was possible to create spaces that responded to the site and its context while making for an interesting living environment. Light penetrates the section as far as the car-parking on the northern elevation. The sculpted topography of the project exploits the available volume, which maintains the local scale.

Under a type of design/build process, a hybrid constructional system emerged. Precast elements (floors) were suspended on frames or cross-walls, clad in solid rendered masonry with internal insulation.

design / completion – 2004–2007
client – Rebarn Ltd

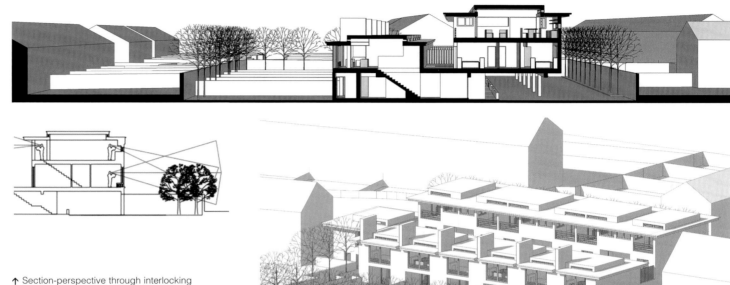

↑ Section-perspective through interlocking maisonettes
↑ Conceptual section – protection of privacy
→ Bird's-eye view of development from south-east
↓ Location map
↘ Ground-floor plan

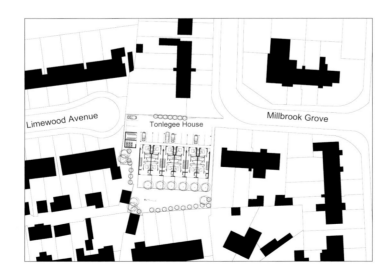

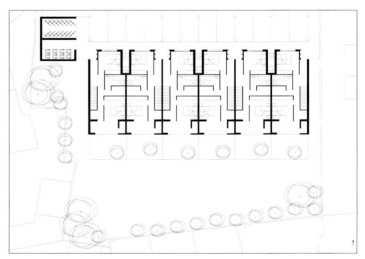

height	mix	percentage	no. of dwellings	site area	density	floor area	bed spaces	site coverage	open space	car spaces	context
2-3 storey	12 x 2-bed apartments	100% residential	12	1,537m²	30 units/acre	848m²	48 (125/acre)	13% (excl. undercroft)	540m² in gardens; also private balconies	15 (1.25 per dwelling)	inner-suburban site in existing residential area

Riverpoint, Bishop's Quay, Limerick

Burke-Kennedy Doyle Architects

Riverpoint is situated on a third-of-a-hectare site on the corner of Lower Mallow Street and Bishop's Quay overlooking the River Shannon. A key feature of the scheme is the signature office tower which marks a crossing point on the river and is a symbol of the regeneration of the Limerick city quays. The challenge was to produce a building with an aesthetically pleasing shape, curving in both plan and section. The 14-storey-high tower uses high-quality glazing to reflect the river flowing by.

The scheme consists of three main blocks grouped around an elevated landscaped courtyard, looking towards the river. The tower houses mainly offices, while the other two blocks contain a mix of two-bedroom apartments and three-bedroom penthouses above restaurants, a crèche, and a leisure centre. All the apartments are orientated towards the garden courtyard and the river.

The flanking limestone wall on Mallow Street is used to step up from the scale of the existing streetscape.

design / completion – 2002–2007
client – Fordmount Developments

→ Model, location map, typical floor plan

opposite

→ Views from Condell Road and across the river
→→ View from Steamboat Quay

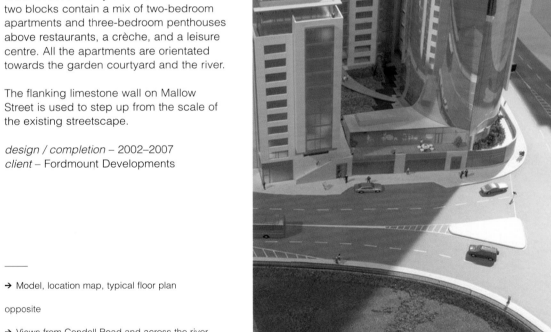

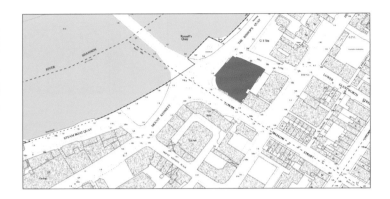

height	mix	percentage	no. of dwellings	site area	density	floor area	bed spaces	site coverage	open space	car spaces	context
8-14 storey	3 x 3-bed penthouses 119 x 2-bed apartments 2 x 1-bed apartments crèche, gym, retail + offices	85% residential 15% other	124	2,800m² (0.7 acres)	172 units/acre	11,800m² residential 6,213m² offices 1,788m² other	249	60% residential	399m² in courtyard 390m² in roof terrace	188 (1.5 per dwelling)	inner-city site adjacent to river

Annaville, Dundrum Road, Dublin 14

Denis Byrne Architects

This private residential project is an example of the possibility of densification in an existing suburban residential area. The vehicular and pedestrian entrance is from Dundrum Road through a gap in the surrounding houses. This narrow neck accommodates the car ramp and the pedestrian bridges that provide access to the various entrance levels.

The 54 residential units are arranged in three blocks over a basement car park. The first block contains 38 apartments and is connected at first-floor level to the pedestrian entrance by a dramatic ramped bridge, in the manner of a ship gangway. This bridge spans the garden, guiding the pedestrian to an arrival area with the choice of entering the lobby of the lower apartments or ascending to the external street at second-floor level. The street gives access to the duplex apartments.

The second block contains twelve apartments, which are approached from a conventional access gallery. The building faces south and overlooks a smaller courtyard garden. This garden provides access to the third block and the four terraced houses.

The integration of the project into this established area is helped by the use of brick as the main material, and the copper cladding of the upper floors.

design / completion – 2002–2005
client – Otranto Partnership

↗ View of development in its landscaped setting
→ Typical floor plan and location map

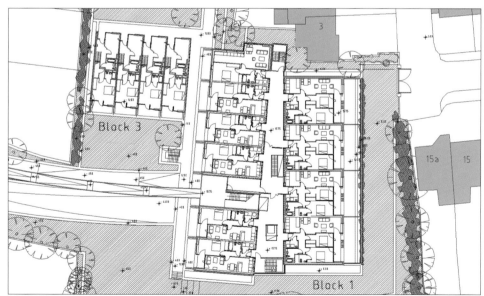

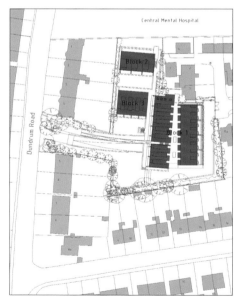

height	mix	percentage	no. of dwellings	site area	density	floor area	bed spaces	site coverage	open space	car spaces	context
2-4 storey	4 x 2-bed houses 16 x 2-bed duplexes 8 x 2-bed apartments 25 x 1-bed apartments 1 x studio apartment	100% residential	54	5,270m² (0.527 ha)	102units/ha	4,540m²	111	40%	615m² in public square; also private balconies	68 (1.25 per dwelling)	town-centre location overlooking historic building and harbour

↑ Views of the completed development
→ Section through site showing bridge and cross-section of block, with duplex apartments above lower-level apartments and underground car park

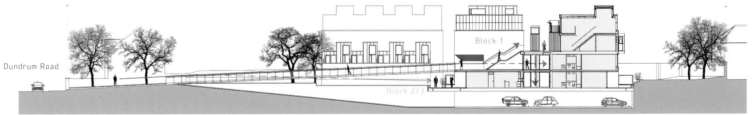

Dundrum Road

Block 1

Block 2/3

Lansdowne Gate, Drimnagh, Dublin 12

O'Mahony Pike Architects

This is a development of 280 apartments on a brownfield site. It includes a crèche, shop and 400m² office suite. It is within walking distance of the Luas Red Line (Bluebell stop) and reinstates part of the Lansdowne Park / Camac river walk.

The blocks are arranged around a courtyard which is open to the south-east to maximise natural daylight and solar-gain. All units are south-facing, either single- or dual-aspect. The site layout minimises exposure by using natural shelter from nearby woodland.

In terms of the building envelope, the following key elements were incorporated:
– the insulation specification is 60% above that in the Building Regulations
– the wall construction is traditional blockwork, drylined on the inside face with 100mm fibreglass insulation, and having a brick outer leaf, thermal mass is used for passive heat storage
– the orientation, glazing positions and detailing were resolved to maximise benefit from solar gain
– draught lobbies at ground floor to avoid heat-loss and extremely high levels of airtightness were achieved through rigorous site practices after the first fix.

A district heating system distributes hot water to the individual apartments. The gas-fired centralised boiler room contains ten modular condensing boilers and the low-energy pumps which control the flow and return pipes. The distribution pipes are highly insulated and supply both the hot-water demand and the space-heating requirement of all the entire development. Residents can enjoy instant hot water. and

the apartments each have an individual meter which monitors consumption; they are then billed bimonthly per kilowatt/hour of energy for the hot water they have used. The gas is bought by the management company at the commercial rate, which allows savings to be passed on to the residents.

Each apartment is ventilated with an individual mechanical ventilation with heat recovery (HRMV) system. The heat-recovery unit is a device that delivers a constant stream of fresh warm air to the

apartment by recycling or recovering the heat from air being vented out of the apartment, and transferring it to the fresh air being drawn in. About 60% of the heat is recovered, which reduces the need for residents to turn on their heating system. The benefits also include a constant supply of filtered fresh air, reduced air moisture and allergens in the air, and reduced condensation and dust.

The individual controls for both the district-heating and ventilation systems have been specifically designed to be user-friendly.

The HRMV control is factory-set, so the 'off' mode corresponds to the background 'trickle' rate of air-changes, and the 'on' mode is a booster setting to be used, for instance, after a shower has been used or after cooking. The heating and hot water operate on simple timer clocks. This project complies with the requirements of the proposed part L regulation.

design / completion – 2003–2008
client – Cosgrave Developments

↖ Location map and site plan

height	mix	percentage	no. of dwellings	site area	density	floor area	bed spaces	site coverage	open space	car spaces	context
2-7 storey	55 x 3-bed apartments 183 x 2-bed apartments 42 x 1-bed apartments crèche, medical, retail	89% residential 11% commercial	280	2.3 ha (5.7 acres)	122 units/ha (49/acre)	27,580m²	1,091 (474/ha)	22.3%	12,000m2 in shared courtyard and landscaped river embankment	326 (incl. visitors) (1 per dwelling)	outer suburban within walking distance of light-rail network

↑ Views of the completed development
↓ Typical floor plan

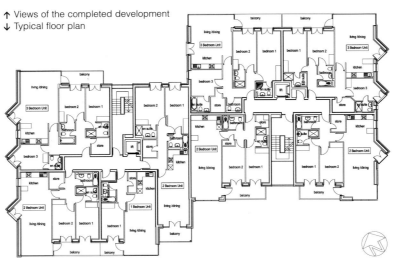

Wyckham Point, Dundrum, Dublin 14

McCrossan O'Rourke Manning Architects

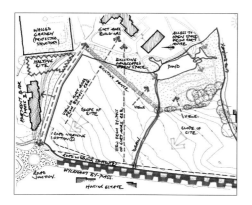

Wyckham Point is the third and largest phase of a residential development totalling approximately 750 apartments. This phase comprises 514 apartments, a crèche and a residents' gymnasium. The development fronts Wyckham bypass, an important local and regional transport route linking Dundrum Town Centre and the M50 motorway, and accessing Balally Luas station. The development lands are part of the Gort Mhuire complex, a protected structure, and include a large wooded area and lake to south-east. The development is arranged in three blocks – two perimeter blocks and one linear building – ranging in height from generally five storeys to local eight-storey zones. The inner street – feeding to a large square at the junction of the three buildings – is formed between the linear building and the adjacent perimeter block. The buildings at this point frame a vista of Gort Mhuire, viewed from the bypass through the square.

design / completion – 2004–2010
client – Dorville Homes / O'Malley
  Construction

height	mix	percentage	no. of dwellings	site area	density	floor area	bed spaces	site coverage	open space	car spaces	context
5-8 storey	17% 3-bed units 65% 2-bed units 18% 1-bed units	100% residential	514	4.8 ha (11.9 acres)	107 units/ha (43/acre)	49,000m²	1,800 (375/ha)	n/a	42% including large wooded area and lake	720 (1.4 per dwelling)	development on lands of protected structure next to transport routes

Mount Saint Anne's, Milltown, Dublin 6

O'Mahony Pike Architects

Mount Saint Anne's is one of the largest private redevelopment projects in inner-suburban Dublin. Built on 22 acres of land previously occupied by a primary and secondary school with a convent, chapel and numerous outbuildings, the scheme adjoins the Milltown parish church and incorporates a new parish centre and priests' housing. It is a mixed-use development with 650 dwellings, and 2,000m² of offices, shops, medical clinic and crèche. It is centred around a 4.5-acre park, and located between the Milltown Road with its bus routes, and the Luas line, with schools and playing fields to the north and south.

A key element is the restoration and reuse of all the major existing buildings, together with the retention of key trees and landscape features. The original 1760 house has been restored for use as offices, retaining all surviving interior plasterwork and staircases. The chapel, dating from the 1880s, has been converted into architects' offices. The convent and former primary school have been converted into apartments, and the original secondary school building, designed by Arthur Douglas in the 1950s, has been converted into special social housing units for St Vincent de Paul. Further special housing for them has been built on the site of the former parish hall, above the medical clinic.

The convent building is combined with new apartments, separated by an atrium. Another atrium apartment building is sited on the other side of the park, which is surrounded by curved buildings, four to six stories high.

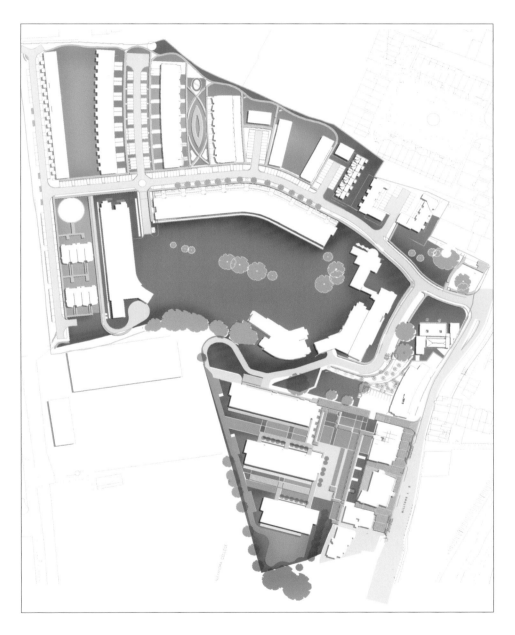

The family housing and duplex units use traditional construction, with stock brick and plaster external walls and tiled roofs, while the apartment buildings are entirely off-site, precast concrete construction, with etched precast façade panels. Underground parking is provided for all the apartments and offices, while the other dwellings have surface parking.

PHASE 2

The second major phase of this development has now been completed. The development is on a 1.75-hectare site which presented a weak frontage to Milltown Road, out of keeping with the surrounding urban grain.

It was the intention to address this issue with the design and placement of new structures along this boundary on either side of the parish church. The resulting space created between old and new serves as the main pedestrian entrance to the site and is the focus of the public uses, including the new parish centre and the play area for the crèche.

Immediately behind this new street frontage, the site rises steeply by 10m before levelling out. Advantage is taken of this to insert the public amenities of basement parking and a crèche, cut into the slope of the site. On the next level behind the crèche, twelve terraced town houses were created in two staggered blocks fronting on to the landscaped roof of the crèche and basement car park, maximising open space. This space sports a series of brightly coloured screens around the roof lights the crèche below.

height	mix	percentage	no. of dwellings	site area	density	floor area	bed spaces	site coverage	open space	car spaces	context
4-6 storey	170 houses and duplexes 480 apartments	74% residential 14% communal 12% commercial	650	9.2 ha (22.7 acres)	71 units/ha (29/acre) (institutional zoning means lower density)	17,000m²	2,124 (231/ha)	23%	4.5 acre park	1.25 per dwelling	restoration project in inner-suburban area

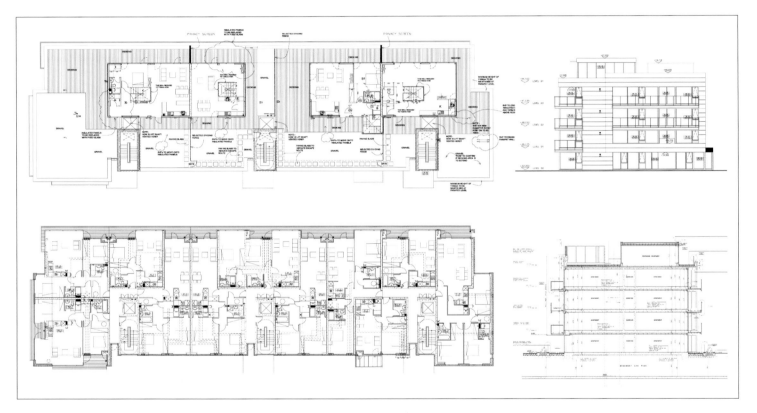

The final level change, to three storeys above street level, defines the wholly residential and, therefore, more private area of the site. The three blocks provide a majority of dual-aspect, two- and three-bedroom units, with a limited number of single-aspect, one-bedroom units where the circulation configuration dictates. Private terraces are provided at ground level, while balconies dominate the southerly elevations.

Landscaped courtyards between the blocks extend out to the rear boundary to the main car park, which is located below ground, under and between the apartments. The courtyards look west over the playing fields of Alexandra College, and east over the parish church to the riverside park along the Dodder.

design / completion – 1997–2008
client – Park Developments

MOUNT SAINT ANNE'S

↑ Section-elevation through site, looking north from Milltown Road
↖ Apartment block R2
   – typical plans – 2nd floor, upper duplex level)
   – east elevation, cross-section
← Cross-section-elevation through site, looking east

opposite

↗ clockwise from top left
   – main entrance to Mount Saint Anne's
   – view to east across amenity area
   – view looking north over amenity area
   – view to east over phase 2 amenity area
   – view to east towards Richmond Hall
   – retail unit at ground floor and Maple Hall facing on to Milltown Road

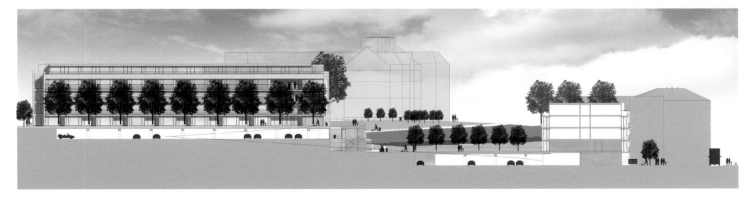

St Brigid's Court, Blanchardstown, Dublin 15

Elliot Maguire Landers Architects

This scheme is on the site of a disused tennis court in an interior corner of a mature council estate, close to the heart of Blanchardstown village. The brief was to design an appropriately scaled development of smaller dwellings in such a way as to give protection to the back-garden walls of adjoining houses and provide a clear public realm and defensible private spaces. The units have own-door access and are easily adaptable for special needs or elderly tenants.

The scheme consists of fourteen one and two bedroom units in a three-sided courtyard arrangement. The larger two-bedroom units are at ground-floor level with the one-bedroom apartments above. All are approached via a gated entrance yard. The ground-floor apartments have individual rear gardens and the first-floor units have a terrace onto which the living room and bedroom open.

The entrance court has excellent natural surveillance as it is overlooked from the living rooms on both levels. Internally, the apartments are simply arranged, with open-plan kitchens and living rooms. They are dual-aspect without unduly overlooking other properties.

The form of construction and materials used are traditional, complementing the existing context while helping to ensure the quality and appearance of the project into the future.

address – St Brigid's Park, Blanchardstown
    Dublin 15
design / completion – 2005–2008
client – Fingal County Council

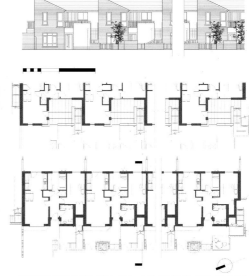

↑ From top: elevation; ground and 1st -floor plans; location map
↖ View of completed development
← Site plan

height	mix	percentage	no. of dwellings	site area	density	floor area	bed spaces	site coverage	open space	car spaces	context
2 storey	7 x 2-bed apartments 7 x 1-bed apartments	100% residential	14	1,982m² (0.49 acres)	28.5 units/acre	747m²	35 (71/acre)	25%	1,659m² in courtyard, gardens and terrace	17 (1.2 per dwelling)	mature suburban Council estate where houses are now mainly privately owned

Hazel Grove, Donabate, Co Dublin

GCA / Gerry Cahill Architects

Sophia Housing Association was founded seven years ago with the aim of providing affordable housing and offering support and educational services to those on low incomes. Their stated aim is to identify specific groups in need of additional support and provide assistance. This particular scheme, developed in conjunction with Fingal County Council, is intended for young families, and offers on-site support services for parents juggling family life with the possibility of re-entering the workforce.

In fulfilling these requirements, the brief for Hazel Grove was to create a new development of twenty residential units, with a particular emphasis on the encouragement of communal interaction while also offering a safe and secure environment for young families.

The development is located on a tree-lined road on the edge of Donabate village, slotted in between two detached bungalows and surrounded at the rear by suburban housing. In order to minimise the impact on this essentially pastoral context, the buildings are set back from the site boundary, and present gable ends to the road, recalling the established rhythm of detached properties in the vicinity.

Entering from the road, one slips between the gables of two terraces into a central garden space. This space is bounded on its north-south axis by two terraces of dwellings, one of which, describing a gentle arc in plan, pivots away from the northern entry point, where administration and education facilities are located, and opens to the south and the light.

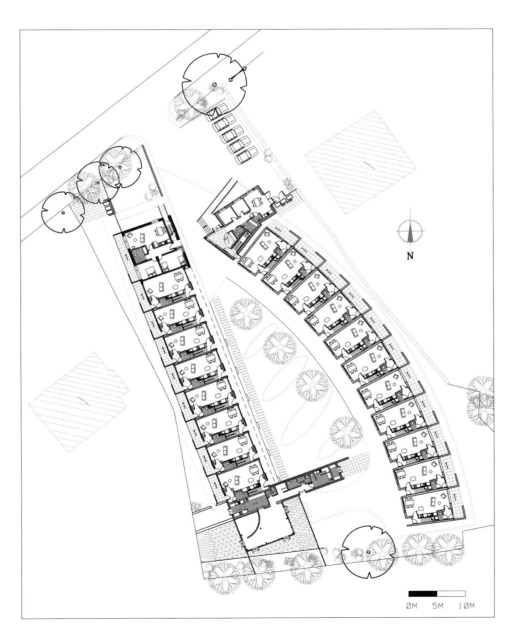

N

↑ Location map
← Site plan

Primary access to all the dwellings is via this central garden space. A three-metre-high brick wall projects along the southern edge of the garden space, screening a more secluded play area and childcare facility to the rear.

All residential units are dual-aspect along an east-west orientation. The standard two-bedroom unit comprises an open-plan living area on the ground floor, with a small utility/wc tucked under the stairs, and two double bedrooms and a bathroom on the first floor. First-floor rear windows look south into external recesses to prevent overlooking neighbouring properties. In addition to the communal garden spaces, each unit has a semi-private patio to the rear of the their unit.

The development is generally of masonry construction, with shallow monopitched roofs of insulated profiled metal sheeting.

ØM   5M   1ØM

height	mix	percentage	no. of dwellings	site area	density	floor area	bed spaces	site coverage	open space	car spaces	context
2 storey	2 x 3-bed houses 17 x 2-bed houses 2 x 2-bed apartments	87% residential 7% communal 6% childcare	21	3,735m² (0.92 acres)	22 units/acre	1,997m²	87 (94/acre)	30.6%	2,590m², including 142m² in semi-private patios	6 (for specific needs)	outer suburban greenfield site, near village centre

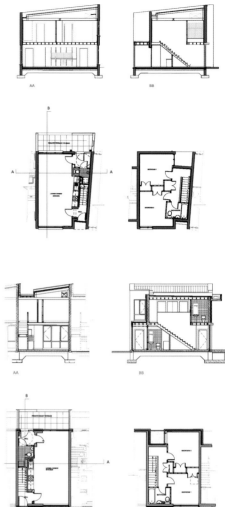

HAZEL GROVE

↑ Central communal garden space

↓ Linear block elevation (top) and curved east block elevation

↗ Typical plans and sections of curved east block (top), and linear block

Terraces have painted rendered finishes. Iroko cladding, windows and doors provide an interesting visual and tactile contrast with the more muscular masonry components of the scheme. The crèche facility is a single-storey steel-frame structure with floor-to-ceiling Iroko windows, glazed in different colours.

design / completion – 2001–2005
client – Sophia Housing Association

opposite

↗ Exterior and interior views of childcare facility
⇥ View of curved east terrace

Kilkenny City Centre Local Area Plan

O'Mahony Pike Architects

Kilkenny is unique among similar-sized cities and towns in Ireland. Its magnificent heritage, its ambient medieval core and its thriving cultural and artistic base make it a major tourist and visitor destination, as well as an attractive place in which to live and work. The city is the main commercial, residential and cultural centre of the county, and the city centre faces major ongoing challenges and opportunities.

The Kilkenny City and Environs Development Plan 2002 recognised that the city centre would be subject to large-scale development within the lifetime of the plan, and so required that a Local Area Plan be prepared for under the 2000 Planning and Development Act (as amended). The LAP would provide a framework that would ensure the continued vitality and viability of the city centre as a place to live, work and visit as future development and growth moved beyond the traditional core retail area. In conjunction with the Development Plan, the LAP will be the main instrument to guide and control development in the area, and thus has major implications for the future growth and development of the city centre.

The client brief determined that the LAP should concentrate on establishing new linkages, improving permeability and determining suitable uses within the city centre. The plan should also assess existing and future needs for car-parking and propose a framework for general directional signage within the city. The brief also required that an urban-design framework, including advice on appropriate land-uses, be prepared for eleven specific sites, including the Kilkenny mart, Bateman Quay, County Hall and The Parade.

This LAP seeks to provide an integrated strategy for the future sustainable development of Kilkenny city centre in

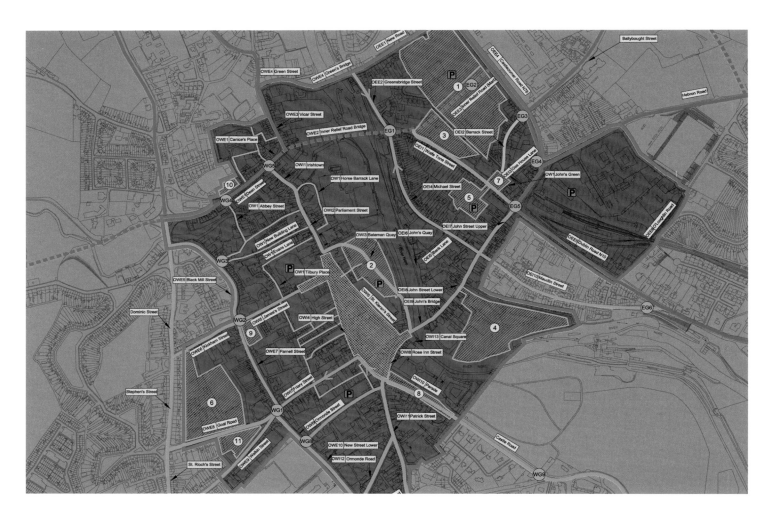

order to ensure its continued vitality and viability, and to strike a balance between preserving its architectural and archaeological heritage, facilitating modern living, and enhancing the quality of life for its existing and future residents.

In order to deliver this strategy, the LAP has a number of principal aims:
– to propose traffic-management objectives to improve existing vehicular and pedestrian linkages within the city centre
– to propose a framework for existing and future car-parking requirements.
– to prepare urban-design frameworks and land-use strategies for key sites
– to assess the core retail area and propose strategies for its future development.
– to develop a general directional vehicular and pedestrian signage strategy
– to propose a network of quality open spaces.

The Local Area Plan is currently being used as intended by both the Borough Council and County Council when dealing with planning applications, as well as by members of the public interested in the future development of Kilkenny city. It has been a valuable resource in the ongoing study for locating an integrated cultural centre on Bateman Quay, and has guided the development of the illustrated proposals for The Parade by GKMP Architects.

design / completion – 2005–2020
client – Kilkenny Borough Council / Kilkenny County Council

→ from top:
View of The Parade leading to Kilkenny Castle
The route into the city past the Castle
View of Bateman Quay
Parade perspective by day and night

→→ from top:
Map of Bateman Quay area
Proposal for The Parade by GKMP Architects
Map of Parade area

↖ Road and street hierarchy map
← Bird's-eye view, with key locations identified
←← Map of Kilkenny city

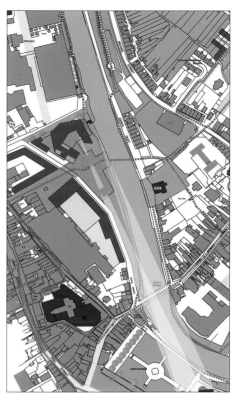

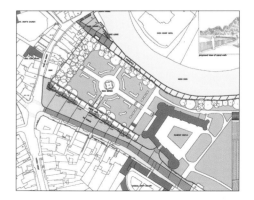

Sexton Street, Limerick

Carr Cotter & Naessens Architects

Part of a convent school in Limerick city, the site is a walled enclosure, once an orchard, but now derelict and unused. The project was an opportunity to knit into the urban matrix while providing a tranquil haven for its occupants. The brief includes housing units for residents requiring various levels of support and care. The retired Presentation sisters will live in a self-contained block. The second requirement was for a regional training and administration centre. The combination of uses will add to the social cohesion within the site. Staff, trainees and residents will interact and contribute to the overall sense of community on the site.

The accommodation is provided in urbane groups, the brick façades modelled to reflect the internal planning whilst defining the central garden. The entrance from Parnell Street leads into a large south-facing garden, an oasis in this gritty urban district. The gardens provide a communal open space that is overlooked by all the accommodation. It provides a buffer between the residential settlement and the more robust territory of the railway station and yards to the south.

The resource centre and the houses have front-door access from the main central space. Block A is accessed via a small private garden linking to the school grounds beyond. Block B is accessed from a small quiet courtyard fronting onto Presentation Court.

The expression of the buildings is determined by the need to define the central garden space. Brick is proposed as the facing material for public façades.

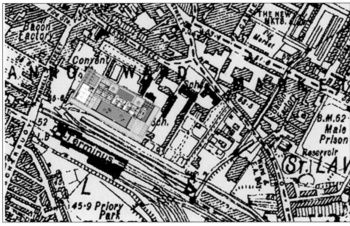

In contrast, render is used for secondary and rear elevations. The overall form of the development is determined by the need to establish formal edges to the open space.

The buildings have traditional front-back relationships. The buildings are low-key without overt detailing and elaboration. Proportions are carefully considered and based on the golden section.

design / completion – 2003–2010
client – Rehab Group /
Newgrove Housing Association

↑ Views of site
↖ Location map
↗ Axonometric

opposite

↗ Elevations and perspective of development
→ Exploded axonometric and ground-floor plan

height	mix	percentage	no. of dwellings	site area	density	floor area	bed spaces	site coverage	open space	car spaces	context
3-5 storey	2 x 5-bed houses 5 x 2-bed apartments 12 x 2-bed apartments 3 studio apartments	64% residential 36% education + administration	22	3,825m²	22 units/acre	2,600m²	36	68% 596m² private	476m² public	23 walled garden in convent	inner city backlands; school

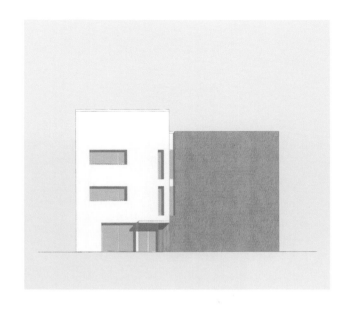

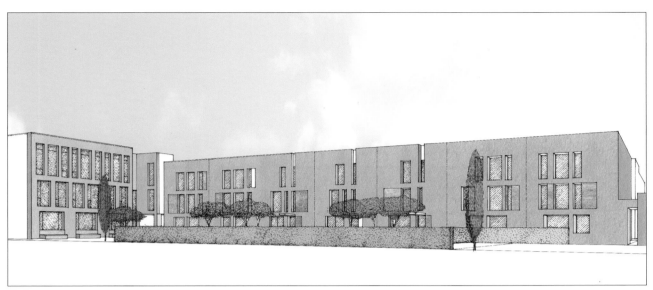

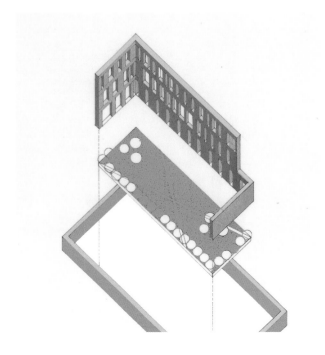

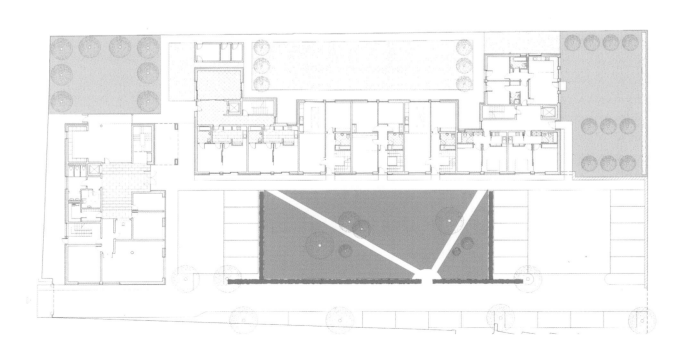

Sarsfield Park, Prospect Hill, Limerick

Elliott Maguire Landers Architects

The brief originally called for a development of 56 housing units with a mix of types and sizes on the site of a former barracks. The brief evolved throughout the design process, and now includes two facilities providing living accommodation for people with learning and physical disabilities.

The existing married quarters building provides a strong and commanding image for the site. This fine limestone building was refurbished, and provides fourteen one- and two-bedroom houses. The building was structurally sound, but required major refurbishment work. It provides a strong anchor point for the entire scheme. The three-storey Health Service Executive buildings are located to either side it.

The terrace of two-bedroom houses at the southern end of the site forms a strong edge and design focus for the scheme. The units are raised on a podium, bringing this part of the development level with the public road. The units use simple forms and clean lines. The elevation is punctuated by steel-framed bay windows with inset timber windows and cedar cladding.

design / completion – 2001–2005
(Phase 1, all works excl. blocks E, G)
client – Limerick City Council

↑ Site plan
↗ Photomontage of development on aerial view
→ Existing married quarters building

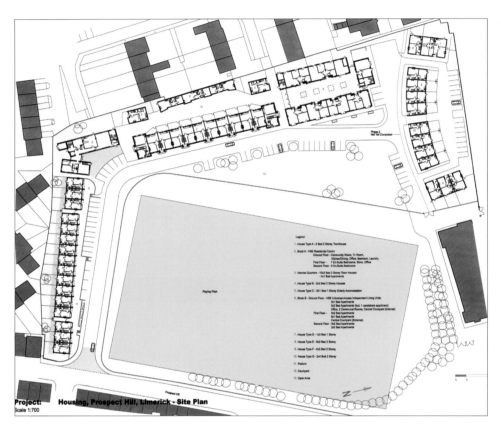

Project: **Housing, Prospect Hill, Limerick - Site Plan**
Scale 1:700

height	mix	percentage	no. of dwellings	site area	density	floor area	bed spaces	site coverage	open space	car spaces	context
2-3 storey	2 x 4-bed houses 13 x 3-bed houses 26 x 2-bed houses 15 x 2-bed apartments 16 x 1-bed apartments	100% residential	72	13,727m² (3.4 acres)	25 units/acre	8,229m²	157 (46/acre)	26%	4,622m², including private gardens and first-floor courtyard	66 (0.92 per dwelling)	city-centre location in existing residential area

HOUSE TYPE'S E & G - FIRST FLOOR PLAN

HOUSE TYPE'S E & G - GROUND FLOOR PLAN

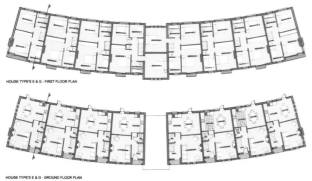

↑ Plans of house types A, E, G
↗ Long elevation of house type A
↑ Plan of block B

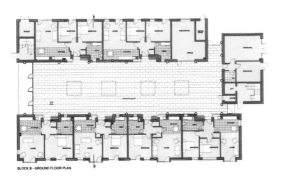

BLOCK B - GROUND FLOOR PLAN

Student Accommodation at Victoria Cross, Cork

DTA Architects

This student residence is located on a highly particular site at the confluence of the South Channel of the Lee and the Curragheen river. Situated along an axis between University College Cork and County Hall, it acts as a prominent urban-scale landmark at the end of the Western Road, adjacent to O'Neill Crowley Bridge.

Consisting of 289 study bedrooms in 59 apartments, with associated reception and communal facilities and a semi-basement car park, all accommodation is contained within a singular extruded and switching zigzag form. This creates a sequence of dynamic and varied external court spaces at a raised-podium level, swapping openness and emphasis alternately between opposite river banks.

A pedestrian access route skewers through the form, cutting a series of double-height external openings in the building volume and culminating in a cantilever at the apex of the site, above the footbridge. This direct experience of the building and the hard surface of the plinth level are contrasted by the casual nature and soft landscaping of the riverbank paths at a lower level, interconnected by an open staircase adjacent to the cantilever. The openings along the access sequence, in conjunction with the stepped profile (from four, to six, to nine storeys over podium level), animate the section in an otherwise generally repetitive and cellular programme.

design / completion – 2001–2004
client – Montgomery Kenneally Partnership

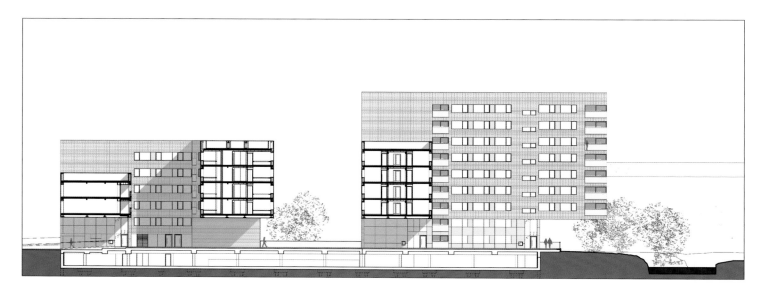

↑ West-east section through the site, and confluence of the Lee and Curragheen rivers
← Location map

opposite

↗ Entrance courtyard
→ View east through courtyards along axis of 'cut-out' volumes
⇢ View from opposite riverbank at dusk

height	mix	percentage	no. of dwellings	site area	density	floor area	bed spaces	site coverage	open space	car spaces	context
4, 6, 9 storey	9 x 7-bed apartments 21 x 6-bed apartments 1 x 5-bed apartments 15 x 4-bed apartments 12 x 3-bed apartments 1 x 2-bed apartments (warden)	100% residential	59	4,510m² (1.12 acres)	53 units/acre	9,236m² (excluding basement)	292 (262/acre)	26% on ground floor 35% on typical floor	3,349m² public	69	prominent suburban landmark site, at convergence of two rivers

VICTORIA CROSS, CORK

↑ View west through courtyards along axis of 'cut-out' volumes, with terrace and balconies overlooking the Curragheen river

↗ Plans (from bottom) – ground, 1st and 4th-9th floors

↓ South elevation to Curragheen river, where it meets the River Lee

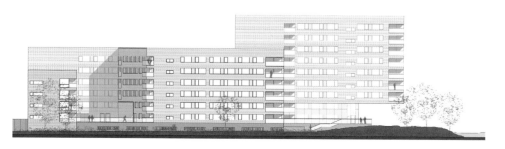

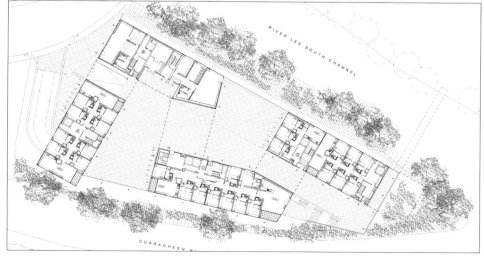

Coppinger Court, Pope's Quay, Cork

Magee Creedon Architects

The site is on a south-facing slope overlooking the River Lee. The scheme includes five existing buildings on the quay, and then steps up in several terraces behind, all overlooked by the distinctive spires of St Anne's, Shandon, and the North Cathedral. The Shandon area is an appealing enclave, characterised by a network of pedestrian-width streets and lanes which crisscross the hill between key public buildings and spaces. Two lanes climb up through the site, one linking through to Shandon Street.

The project knits itself into the existing grain of Shandon. It uses the sloping section to separate commercial uses and car-parking from the residential areas, giving a pedestrian character to the residential zone, but with easy lift access to the upper terrace. The existing routes have been substantiated, and new links opened up, creating an experience of unfolding vistas as one walks through. Surfaces capture changing sunlight patterns throughout the day. Use of render and timber elements give a sense of domesticity, and zinc roofing has allowed flexibility of form, providing for an inhabited roofscape and contrasting new with old. The quay-front buildings have been refurbished using hardwood sash windows and natural slate. All apartments have front-door access, either from the quay front or laneways. Amenity spaces include shared courtyards with 'back-door' access, and private balconies and roof gardens. Each apartment is individually designed to suit its location and orientation.

design / completion – 1999–2004
client – Westboro Developments Ltd

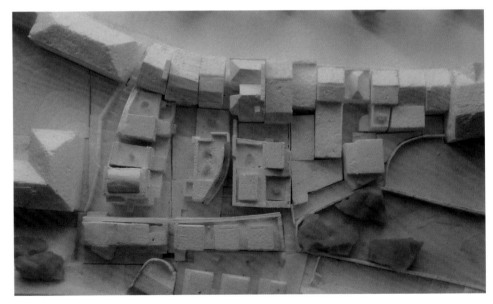

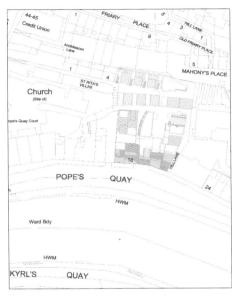

↖ Bird's-eye view of model, with the refurbished quayfront buildings in the foreground
← View of model from above
↓ Site plan

height	mix	percentage	no. of dwellings	site area	density	floor area	bed spaces	site coverage	open space	car spaces	context
3-4 storey	1 x 3-bed apartment 28 x 2-bed apartments 13 x 1-bed apartments retail units	95% residential 5% commercial	42	1,840m² (0.45 acres)	88 units/acre	2,900m²	72 (158/acre)	65%	598m²	12	inner-city site on river

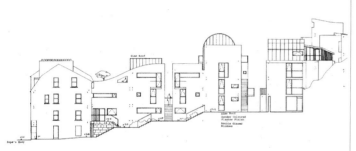

COPPINGER COURT

↖ Plans – levels 3, 4, 5
← Longitudinal section through site along Coppinger Lane, looking west
→ Cross-section through site, with elevation of northern block
↙ Plans – levels 0, 1, 2

opposite

→ Close-up views of the completed development
⇢ View of the completed development, with the refurbished Pope's Quay buildings in the foreground

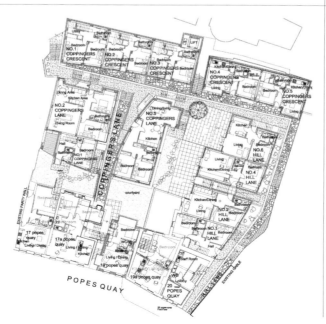

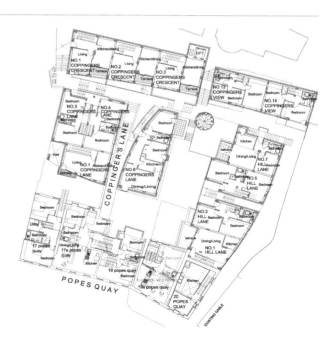

Social Housing, Gerald Griffin Street, Cork

Paul Keogh Architects

The aim of this proposal for a derelict site on Gerald Griffin Street, adjoining SS Mary's and Anne's Cathedral (North Cathedral), was to produce a quality design which would contribute positively to the streetscape and the setting of the cathedral. The scheme consists of eight housing units in three separate blocks. It comprises four two-storey maisonettes and four single-storey apartments, connected by an external staircase from a shared courtyard at ground level.

Entry from Gerald Griffin Street is gated to provide a secure courtyard, which the residents, taking advantage of its south-facing orientation, have landscaped and furnished, making it into a pleasant communal open space.

The scheme has provided the street and cathedral with a new image in place of the previously derelict look of this strategic site. It achieves a quality design response to its site and brief, providing social housing that is secure and attractive yet responsive to its historic urban context.

design / completion – 1998–2002
client – Cork City Council

SITE PLAN
0   5   10   20m

↗ The North Cathedral, with this scheme to its right
→ Location map
→→ Plans – 1st, 2nd, 3rd floors

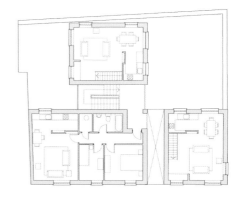

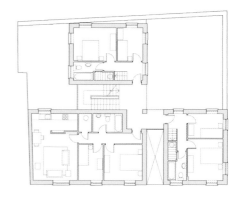

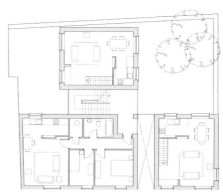

height	mix	percentage	no. of dwellings	site area	density	floor area	bed spaces	site coverage	open space	car spaces	context
4 storey	4 x 2-bed maisonettes 4 x 2-bed apartments	100% residential	8	291m² (0.07 acres)	111 units/acre	488m²	24 (333/acre)	63%	110m² at ground level	0	derelict inner-city site

↑ View of the North Cathedral from balcony
↗ Looking down Gerald Griffin Street
➡➡ Plans – 1st, 2nd, 3rd floors
↘ View from the grounds of the cathedral
↓ Ground-floor plan and section-elevation

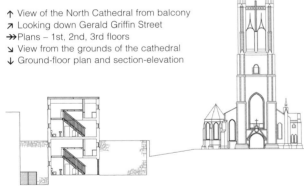

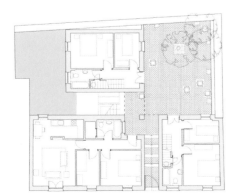

209

Block D, Knocknaheeny, Cork

Knocknaheeny is an isolated hilltop site located 1.2km from Cork city centre. Cork City Council, wishing to improve the Knocknaheeny housing stock, began a series of refurbishments in 1997. It became evident that an in-depth study of the area was essential in order to simultaneously treat the problems of urban quality and social deprivation.

The City Council engaged planners and urban designers to carry out a diagnostic study on the area with a view to preparing a master plan document. The aim is to bring the north-western part of the city back into the urban mainstream.

During the initial research, it quickly became evident that the area had experienced an accumulation of major social and physical handicaps since its creation in the 1970s. These included:
– no centre to the area
– poor, monotonous housing stock
– high unemployment with low prospects for funding jobs
– low income sufficiency
– high population of single-parent families
– little or no facilities for childcare, youth-care, healthcare, social welfare, care for the aged, association or club activities
– no social mix
– physical and social isolation from the rest of Cork city.

Despite these factors, a community exists which endeavours to thrive against the odds. An analysis of the topographic, demographic and urban-planning environment was carried out, and recommendations for implementation by Cork City Council were prepared.

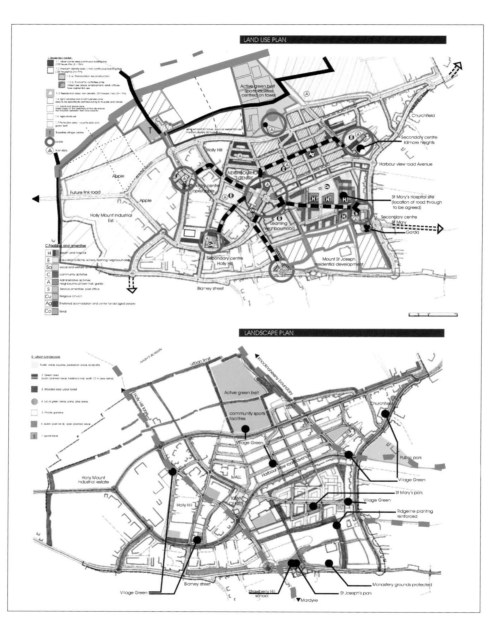

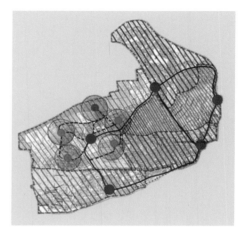

This firm of architects was appointed to design a Youth Link drop-in centre catering for 12 to 18 year-olds, the Strawberry Hill facility, which caters for 12 to 15 year olds, and the HSE Spring Board offices and facilities. This scheme also includes a crèche and family centre in a separate structure, and major infrastructural housing, sheltered housing and community-care services. The community care complex is physically linked to the sheltered housing, and provides for dedicated community facilities – a doctors' surgery and a HSE primary care unit.

design / completion – 1997–2009
client – Cork City Council

↖ Early master-plan exercises which were adopted by Cork City Council, and have influenced development since
→ Computer perspectives of development

height	mix	percentage	no. of dwellings	site area	density	floor area	bed spaces	site coverage	open space	car spaces	context
2-3 storey	8 x 4-bed houses 81 x 3-bed houses 10 x 2-bed houses 24 x 1-bed sheltered house	95% residential 5% communal	123	6.25 acres	20 units/acre	10,523m²	421 (67/acre)	42%	1,340m² (5.3%)	123	isolated suburban hilltop location, poorly serviced by infrastructure

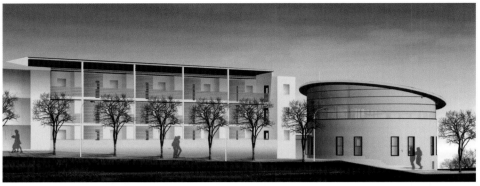

A2 SECOND FLOOR PLAN B1 SECOND FLOOR PLAN B2 SECOND FLOOR PLAN C1 SECOND FLOOR PLAN C2 SECOND FLOOR PLAN

D1 SECOND FLOOR PLAN D2 SECOND FLOOR PLAN E2 FIRST FLOOR PLAN E2 SECOND FLOOR PLAN

G FIRST FLOOR PLAN

A2 FIRST FLOOR PLAN B1 FIRST FLOOR PLAN B2 FIRST FLOOR PLAN C1 FIRST FLOOR PLAN C2 FIRST FLOOR PLAN

D1 FIRST FLOOR PLAN D2 FIRST FLOOR PLAN E1 FIRST FLOOR PLAN E2 FIRST FLOOR PLAN

G GROUND FLOOR PLAN

F FIRST FLOOR PLAN

A2 GROUND FLOOR PLAN B1 GROUND FLOOR PLAN B2 GROUND FLOOR PLAN C1 GROUND FLOOR PLAN C2 GROUND FLOOR PLAN

D1 GROUND FLOOR PLAN D2 GROUND FLOOR PLAN E1 GROUND FLOOR PLAN E2 GROUND FLOOR PLAN F GROUND FLOOR PLAN

BLOCK D, KNOCKNAHEENY, CORK

↑ Some of the many community facilities being provided on site, including a family centre, a youth centre, and HSE offices and facilities

↑ Some of the many house-types developed for this project

↓ Cross-section through site

Athlone Town Centre, Co Westmeath

Murray Ó Laoire Architects

This seven-acre site in the centre of Athlone is an assemblage of infill and backland plots, brownfield areas and semi-derelict structures. Its location and physical attributes are fundamental to the architectural and urban-design approach. The challenge – to insert a large mixed-use development into a historic setting – was assisted by the shape, topography and particular features of the site. The project is about 'stitching' and 'mending' existing streetscapes, and making connections and spaces, as much as it is about giving appropriately authentic contemporary expression to its core, retail function.

Exploiting the site gradient effectively conceals all car-parking, servicing and delivery facilities on two subterranean levels, eliminating vacuous expanses of surface parking and allowing the range of new buildings to integrate with existing development on all edges. A new order is overlaid on the site, imposing a pattern of streets and lanes, squares and courtyards on land that was hitherto excluded from the fabric of the town. The project creates a new urban quarter, accommodating a diverse mix of over fifty retail units; 150 residential units in disaggregated blocks of apartments and town houses set around squares, courtyards and playgrounds; restaurants and cafés; a crèche and a primary healthcare facility; and a 167-bedroom hotel, rising to an eleven-storey signature tower at its core, heralding the commercial centre of town.

↗ Location map; retail uses
→ Hotel and residential uses
⇢ Residential buildings

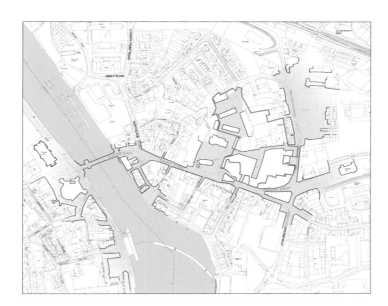

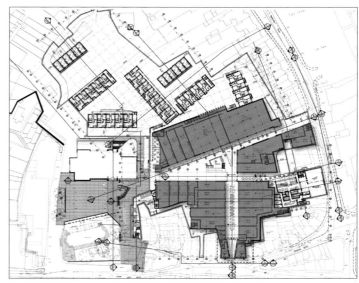

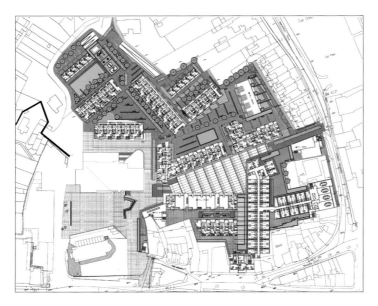

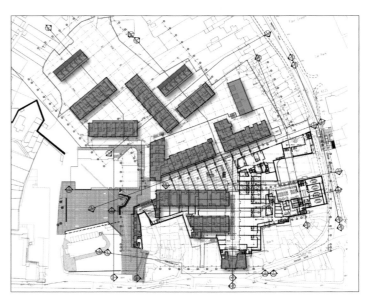

height	mix	percentage	no. of dwellings	site area	density	floor area	bed spaces	site coverage	open space	car spaces	context
3-5 storey 11-storey hotel	150 town houses + apts 52 retail units 167-bed hotel offices, community facilities, restaurants + car park	15% residential 27% commercial 15% hotel 40 % car park 3% communal	150	8.1 acres (3.3 ha)	20.5 units/acre	97,000m²	592 residential	70%	3,117m² in covered streets and square	1,140 (+ 7 coach spaces)	brownfield site with narrow street frontage

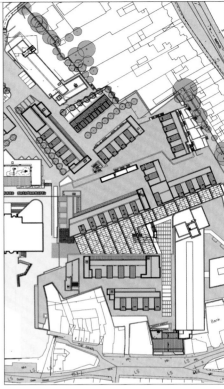

Organised as intimately scaled streets or around sunny courtyards, the residential element of the development has generous private and communal space. Landscape treatments and high levels of planting define, in comprehensible degrees, the transition from public to private space. All residential accommodation is easily accessed, and is permeable, yet secure.

address – Mardyke / Gleeson / Church
Street, Athlone, Co Westmeath
design / completion – 2004–2008
client – Gallico Development

ATHLONE TOWN CENTRE

↖ Study model of town-centre redevelopment
↑ Residential area of redevelopment
← View from Civic Square facing east, with existing town hall and library complex in the foreground, and new pedestrian street and hotel tower in the distance

opposite

↗ Views of the town centre redevelopment as it nears completion
→ Sections through development

The Arches, Gas House Lane, Kilkenny

John Thompson + Partners

This is a mixed-use development located within Kilkenny's historic city-centre IAP site. This complex urban-infill site forms a triangle bounded by Barrack Street and Gas House Lane, with a corner fronting onto the busy Castlecomer New Road. The site is also bounded by stone railway arches carrying the disused rail line. These are protected structures and are key to the identity of the development.

A total of 76 one-, two-, three- and four-bedroom residential units are arranged onto Barrack Street and Gas House Lane, forming an internal court for parking. Mixed commercial units are at ground-floor level, with a café court located at the junction of Gas House Lane and The Arches.The railway arches have been opened up to create an entrance and a connection between the café court and John's Green. A large south-west-facing communal roof garden onto Gas House Lane gives views over the city.

Working in historic contexts with an existing residential pattern of individual, small-scale units is one of the main challenges to increasing densities in towns and cities. A rational approach to expression was explored from the outset. Forms are broken down to a scale reflecting the surrounding buildings, materials are traditional render and stone, but are detailed in an uncluttered, non-stylistic manner.

Discussions are currently under way with the Local Authority to include an art gallery and café over the existing railway arches.

design / completion – 2003–2005
client – McInerney Homes Ltd

height	mix	percentage	no. of dwellings	site area	density	floor area	bed spaces	site coverage	open space	car spaces	context
3-5 storey	1 x 4-bed apartment 6 x 3-bed apartments 61 x 2-bed apartments 8 x 1-bed apartments	80% residential 20% commercial	76	4,887m² (1.2 acres)	63 units/acre	5,236m²	291 (242/acre)	50%	300m² in café court 200m² in roof terrace; also private balconies	74 (0.97 per dwelling)	urban site facing public square, adjacent to old railway bridge

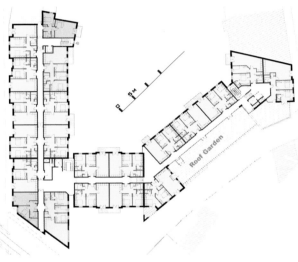

Maynooth Harbour Area Development, Co Kildare Weber & Company Architects

Located 24km west of Dublin, the 18th-century village of Maynooth is enjoying renewed growth and development as a thriving university community and urban centre within easy commuting distance of Dublin. This project for Maynooth Harbour is a response to the desire for the expansion of the town centre.

The development area encompasses a seven-hectare underutilised tract of land east of St Patrick's College, between the village centre and the Royal Canal and railway station. In the first half of the 20th century, this swathe of land became, increasingly, a backland area, as canal and railway usage declined as a result of road improvements. Today, with recognition of the vast canal network as an amenity for pleasure boating and the resurgence of commuter rail travel, these former backlands have taken on renewed importance. As such, the development of Maynooth Harbour presents the opportunity for the town centre to reorient itself back towards the canal and railway station through balanced use and pedestrian-friendly planning.

The planning intent of this development is for the creation of a communal environment to serve as both portal and link to the historic town centre. Incorporated into the plan are programme elements for residential, retail, commercial, civic and cultural usage. Traffic limitations and underground car-parking would reinforce the pedestrian nature of the plan. The principal organising element of the site is an axial, tree-lined avenue, reminiscent of the original 18th-century Maynooth town plan. This avenue originates at the canal

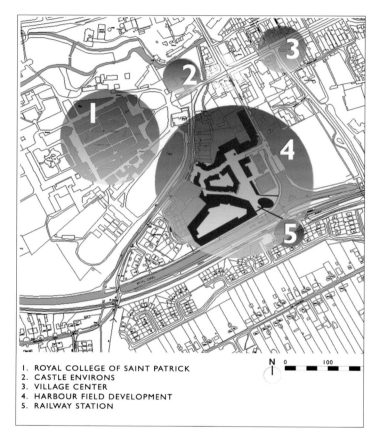

1. ROYAL COLLEGE OF SAINT PATRICK
2. CASTLE ENVIRONS
3. VILLAGE CENTER
4. HARBOUR FIELD DEVELOPMENT
5. RAILWAY STATION

N   0   100

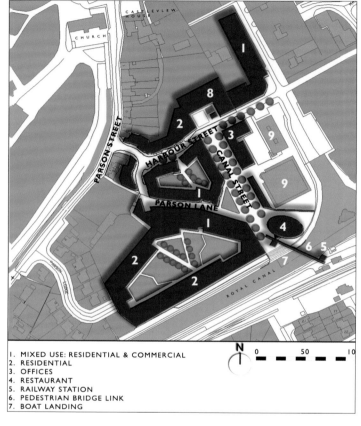

1. MIXED USE: RESIDENTIAL & COMMERCIAL
2. RESIDENTIAL
3. OFFICES
4. RESTAURANT
5. RAILWAY STATION
6. PEDESTRIAN BRIDGE LINK
7. BOAT LANDING

N   0   50   10

and rail station at one end, and terminates at the proposed new Government Centre Civic Plaza at the opposite end. In contrast to the linear avenue are a series of smaller, irregular streets which circumvent the site, providing natural paths of circulation to the town centre and university, recalling the organic nature of earlier medieval town plans. Buildings which define these streets incorporate retail and commercial uses at ground level, serving those who transverse

the site as part of their daily commute, as well as those who reside in the apartments above. Where these streets intersect, nodes of public space are created for community activity and interaction. The larger, more central building-block island allows pedestrians to pass through its perimeter at ground level, and introduces them to an internal courtyard plaza, populated by retail units and cafés, thus creating yet another urban experience.

Responding to neighbouring built conditions and sight-lines to the university belfry, the buildings vary in height and volume, creating an animated streetscape reminiscent of smaller villages where civic spaces and landmarks provide a framework for the communal experience. Buildings are characterised by a plinth base of dimensional Irish blue limestone, upon which rest pristine, white plasterwork apartment blocks which shift in response to

height	mix	percentage	no. of dwellings	site area	density	floor area	bed spaces	site coverage	open space	car spaces	context
2-5 storey	9 x 3-bed apartment 57 x 2-bed apartments 24 x 1-bed apartments	80% residential 20% commercial	90	1.64 acres (0.66 ha)	55 units/acre (136 units/ha)	11,932m²	165 (100/acre)	46%	1,307m² in courtyards, private gardens and balconies	74 (0.97 per dwelling)	town centre expansion through development of canal harbour

views and the streets below. Suspended from the upper volumes are projecting bays, clad in weathered copper, adding further dimensionality and reduction in overall building massing. Utilising this simple palette of materials, a direct correlation is established between the indigenous medieval and 18th- and 19th-century architecture of the local environ and the new intervention.

A complex mix of one-, two- and three-bedroom apartments are arranged throughout the development, offering a variety of living arrangements, from sweeping penthouses to traditional town houses. All units are dual-aspect, maximising external exposure for sunlight, cross-ventilation and changing views. Furthermore, all apartments are provided with varying amounts of open space, consisting of private yards, terraces and balconies, which overlook landscaped gardens, plazas and the streets below.

It is anticipated that the proposed development will not only serve the intended pragmatic roles of expansion and connection between the town centre and harbour, but also serve as a cultural bridge connecting Maynooth's rich history and its future.

design / completion – 2005–2008
client – P&G Dormer

↗ View of Civic Square
→ View of Harbour Street, looking east

opposite

→ Development site plan
↞ Area site plan

Garden Court, Tone Street, Ballina, Co Mayo

A & D Wejchert & Partners

Located on one of the main shopping and pedestrian areas of the town, this mixed-use infill scheme forms a meaningful modern addition to the town centre. It consists of a retail centre at ground level, entered by means of an arched laneway from the street and also connected to a rear laneway leading to a public car park.

The apartments are accessed from an open gallery at first-floor level, which looks onto the courtyard below – the central focus of the development. They are also provided with private balconies or terraces. Careful use of angled bay windows to capture sunshine, and translucent glazing and planted terraces create well-lit apartments whilst minimising overlooking between apartments.

The apartments are orientated to ensure they all receive sunshine during some or all of the day. Duplex apartments have living accommodation on the lower level and sleeping accommodation above. This is reversed in some apartments, with living accommodation on the upper level to maximise southern light through the use of rooflights.

To promote sustainability, the following measures have been taken:
– use of natural materials with low-energy production
– orientation and use of light-coloured wall finishes to maximise daylight
– high levels of insulation
– extensive planting
– solar panels on the south-facing roof.

design / completion – 2003–2006
client – James Geraghty

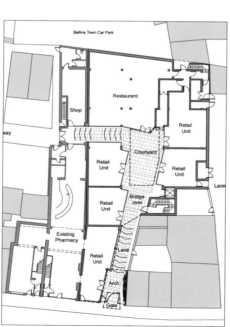

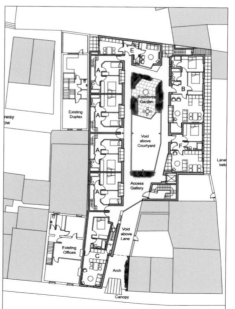

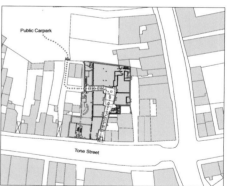

↖ View from Tone Street
↗ View of apartments arranged around landscaped courtyard
↑ Location map
← Plans – ground, 1st floor

height	mix	percentage	no. of dwellings	site area	density	floor area	bed spaces	site coverage	open space	car spaces	context
2-3 storey	5 x 2-bed duplexes 2 x 2-bed apartments 2 x 1-bed apartments retail units	66% residential 34% commercial	9	740m² (0.18 acres)	50 units/acre	1,200m²	24 (133/acre)	66%	180m² in courtyards; also private balconies	0 (adjacent to public car park)	infill scheme in town centre

Avenue Residential Development, Killarney

Murray O'Laoire Architects

The development comprises 104 cedar-clad, dual-aspect apartments, duplexes and penthouses, eleven holiday houses and a crèche for up to sixty pre-school children on a sensitive four-acre site in the centre of Killarney. The site, behind the former Great Southern Hotel, was formerly part of the estate of Kenmare House. It has an important avenue of lime trees and some significant stands of oak, planted between 1750 and 1780, hence the name of the development. The main driving force behind the design was to ensure that the existing trees were not only maintained, but became a strong feature of the development.

This development has removed the high wall along the Countess Road and has opened up these trees to view for the first time in generations. The one-storey creche is the only building located in front of the limes, as it addresses Countess Road and provides access to this facility for non-residents. The remainder of the site in front of the limes is landscaped and provides public open space.

The apartment scheme consists of six separate four-storey blocks arranged in an east-west axis to accommodate the trees and maximise aspect. The apartments are large dual-aspect units with access to private balconies. The upper levels consist of duplexes and penthouses with access to private terraces. The areas between buildings form private open space which is landscaped to accentuate the existing mature trees. The site is opened up to view from Countess Road, with the principal elevation screened by the avenue of tall limes.

↑ Site plan

The holiday home scheme of eleven terraced houses to the rear of the site is arranged around shared open spaces to form a *sráid bhaile* (i.e. a single-street village), with pedestrian and the limited vehicular traffic sharing the public open space of this cul-de-sac.

address – Countess Road, Killarney, Co Kerry

design / completion – 2002–2007
client – Sundays Well Properties Ltd

height	mix	percentage	no. of dwellings	site area	density	floor area	bed spaces	site coverage	open space	car spaces	context
2-4 storey	104 apartments / duplexes 11 holiday houses crèche	95% residential 5% communal	115	1.6 ha (4 acres)	72 units/ha (28.7/acre)	12,324m²	283	26%	15.3% of site also courtyards, balconies and roof-top terraces	148	on the fringe of town

AVENUE ROAD

↑ View of apartment blocks from the south
↗ View of shared open space
↓ View of the main entrance to the development from Countess Road
  – buildings are set back from the road and screened by tall lime trees
↘ View of the holiday village

opposite

→ Plans of 'Bookend' apartment building – ground, 1st, 2nd floors
↠ View of shared open space
↘ Cross-sections through apartment block
  – typical section through circulation
  – typical section through accommodation

TYPICAL SECTION THROUGH
CIRCULATION

TYPICAL SECTION THROUGH
ACCOMODATION

What does building new communities mean?

SEÁN HARRINGTON

Over the last few years, we have been in a mad rush to satisfy the Celtic Tiger's demand for housing, but it is now worth reminding ourselves what building communities should really be all about. It should not primarily be about maximising the number of saleable units (or 'assets'), or the provision of 'housing' by itself. Rather, it should be about creating good neighbourhoods that can engender sustainable communities. A good neighbourhood is a place to call one's own, a place to be proud of, and a place to invest energy, emotion and resources into. It's a place where people can live life.

WHAT'S GONE WRONG ?

In the current economic downturn, it is worth stopping to examine the reasons why things went so wrong. The economic boom enabled development at an unprecedented rate and scale. But why have we failed so miserably to create good, sustainable new communities? In October 2005, a European Environment Agency report cited recent development in Ireland as the 'worst case scenario' and an example to new EU member states of how not to develop.

As we can all see, Dublin, Cork, Galway and other places have developed out of control. As our city-centre populations decline, the suburbs sprawl. Even now, we have the fastest growing population in Europe, and space is running out in our cities. Accessibility to any kind of housing, never mind in good-quality neighbourhoods, is getting more difficult and expensive, even for well-paid young professionals, so people are forced to move further and further away from their place of work.

With the lack of efficient public transport, it has become the norm to use cars to get to work, school or the shops. Community life is suffering; there's been an increase in social isolation and fragmented families. Disturbingly, but not surprisingly, a recent Institute of Public Health report confirmed the physical and emotional health problems brought about by suburban sprawl, commuting long distances and car-dependency, with obesity levels rising. Hours spent travelling eats into time for exercise and neighbourly interaction, leading to social exclusion. This over-reliance on the car contributes to our environmental

footprint being one of the worst in the developed world.

On the whole, our quality of life is decreasing. The fundamental problem is that we have been building in the wrong way – at too low a density and with a lack of concern for the required infrastructure and facilities – with the shortsighted view that it is the commodity of the house that matters, to the detriment of developing sustainable new communities.

THE SUBURBAN NIGHTMARE

Our national love affair with the suburbs is understandable. In theory, at least, they allow us to escape the perceived dangerous, overcrowded, dirty city, and have the benefits of both town and country by being closer to nature. We can have a garden, front drive, garage, a place for the kids to play... And in recent years it has become the only place that we can afford.

The problem with suburbs is that the more of them you have, the more self-defeating they become. A limited number of small, low-density suburbs close to the city centre provides all of the perceived advantages. However, low-density suburban living is now the norm, each newly built scheme being further and further away from town. It is reported that by 2015, the Greater Dublin Area will have the same footprint as that infamous sprawling car-city Los Angeles, except with only a quarter of the population. As Eugene Gribbon outlines in his excellent 1998 paper 'The Housing Crisis – Is Higher Density a Solution?', building at densities as low as five to six houses an acre means that more land is used up and, critically, there are fewer people to support shops, services, public transport, schools and health centres. These end up being further apart and only accessible by car.

Many of our suburban housing estates are big cul-de-sacs, leading nowhere and laid out to suit cars. This arrangement is unlikely to create a feeling of belonging and a sense of place with character or local distinctiveness. Most of suburbia is single tenure and single use, with a common household size. It can, indeed, be a place of isolation, being boring, monocultural, lacking in neighbourliness and a sense of community.

OUR CHALLENGE FOR CHANGE

To undo this legacy will be nigh on impossible, although the upcoming rise in energy and transport costs may prove to be a suitable catalyst for serious change when the economy allows. In the meantime, consolidation of our inner cities and existing suburbs is difficult, but essential. Furthermore, there will be limited opportunities in the future, due to a shortage of land remaining near urban centres or on public transport corridors, to create the new communities. It is vital that we get it right.

But are we ready to change our patterns of behaviour and face up to the challenge on a political, community and personal level? Are we ready to understand and embrace the notion of the common good in place of personal liberty and commercial gain? And can we modify rampant free-market capitalism, which drives most development, to ensure access to good neighbourhoods and communities, for all? The stakes are massive, our responsibilities are huge. Will we be known as the generation that squandered the opportunities or the one that created an enlarged, cohesive and fair society for our children, and theirs?

NEW NEIGHBOURHOODS

Creating good places to live is about quality of life. In creating these new communities, we need streets and squares instead of roads and roundabouts, and parks instead of wastelands. Children need to be able to walk to school, and live within easy distance of their school friends. Shops, too, need to be within walking distance, and efficient public transport must be easily available. This can only be done by building at higher densities, providing adequate infrastructure and facilities, and ensuring the proper management of new neighbourhoods.

We must also design for a more sustainable mix – mixed use, mixed tenure and mixed household size. We invariably build single-use projects, large housing schemes that are for one tenure-type only. These lack the variation and complexity of established communities, and encourage the development of ghettos, either perceived or actual.

Where possible, public and private should be mixed, along with housing association and affordable dwellings, to create a mix of socio-economic groups, family sizes, ages and tenure. In Holland and Denmark it is often very difficult to distinguish between local authority and private housing, and in Finland it is enshrined in law that private and public housing must be indistinguishable.

That is the way it should be. We should not build housing in isolation. Shops, schools, crèches, doctors' surgeries, workplaces and public transport should be integrated from the beginning. The best parts of towns and cities have a richness and interest derived from the complexities of multiple uses. With a good mix comes variety in building form. Buildings then have the potential to be interesting, memorable and distinctive. With judicious arrangements of buildings, places can be made. With place comes identity – a far cry from the monotonous sameness of much of our recent developments.

INVOLVING THE COMMUNITY

Consideration of the process of creating new communities is vital. Consolidation of existing suburbs with large new high-density neighbourhoods is threatening to locals. This must be dealt with delicately; in our experience, change is always initially resisted. There is ample evidence that community consultation, although time-consuming, costly and draining, can be immensely beneficial in helping to create an inclusive and cohesive new community.

To start with, all the residents of any new place are strangers to each other. To develop a successful community, they will need all the help they can get to bond, organise and take psychological ownership of their new neighbourhood. We can learn from the examples of other European countries. For many decades it has been the norm in Finland that all apartment buildings of a certain size have basic communal facilities such as a club or meeting room, a laundry, a sauna

→ left to right:
– The next generation
– A bicycle culture
– Playgrounds for children

(sometimes with a pool), and generous basement storage space. Each block or small group of blocks has a live-in caretaker who regularly maintains the buildings and deals with any relevant daily issues concerning the residents. Each resident has a share in the management company, which meets regularly to agree how to deal with maintenance and other matters. The need to maintain the buildings and immediate surroundings to an acceptable standard is enshrined in law. This example shows that when good provision is made and reasonable standards of maintenance are enforced, a sense of social and civic pride is engendered.

GOOD DESIGN

So what kind of places do we want? Design cannot, on its own, create a good community, but bad design can definitely prevent a community from developing. With higher densities, new issues arise that must be dealt with, like the maintenance of privacy, protection from noisy neighbours, and the need for more complex building types beyond the standard semi-detached or short terrace form. For these reasons, if we are to build at higher or middle-level densities – vital for the sustainability of our cities and towns – good design becomes much more important.

We need to be providing bigger apartments, particularly aimed at families, as an alternative to the suburban semi-detached, and all dwellings should be capable of lifetime change. They should have generous storage, big balconies, a place for bikes and recycling facilities. Both site and apartment layouts must respond sensibly to orientation. We should fully embrace sustainable design and technology, not just pay it obligatory lip service. Apartments that do not receive adequate sunlight must have access to compensatory amenities like a wonderful communal roof garden.

Higher densities needn't mean high-rise. Some of the most attractive and livable places in Dublin for instance, like Phibsborough, Ranelagh, Portobello and Rathmines, have buildings of between two and four storeys, but have densities of thirty to fifty dwellings per acre. They are made up of ordinary streets and squares, are rich in variety, form and mix, and the fine urban grain allows room for change. They are of a human scale, generally made from attractive materials, have intricacy, interest and a great sense of place. We must hope that in the new city-fringe developments, the impetus to maximise profits and minimise delivery times does not create overly industrialised, repetitive, large-grained and out-of-scale buildings sitting in a sterile public realm. The value of good design, careful consideration and delight in detailing – which all takes time and costs money – should never be underestimated by private or public developers.

ILLUSTRATED SCHEMES.

There are a host of new developments about to happen that, it is hoped, have the potential to develop as viable, sustainable neighbourhoods. In Dublin, these are largely located on a concentric ring either side of the M50 orbital. To the north-east of the city, the North Fringe Action Area Plan involves a massive 200-hectare scheme, complete with a train station (on the Belfast-Dublin line) and the Fr Collins Park (currently being developed). To the east of the park is Clongriffin, designed by Conroy Crowe Kelly Architects, and to the west is Balgriffin by McCrossan O'Rourke Manning, totalling around 7,000 new dwellings. Each has its own town centre and includes a mix of apartments, houses, offices, shops and community facilities. Further west, on the other side of the Malahide Road, is the Darndale/Belcamp area. Here, DMOD have built their competition-winning village centre, striking a difficult balance between robustness and openness.

In Finglas, Anthony Reddy Associates' Prospect Hill scheme is just complete. This follows a less urban, more landscaped campus-like approach, albeit with a high-density 52 dwellings an acre. Continuing in an anticlockwise rotation around the city are the developments at Pelletstown and Royal Canal Park by McCrossan O'Rourke Manning, O'Mahony Pike and Murray Ó Laoire. These are laid out along the north bank of the Royal Canal and adjacent to the mainline and commuter train line from Maynooth.

Next to this, just south of the N3 Navan Road, is the new scheme at the old

← left to right:
– A sense of place
– Marino, Dublin
– Desigining for private and shared space

Phoenix Park Racecourse, Castleknock, by OMS Architects. Again, on a vast scale, it is 98% residential, with over 2,300 dwellings. Further south and just to the west of the Liffey Valley Shopping Centre and Quarryvale Park, McCrossan O'Rourke Manning have designed another predominantly residential scheme of nearly 600 new dwellings at St Loman's Road, while south of this, ten hectares at Cherry Orchard is being master-planned and co-ordinated for Dublin City Council by Anthony Reddy Associates. This scheme is fairly unique in that seven architecture practices are collaborating to create a more varied result.

Finally, just west of Dublin is Adamstown. This ambitious project for a new town of up to 10,000 homes, with the full gamut of shops, work places, leisure, civic and cultural facilities, is focused around a new railway station. Adamstown is being built on a phased basis, with the provision of schools and other essential community facilities keeping pace with the demand generated by new homes. O'Mahony Pike Architects collaborated with South Dublin County Council and others in the preparation of the Strategic Development Zone master plan, which is to be complemented by a public realm design guide by Camlin Lonsdale Landscape Architects and our own practice.

All of these new Dublin schemes have similarities. First, they are all on a vast scale, often created by one developer with just a single architectural practice. They are all at higher densities, ranging from 25 up to 75 dwellings per acre. Most are adjacent to existing public transport routes, and are mixed use but with an overwhelming preponderance of private-sector dwellings, mainly apartments.

Outside Dublin, where good-quality sustainable developments are essential to help counterbalance the overbearing economic and cultural influence of the capital, some interesting schemes are emerging. Two projects by Simon J Kelly & Partners in Westport, provide a welcome contemporary interpretation of neighbourhood place-making, as does Stag Park in Mitchelstown, by Stratagem Planning & Design and Wain Morehead for Cork County Council. This mixed-use project includes 362 homes, laid out around streets, squares and small parks.

In 2005 Tipperary Town Council hosted a design competition for high-quality low-density rural housing. This was won jointly by three architectural practices, including MCO Architecture and Carew Kelly Architects. With the future of the project uncertain, let's hope something comes out of it.

CONCLUSION

I look forward to all these schemes coming to fruition, but their success as good new neighbourhoods with thriving new communities depends on many complex factors, some outside of the control of the architects. These include:
– engendering a sense of pride amongst the residents so that they participate in the collective care of their neighbourhoods

– having a fairer, just and better-educated society with a more even distribution of wealth and opportunity. This will reduce exclusion, resentment and crime.
– wherever possible, to be encouraging mixed-use, mixed-form, mixed-tenure, mixed-size, complex, intense and interesting new urban neighbourhoods
– having a complementary provision of essential public facilities such as good public libraries, community centres, parks, playgrounds, sports facilities and swimming pools
– greatly investing in and carefully managing the public realm
– continued and increasing investment in public transport so that it keeps pace with new developments in order to give us efficient, accessible, cheap and clean services
– safe, extensive and continuous cycleways to provide an alternative to car travel for short journeys
– the ability of the buildings to be adapted to the demands of future and inevitable lower carbon-emissions targets
– the ability of the sites and buildings to cope with the ravaging effects of global warming, such as increased flooding and extreme weather conditions.

We need new neighbourhoods which future generations will be pleased, rather than feel burdened, to inherit – places that provide more than a roof over your head or an investment opportunity. Indeed, we are hoping for places that may even lift peoples' spirits. As the great master le Corbusier said:

You employ stone, wood, concrete, and with these materials you build houses and palaces. That is construction. Ingenuity is at work. But suddenly, you touch my heart, you do me good, I am happy and I say 'This is beautiful.' That is architecture. Art enters in.

My house is practical. I thank you, as I may thank railway engineers, or the telephone service. You have not touched my heart. But suppose that walls rise toward heaven in such a way that I am moved. I perceive your intentions. Your mood has been gentle, brutal, charming, or noble. The stones you have erected tell me so. You fix me to the place and my eyes regard it. They behold something which expresses a thought. A thought which reveals itself without word or sound, but solely by means of shapes which stand in a certain relationship to one another. These shapes are such that they are clearly revealed in light. The relationships between them have not necessarily any reference to what is practical or descriptive. They are a mathematical creation of your mind. They are the language of architecture.

By the use of raw materials and starting from conditions more or less utilitarian, you have established certain relationships which have aroused my emotions. This is architecture."

— *Towards a New Architecture* (Architectural Press, London, 1927)

Seán Harrington is the principal of Seán Harrington Architects

Adamstown, Co Dublin – History and Process

O'Mahony Pike Architects

In 1997 O'Mahony Pike Architects (OMP) were asked by developers Castlethorn Construction to advise on the potential of a 500-acre greenfield site located north of the railway line in west Lucan. Since then, much collaborative thinking has fuelled the delivery of the Adamstown project. The local authority, landowners and designers have all worked together in an effort to create an environment of best practice. The three principal landowners collaborated on a joint rezoning submission, which led to the creation of a joint venture infrastructural delivery company.

The planning process started with the preparation of an Action Area Plan, followed by the approval of a Local Area Plan in April 2001, prepared by South Dublin County Council (SDCC). The area was given priority by the granting of a Special Development Zone designation in June 2001. The planning scheme for the SDZ, prepared by SDCC and OMP, was ratified by An Bord Pleanála in September 2003. As the SDZ was being prepared, a Sustainable Energy Ireland-sponsored study was undertaken to establish energy priorities in the master-plan lands.

An opportunity was identified at an early stage to re-engage with the railway at the heart of a higher-density town centre, based on the principles of the Transit Village. OMP prepared a planning application to deliver a suburban station on the Dublin-Kildare line to coincide with the upgrading of the line. It became operational in 2007.

As the first-phase housing was being completed by OMP, a study of the District

↗ The different stages in the planning process for the new town of Adamstown

228

Local Area Plan, 2001

SEI study, 2003

Strategic Development Zone scheme, 2003

Railway station planning application, 2004

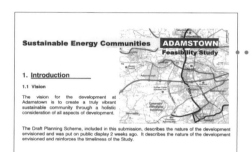
Phase 1 planning application, 2005

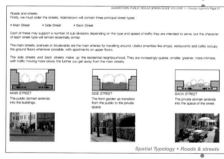
Adamstown public realm, 2005

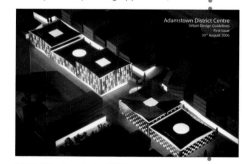
District Centre study, 2006

Adamstown parks competition, 2008

District Centre planning application, 2008

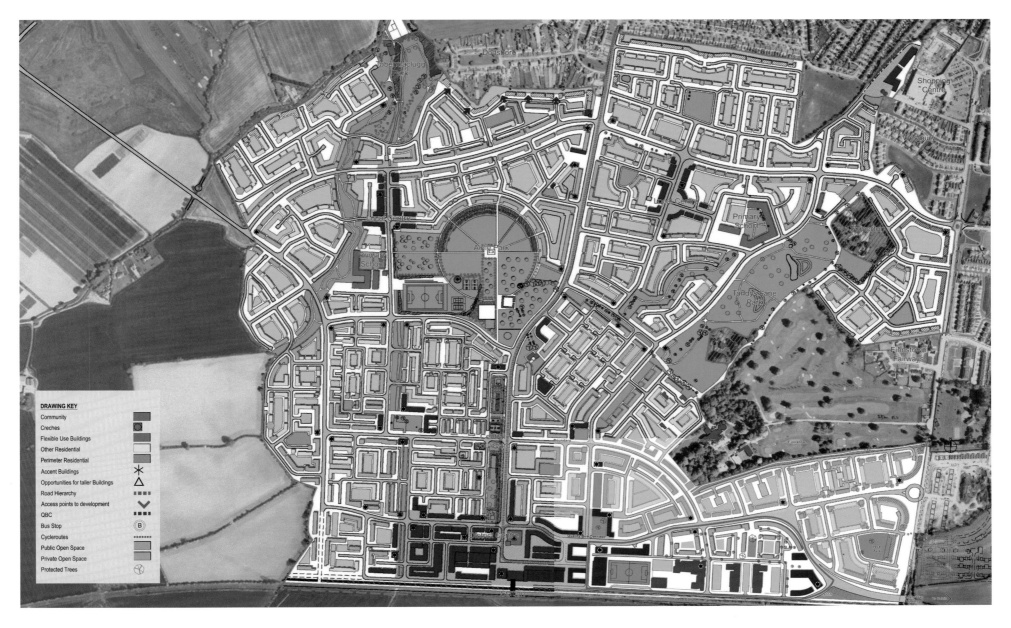

DRAWING KEY

Community
Creches
Flexible Use Buildings
Other Residential
Perimeter Residential
Accent Buildings
Opportunities for taller Buildings
Road Hierarchy
Access points to development
QBC
Bus Stop
Cycleroutes
Public Open Space
Private Open Space
Protected Trees

Centre was being prepared in 2005 by Metropolitan Workshop to agree the urban-design principles and organisation of the new town centre at Adamstown. The planning application which evolved from these design principles was given approval in 2008.

A similar process was undertaken for the public realm through a study by Howley Harrington Architects and Camlin Lonsdale Landscape Architects, agreeing the detailed principles for the creation of

Key

Motorways
Motorways (Under Construction)
Railways
Main Roads
Airports
Built up Areas
Parks and Amenity Areas
Adamstown Lands

successful streetscapes and public open spaces. These principles were delivered upon through a competition that was organised for the design of the parks, which was won by Foley & Salles Landscape Architects in 2008.

↑ The Strategic Development Zone scheme, 2003
← Map showing the location of Adamstown near Lucan on the west side of Dublin

Adamstown – Strategic Development Zone

O'Mahony Pike Architects

Through the Strategic Development Zone (SDZ) structure, South Dublin County Council (SDCC) became the development agency for the Adamstown planning scheme. A steering group of SDCC senior directors, developers' representatives and design team representatives was set up to work with the developers' design teams. The steering group ensured that the Government departments and agencies and the various public transport representatives were now involved in the delivery of a planning scheme informed by an extensive public consultation process and best-practice urban-design schemes from around Europe and the United States.

The principles set down in the Local Area Plan did not substantially change. and the general arrangement of roads, parks and density zones remained the same. However. an immense level of detail was added to both the design of the services infrastructure and the built environment in the SDZ planning scheme.

The master plan was organised around a hierarchy of district and local centres and a series of landmark elements and

↗ from top: (1) Road network, (2) Green network, (3) Destinations, (4) Key frontages
➡ Perspective of Airlie Park master plan
↓ Plan of the neighbourhood

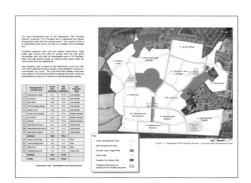

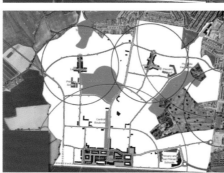

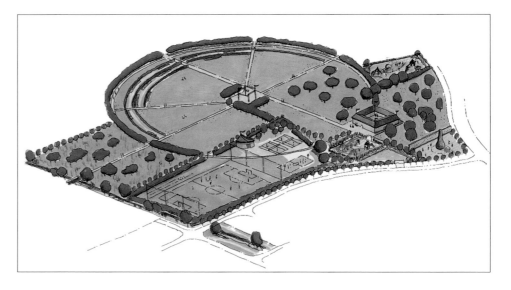

destinations, which responded to specific site characteristics. The proposed streets and squares around the station make up the town centre, with two smaller village centres at Tobermaclugg to the north-west and Tandy's Lane to the north-east. Schools and parks activate the village centres. More local parks appear along a network of amenity linkages and residential streets.

For clarity, the lands were divided into eleven neighbourhoods and three amenity areas. The essence of each of these neighbourhoods is described in the planning scheme master plan through
- a detailed indicative layout
- urban-design principles
- facilities
- access and movement layout
- location of key buildings and amenity spaces
- a checklist of development standards applying to the area.

The draft scheme took about sixty weeks to prepare. This was the first document of its kind in Ireland, and it constituted a detailed design for a new town with a potential population of 25,000 people and 8,000 to 10,000 dwellings, together with all the other non-residential uses supporting an integrated community of this scale. It was required to be robust, comprehensive and detailed in its content, and, where possible, be future-proofed, equitable, deliverable, sustainable, marketable and affordable.

Schools, housing, roads, and both hard and soft infrastructure continue to be delivered in line with the phasing targets. The delivery process of the new community is chronicled on the South Dublin County Council website, www.adamstown.ie.

design / completion – 1998–2003
client – South Dublin County Council / Chartridge Ltd

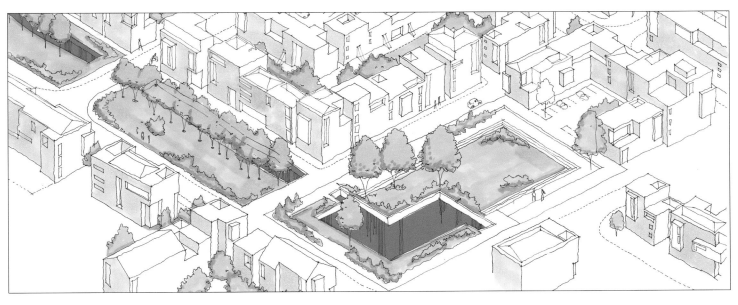

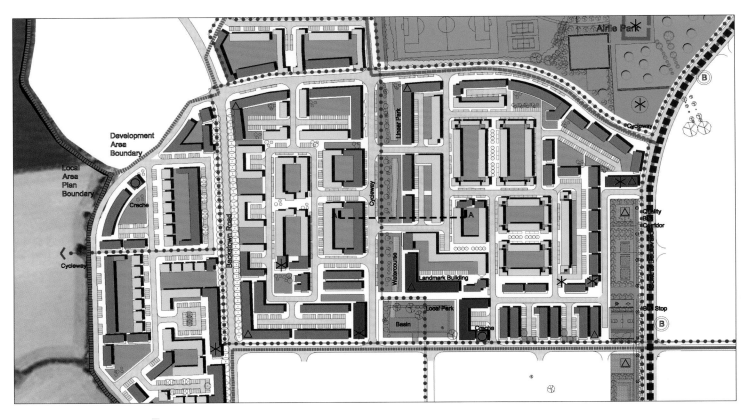

↗ Perspective and section of Aderrig Park
→ Part-plan of Aderrig Park

231

Adamstown – Housing

O'Mahony Pike Architects

Following the adoption of the Adamstown Strategic Development Zone master plan, the design of the first phase of housing was seen as being a critical factor in the future success of the new Adamstown urban village project.

Adamstown Castle is a cradle-to-the-grave community, with the first phase of 650 dwellings incorporating a wide variety of dwelling types, from four-bedroom family houses to one-bedroom corner apartments. The built environment is distinctly different from neighbouring housing, with three- to four-storey street edges, extensively landscaped pocket parks, high-quality finishes to buildings and access points. The railway station, primary schools and a leisure complex were in place within six months of completion of the project.

design / completion – 2005–2008
client – Charterbridge Ltd /
    Castlethorn Construction

↗ Views of newly completed housing
↓ Phase 1 – part-plan
↘ Phase 1 – site plan
↘ Illustrative layout from SDZ planning scheme

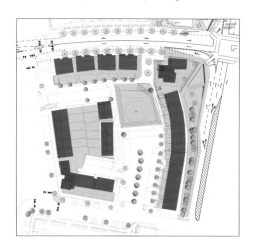

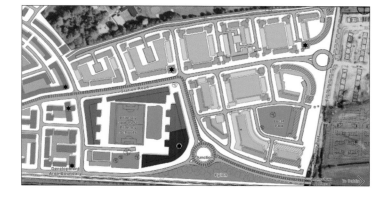

Adamstown – Parks

Foley & Salles Landscape Architects

Airlie Park and Tandy's Lane Park make up 48 acres of a 74-acre network of public open space in Adamstown. Both parks were designed in tandem in response to the brief for an international design competition. Although the parks differ, offering a range of play and recreational experiences, they have been designed using similar materials and detailing in order to achieve a sense of connection. Repetition, similarity and recognition assist in strengthening the impact of one park by association with the other, and vice versa, even though the location, topography and orientation of each park is different.

The design intent also stretches beyond the boundaries of the parks to include the streetscape and to ensure that the park experience continues even after the park is closed. In this way, the parks contribute strongly to a landscape network within which built development will proceed.

The way in which the parks address their immediate context was considered in detail at the conceptual stage. Airlie Park is subdivided into three main zones, the southern and northern zones addressing the adjacent residential neighbourhoods, and the central zone facilitating recreation within the park along its central spine. Activity in Tandy's Lane Park is along its western flank in the form the 'active strip', where park activities are concentrated and available for use after the park is closed at night. This strip forms part of a connecting route from the northernmost residential districts in Adamstown to Adamstown Central and the train station. The eastern side of the park is treated with less intensity, responding to the quieter condition of Tandy's Lane.

↗ View of the main entrance to Airlie Park
→ View of the dykes within the woodland area of Tandy's Lane Park

233

Adamstown – District Centre

The District Centre is the heart of this new community of 25,000 people, conveniently located beside the new railway station and a fifteen-minute journey to Heuston Station. The urban design for the District Centre includes the outline design for 25,000m² of retail space, 23,000m² of other non-residential facilities, and more than 700 new homes. From the outset, it was agreed that the retail layout should be based on open streets and not a covered mall. Defining those streets and places will give Adamstown its identity and distinctive character.

The design process entailed assembling the commercial brief, then testing numerous layouts to find the optimum configuration that fulfils good urban-design practice in terms of permeability, and conforms with the Strategic Development Zone planning scheme.

The parking arrangements for 2,400 cars, and their relationship to the station for commuter parking and to the two anchor stores, was the strategic decision that needed most testing. The podium parking layout utilises a multifunctional car-parking strategy that satisfied retail demand and evening use for leisure and residential parking. This vertical separation of the parking helps create a pleasant public domain, activated by pedestrians, buses and taxis, and streets that can be open in the evenings for residential traffic. The podium also absorbs loading bays and suppresses the anchor-store volume so that there can be a public square above it.

design / completion – 2005–2008
client – Castlethorn Construction

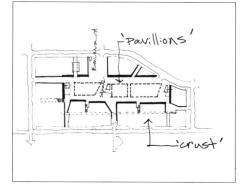

↗ Part-plan of District Centre
→ Early station concourse view / Concept drawing /
   Developed station concourse view

↑ Landmark building by O'Donnell + Tuomey Architects
↗ Section-elevation through station concourse, looking east
↓ Retail street, looking west
→ Library by Grafton Architects

Clongriffin, Dublin 13

Conroy Crowe Kelly Architects

The North Fringe forms a new development edge to the Dublin city area, between the M50 at Santry and the sea at Baldoyle. When complete, it will accommodate up to 35,000 people and a number of new mixed-use employment and service centres. Development is guided by an Action Area Plan prepared in 2000 by Urban Initiatives on behalf of Dublin City Council. This plan envisaged two prime urban centres, one at Malahide Junction, the head of the Malahide Road quality bus corridor, and the other at Clongriffin, on the Dublin-Belfast railway line. Main Street, with public-transport priority, is the organising spine for the district, connecting the mixed-use centres.

Clongriffin, granted planning permission in 2003, is a large mixed-use residential district incorporating a new town centre which seeks to balance the existing surrounding neighbourhoods of mainly two-storey semi-detached houses, increasingly occupied by empty-nesters. The Dublin-Belfast railway forms the district's eastern boundary and a new DART station serves the development. Adjacent to the station is the Town Square, where the main street and all the principal routes culminate.

Pedestrian desire-lines through the site inform the route layout and open-space network. The major pedestrian route runs diagonally from Fr Collin's Park to the town centre. The major vehicular routes run east-west, north and south of the park, to the Town Square; Main Street is the most southerly of these routes. Local parks of varying size and function give character and identity to the residential districts that are formed by these movement spines.

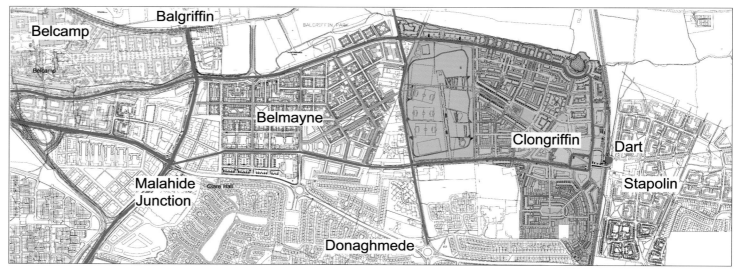

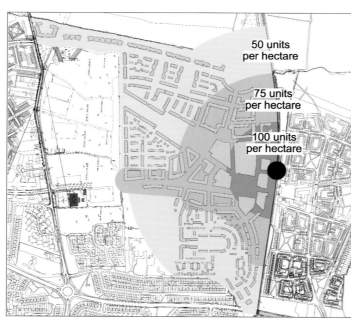

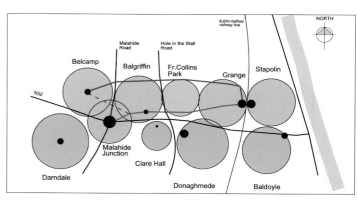

↑ North Fringe context map
← Density study
↗ Neighbourhood areas
→ Route classification

height	mix	percentage	no. of dwellings	site area	density	floor area	bed spaces	site coverage	open space	car spaces	context
2-7 storey 13-storey tower	25% 3/4-bed units 75% 1/2-bed units	76% residential 24% commercial	3,590	53 ha (130 acres)	68 units/ha (28 units/acre)	281,992m² residential 89,918m² commercial	10,908 (206/ha)	26%	10% public	1.25 per dwelling, with additional public parking	established 2-3 storey residential area

Residential perimeter blocks increase in density and height towards the town centre. The design of the town centre consists of urban perimeter blocks defining a strong building line, with active commercial frontages and a fine grain. The traditional urban format of the town centre rejects the single-use enclosed shopping-centre concept.

Retail uses and services are located at street level, with residential or other commercial uses overhead. The success and vibrancy of such proposals relies heavily on Local Authorities actively discouraging car-based, single-use enclosed shopping centres which displace footfall away from the public realm.

The Town Square has been designed as the civic focus for Clongriffin, and is essentially a hard public place with a large raised grass table, space for a local market, and broad pavements surrounding it so that street-level uses can spill out into the space. A large, sculptural, coloured-glass canopy occupies one side, forming a covered cycle park, and contains the entrances to the Park & Ride car park located under the square.

design / completion – 2001–2013
(Phase 1 completed 2006; Phase 2 completed 2009)
client – Gannon Homes Ltd, Pennon Homes, Menolly Homes, Killoe Developments, Pierse Homes Ltd, Barina Construction Ltd

↗ Computer perspectives of Town Square
⇥ Site map
↓ Models of Town Square and Main Street →

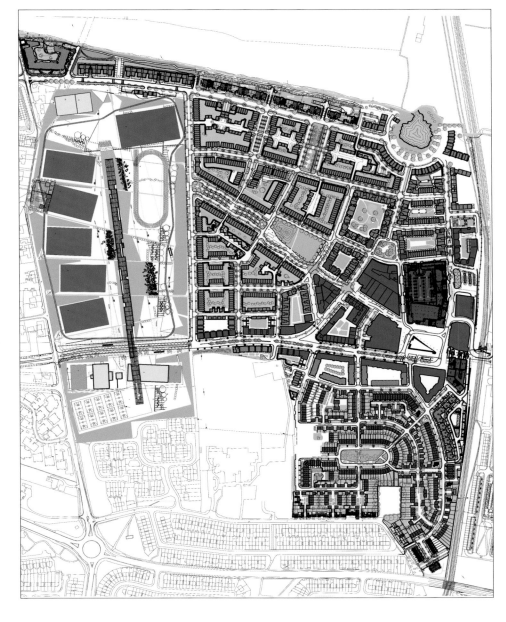

237

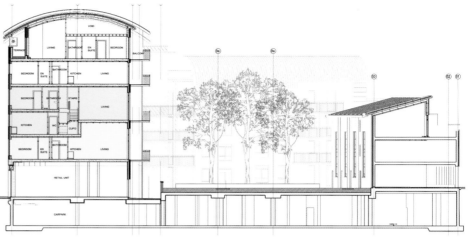

0m   10m   20m

CLONGRIFFIN

↘ Views of Main Street and Town Square
↙ Views of Station Street and steps to station

↑ Duplex plans and cross-section
↓ From top:
   Context section through main street
   and mews lane, looking east
   Elevation along Market Street
   Elevation along Clongriffin Road

JUNE 21st
ANGLE OF NOON SUN
56 DEGREES

Balgriffin, Malahide Road, Dublin 17

McCrossan O'Rourke Manning Architects

Balgriffin in north Dublin is a residential and new town centre with associated facilities and amenities, including shops, cafés, bars, crèches, health centre, community centre, post office, offices, etc. The area forms part of the North Fringe Action Area Plan which comprises 200 hectares of land, incorporating a regional-scale park and a train station.

The project involved the design of a range of dwelling types contained in town blocks and different precincts, served by a new main street and town centre, and with a quality bus corridor linking to the train station. Balgriffin is to be considered as a 'piece of town' rather than a segregated suburban housing estate, delivering a model of development very different from that which has dominated our suburbs over the past fifty years.

High priority is given to the urban-design quality of development. All elements of successful urban design have been considered, such as strong streets and parks; clear definition between public and private spaces; no ambiguous leftover areas; legible and coherent block layouts; considered vistas and focal points. This, coupled with a number of different precincts, each with their own character, is designed to give residents and workers a sense of place, ownership and identity. A new approach to apartment living has been established in order to encourage more apartment owner-occupiers.

———
↗ Master plan (with location map inset)
→ Framework plan
⇉ Walking distances

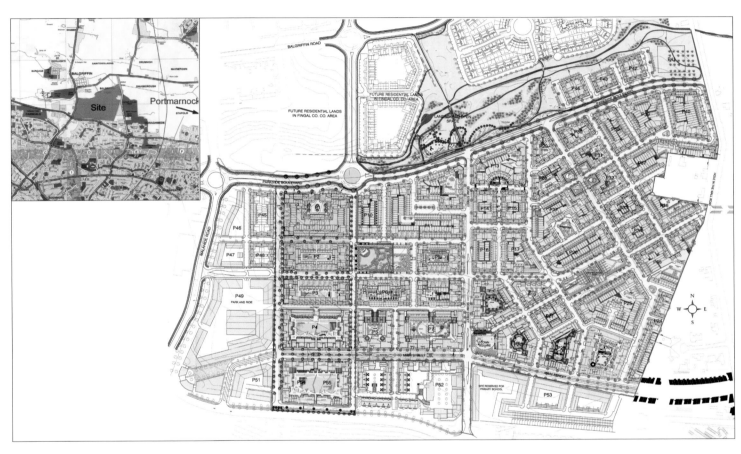

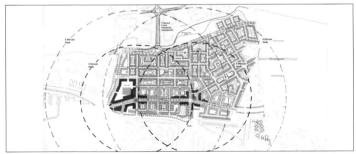

height	mix	percentage	no. of dwellings	site area	density	floor area	bed spaces	site coverage	open space	car spaces	context
2-7 storey	6% 4-bed units 34% 3-bed units 51% 2-bed units 9% 1-bed units	95% residential 5% commercial + community	2,817	46.3 ha (114 acres)	61 units/ha (25 units/acre)	267,296m²	9,493 (205/ha)	n/a	9%	1.5 per house 1.25 per apartment	major greenfield urban extension, part of DCC North Fringe Action Area Plan

239

The scheme provides a large range of housing types to cater for different socio-economic groups and family types (20% social, affordable and shared ownership, and 80% private). Dwelling types range from one-bedroom to four-bedroom units; heights vary from two storeys to eight storeys in the town centre.

address – Balgriffin, Malahide Road / Grange Road, Dublin 17
design / completion – 2006–2012
client – Stanley Holdings

BALGRIFFIN

← Garden precinct
↙ Garden precinct plan
↙ Views of garden precinct
↓ Turning corners
   Ground and 1st-floor plans of corner block

opposite

→ Site plan of nodal point
→→ Perspective of new town square
↘ View and elevation to main street

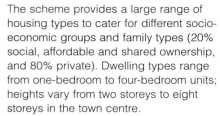

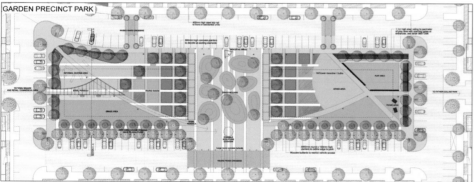

GARDEN PRECINCT PARK

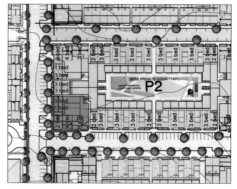

P2

TYPE J
TYPE H
TYPE J1

TYPE J
TYPE H
TYPE J1

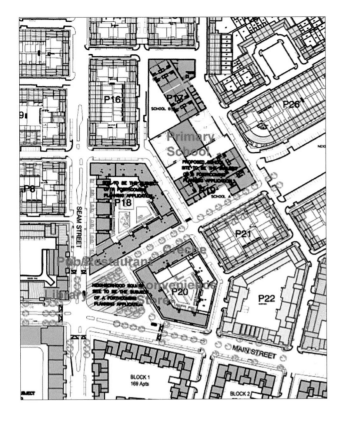

Pelletstown, Dublin 11 – Master Plan

O'Mahony Pike Architects

The early master-planning of this new urban development of 4,000 dwellings on 106 acres between the Tolka Valley and the Royal Canal and Dublin-Sligo railway line was set out in the first *New Housing* publication. The project is now well advanced, with half the projects built and the balance in the planning process.

The original master plan and tissue studies were prepared for the whole site by O'Mahony Pike Architects. An Action Area Plan was then prepared for Dublin City Council by Urban Initiatives. More detailed master plans were then prepared by OMP for Castlethorn and by the London practice C2WG for Ballymore.

The plans provide for two local centres, one at each end of the site. The west end has the existing Ashtown station, and the first element, Market Square, has already been completed. The east-end railway station has not yet been built, and the local centre is only at planning stage. Other elements include a central semicircular open space which has been completed, and an interconnecting series of boulevards, which have been completed to the extent that a Dublin Bus route now serves the whole site and terminates adjacent to Market Square.

Recreational open space is in abundance in the area, with the Martin Savage Playing Fields to the south and the Tolka Valley to the north, where substantial playing pitches and other facilities are planned. Land is allocated for a primary school at the centre of the site, and crèches are already in place, as are a range of local shops and other facilities.

This part of Dublin, with its local advantages and first-class transport links, has allowed for the development of a relatively high-density community, while

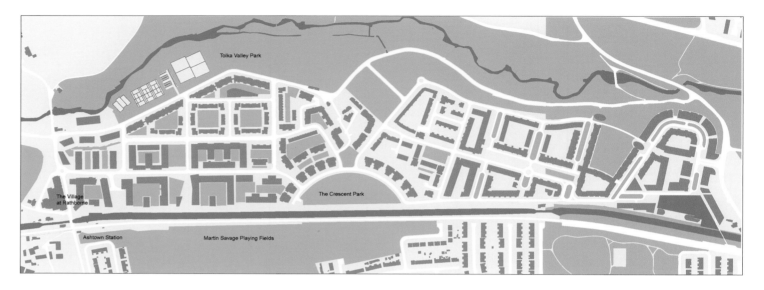

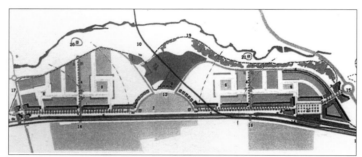

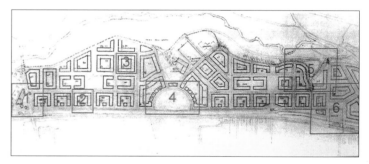

keeping a balanced housing mix, which includes families with children.

Four individual schemes which have been completed are illustrated on the following pages – two at either end of the area. Further smaller schemes or parts of schemes have also been completed, but most of the remaining development is at planning stage, with some already approved. The schemes illustrated are the Rathborne Village Centre and the Rathborne Phase 1 housing schemes, both by O'Mahony Pike, following closely the general designs shown in the original tissue studies. The other schemes illustrated, Phases 1 and 2 of the Royal Canal Park, designed by McCrossan O'Rourke Manning, closely follow the master plan prepared by C2WG. Also illustrated is the revised project for the eastern town centre and canal basin being designed by Murray O'Laoire Architects.

Also shown on this page is a block model of the western end of the site showing the two completed projects and the practically completed scheme by Capel Developments, who purchased a substantial part of the site from Castlethorn Construction. A master plan for the final twelve-acre project along the Royal Canal bank, adjacent to Rathborne Village Centre, was prepared by O'Mahony Pike for Capel Developments, as well as the final element of the eastern village, designed by McCauley Daye O'Connell and now approved.

design / completion – 1998–2015
client – Castlethorn Construction / Capel Developments / Ballymore Homes

↑ Model of western end
↗ Tissue study
→ Master plan of Royal Canal Park

opposite

↑ Plan as now proposed
↖ Original master plan and Dublin City Council master plan (by Urban Initiatives)
← View of model

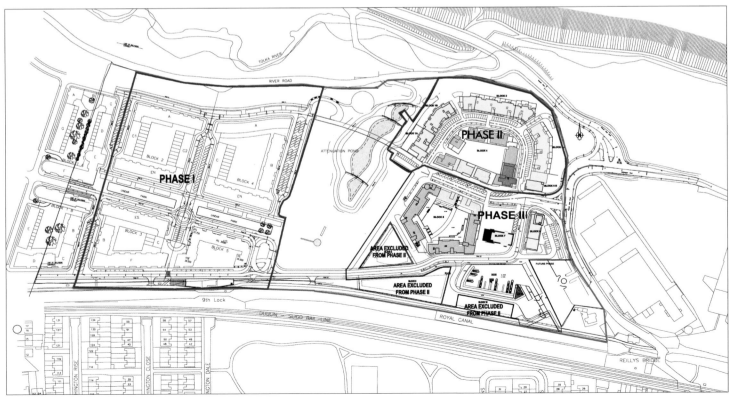

Pelletstown – phase 1

O'Mahony Pike Architects

Phase 1 provides a substantial proportion of family housing units. There are two squares with central shared gardens, accessed from the small private gardens of the perimeter houses and duplexes. These blocks are framed by four-storey apartment buildings. The curved four-storey edge block defines the boundary of the site along the Tolka Valley Park, and follows closely the original tissue study.

The detailed design was shown in the original *New Housing* book, and consists of two-storey three-bedroom duplexes with apartments above, accessed from an atrium running the full length of each block.

The residual areas between the edge blocks and the squares have a local centre with shops, gym, crèche and other amenities, and a triangular housing block.

address – Pelletstown, Dublin 11
design / completion – 1999–2005
client – Castlethorn Construction

↑ Aerial view of development
← Elevation to River Tolka
↓ Tissue study

opposite

↗ Views of edge block
↘ Views of (left to right)
 – Main traffic street
 – Aerial view of a communal courtyard
 – Local centre with shops, gym, crèche and other amenities

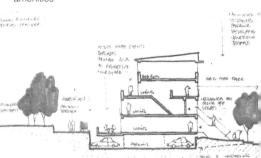

height	mix	percentage	no. of dwellings	site area	density	floor area	bed spaces	site coverage	open space	car spaces	context
3-5 storey PHASE 1	35 x 4-bed houses 323 x 3-bed units 122 x 2-bed units 95 x 1-bed units	70% residential 20% commercial 10% communal	575	20.5 ha (50.6 acres)	28 units/ha (11 units/acre)	31,000m²	2,300 (112/ha)	30%	1.5 ha in a crescent park	879 (1.5 per dwelling)	greenfield site

Pelletstown – phase 2 – The Village Square

O'Mahony Pike Architects

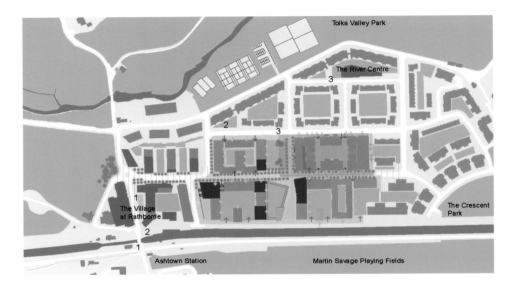

Tolka Valley Park

The River Centre

3

2   3

1

The Village
at Rathborne

2

1

Ashtown Station

Martin Savage Playing Fields

The Crescent
Park

The Village Square is at the western end of Pelletstown, next to Ashtown railway station. It forms the core of the first of two neighbourhood centres planned for the area.

The plan of the development closely follows the original tissue studies for the master plan, with a public square surrounded by shops and landmark building on the Royal Canal bank, facing the railway station. To the east is a residential square with six-storey apartment buildings surrounding a private garden square, open to the south.

A pavilion restaurant bar is placed between the square and the canal. The café below the landmark building, and the restaurant bar face the waterfront on the canal tow path, with a new docking bay for barges.

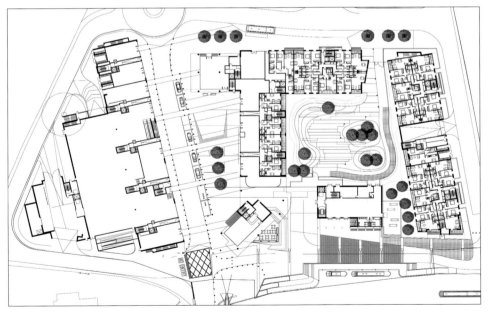

The waterfront seating in front and the café and bar have proved a popular open-air venue.

The village centre comprises 2,800m² of retail space, including a supermarket and a medical centre. There are 259 apartments, with private, shared space, in the eastern square, and at first-floor level, over the supermarket, on the western side.

address – Pelletstown, Dublin 11
design / completion – 2003–2008
client – Castlethorn Construction

↖ Location map
↑ Computer perspective of Village Square
← Site plan

→ opposite – Views of completed development

height	mix	percentage	no. of dwellings	site area	density	floor area	bed spaces	site coverage	open space	car spaces	context
6-8 storey	26 x 3-bed apartments 171 x 2-bed apartments 62 x 1-bed apartments medical centre / retail / bar	95% residential 5% commercial	259	1.9 ha (4.6 acres)	133 units/ha (66 units/acre)	33,510m²	n/a	29.3%	n/a	n/a	greenfield site

Pelletstown – Royal Canal Park, phases 1 + 2   McCrossan O'Rourke Manning Architects

Phases 1 and 2 of Royal Canal Park, west of Dublin city, form part of a new mixed-use town centre and residential development with retail, commercial, community, leisure and recreational facilities. Phases 1 and 2 are located to the eastern side of the overall Pelletstown development.

The master plan for phases 1 and 2 covers an area of nine hectares (five hectares for Phase 1, four for Phase 2). An indicative plan was produced by the two main landowners to provide a co-ordinated and coherent approach to implementing the Dublin City Council's Action Area Plan for the lands.

The development ranges from a small number of three-storey houses to predominantly four-to-six-storey apartment buildings and commercial buildings, with local wight-storey elements in the town centre. The town centre is focused around quality public-transport links, ensuring all those living and working in Pelletstown are within a few minutes' walk of a bus route or train station. Architecturally strong boulevards and a new town square deliver identity and place-making to the scheme.

Residential blocks were built in an innovative fast-track construction process involving the off-site production of precast concrete internal structures and external wall elements. All external materials – zinc, terracotta tiling, self-coloured render, etc – are low maintenance and chosen for longevity.

design / completion – Phase 1: 2001–2005; Phase 2: 2005–
client – Ballymore Properties Ltd

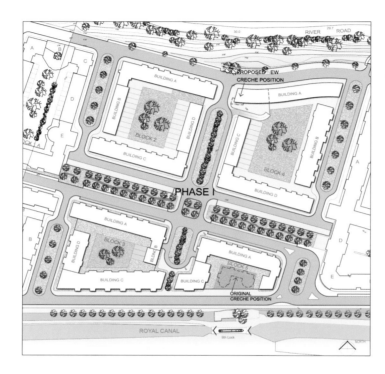

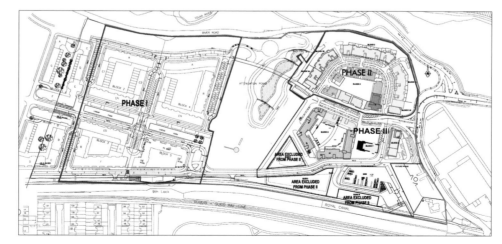

↑ Elevation study
↖ Site plan for phase 1
← Master plan for Royal Canal Park at the western end of Pelletstown, showing this scheme in context

opposite

→ Views of completed development

height	mix	percentage	no. of dwellings	site area	density	floor area	bed spaces	site coverage	open space	car spaces	context
5-8 storey PHASE 1	22% 3+-bed units 56% 2-bed units 22% 1-bed units	73% residential 27% commercial + communal	552	5 ha (12.6 acres)	104 units/ha (42 units/acre)	53,122m² (approx)	1,650	n/a	10%	1.25 per dwelling	new town on greenfield site on north bank of Royal Canal

Pelletstown – Royal Canal Park, phase 3

Murray Ó Laoire Architects

This mixed-use development, surrounding a large south-facing marina will generate an active semi-urban centre with local shops, cafés and dining areas, and a residential quarter comprising apartments, townhouses, and live-work units.

This scheme proposes that Royal Canal Park should have a 'town centre' distinguishable from its residential quarters, achieved by the employment of analogous architectural means – change in use, density, height and architectural language, a coherent and continuous streetscape, and a main square marked by a vertical landmark. It offers a lively civic space of strong character, a place where people will gather, meet and spend time.

The residential element is substantial – a residential quarter in its own right. The scheme seeks to provide for a residential environment of high quality in which all residents will enjoy the generous provision of private, communal and public open space, sunlight and daylight, good aspect regardless of orientation, and, for the majority of residents, views over the water and distant mountains.

This scheme seeks to ensure that this final phase of Royal Canal Park will provide a successful and even memorable commercial and civic heart for Royal Canal Park both by day and night, that it will serve as a focal point for a wider community and as an exemplar in the design of new such urban environments.

design / completion – 2003– (on site 2006)
client – Ballymore Properties Ltd

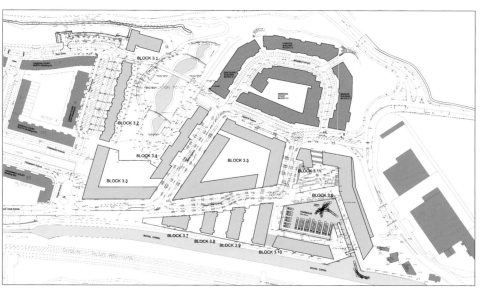

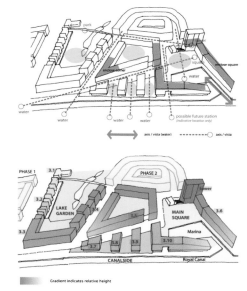

height	mix	percentage	no. of dwellings	site area	density	floor area	bed spaces	site coverage	open space	car spaces	context
5-17 storey	19 x 5-bed apartments 11 x 4-bed apartments 100 x 3-bed apartments 213 x 2-bed apartments 94 x 1-bed apartments	75% residential 25% commercial	437	6.63 ha (16.38 acres)	66 units/ha (27 units/acre)	86,750m²	n/a	28%	n/a	542	greenfield development along Royal Canal

Phoenix Park Racecourse, Castleknock, Dublin 15

OMS Architects

Fingal County Council adopted an Action Area Plan in 2001 for the former Phoenix Park Racecourse lands. A planning application for the lands was lodged in 2002, and was granted planning permission by An Bord Pleanála in 2003.

The master plan continues to evolve in co-operation with the County Council to respond to changing context, regulation and market. There are approximately 500 units constructed to date, along with a new railway station and N3 interchange.

Urban-design objectives of the scheme include:
– the creation of a quality living environment with a strong sense of place for a new community, integrated into the existing community of Castleknock
– the provision of an urban-design framework with high-quality public space that ensures a sense of security, accessibility and ease of movement
– the provision of urban nodes which facilitate community amenities and encourage social interaction
– the delivery of diversity through a mix of dwelling types that embody high-quality architectural design.

Apartments are designed over four and five floors around courtyards, over naturally ventilated car-parking for residents, with surface car-parking being provided for visitors. Pedestrian movement is

→ Master plan
→→ View of model, looking west, with the Phoenix Park in the foreground

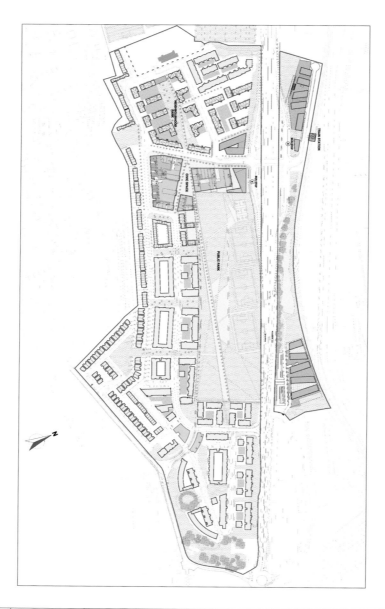

height	mix	percentage	no. of dwellings	site area	density	floor area	bed spaces	site coverage	open space	car spaces	context
3-5 storey	4 x 5-bed houses 83 x 4-bed houses 239 x 3-bed houses 69 x 3-bed apartments 1,691 x 2-bed apartments 241 x 1-bed apartments	98% residential 2% commercial	2,327	118 acres (47.7 ha)	20 units/acre (50 units/ha)	213,818m²	7,222 (64/acre)	17%	33 acres Class 1 open space; 13.8 acres Class 2 open space; also private balconies	3,317 (1.4 per dwelling)	outer-suburban site adjacent to Phoneix Park

encouraged through links connecting the courtyards to the public park and civic areas.

To lessen the impact of car-parking on the site, a number of housing types were devised, including one which allows for back gardens to be provided at first-floor level on a deck above residents' car-parking.

design / completion – 2000–2013
client – Flynn & O'Flaherty Ltd

PHOENIX PARK RACECOURSE

↖ Views of completed scheme

Mixed-use Development at Cherry Orchard, Dublin

Anthony Reddy Associates

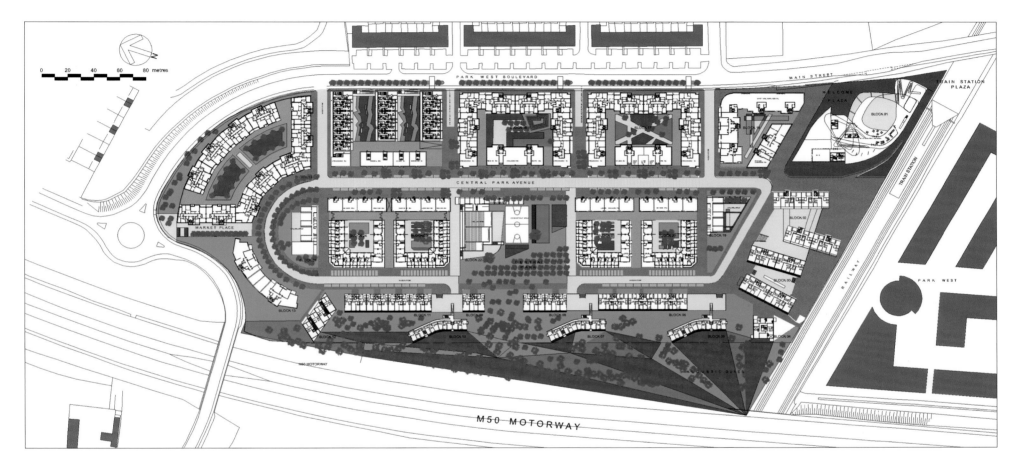

The 25 acres of land at Cherry Orchard, owned by Dublin City Council, are located at the western edge of the city, bounded by the M50 motorway and adjacent to a major new railway interchange on the Dublin-Cork line. Due to its strategic location, the site was the subject of a competitive tender-and-design process (prepared by DCC in 2004) for the creation of a new urban centre at Cherry Orchard.

Given the extent of the lands and the opportunity to create a new and varied urban landscape, a decision was made at the outset to involve seven architectural practices in the competition. These architects would be retained thereafter, with ARA acting as master-planners.

The project has offered the various designers an opportunity to realise many

new urban-design principles involving the creation of a quality public realm, dwelling units that exceed the stringent DCC standards, and homes that serve a wide variety of users, sustaining the new neighbourhood into the future.

The new neighbourhood is clearly structured with a hierarchy of streets and open spaces. A new main street will connect the

railway interchange to the south to the new retail uses at the northern end of the lands.

other architects involved – Bucholz McEvoy, de Paor, Donnelly Turpin, Henchion Reuter, McGarry NíÉanaigh, MCO
address – Cherry Orchard, Dublin 10
design / completion – 2004–2014
clients – Durkan New Homes Ltd and Bennett Construction Ltd

height	mix	percentage	no. of dwellings	site area	density	floor area	bed spaces	site coverage	open space	car spaces	context
4-20 storey	495 x 3-bed apartments 1,155 x 2-bed apartments 300 x 3-bed apartments	85% residential 15% commercial	1,950	24.7 acres (10 ha)	79 units/acre (195 units/ha)	225,315m²	7,900 (320/acre)	12%	5.4 acres public; also semi-private courtyards, private balconies / terraces	3,100 (1.6 per dwelling)	greenfield suburban site adjacent to major transportation node

CHERRY ORCHARD

Seven architectural practices are involved, with ARA acting as co-ordinator.

← Working-living tower by de Paor Architects

↑ Mixed-use block near railway station by Henchion Reuter Architects
↗ Landmark tower at railway station by Bucholz McEvoy Architects
↓ Residential block at Central Park by Donnelly Turpin Architects

opposite – projects by ARA

→ Birdseye view
Looking towards Market Square
↠ View along Central Park Avenue
Family units overlooking Central Park

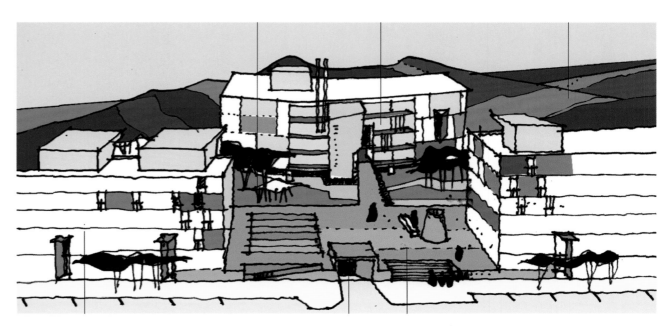

Cherry Orchard, Dublin 10

O'Mahony Pike Architects

The site is triangular in shape, bounded on the west side by a local distributor road. An estate road bounds the east side and the northern edge is the site for an equestrian complex, with a single large-scale arena building dominating the site.

The site is flat. A large, expansive green space adjoins the full length of the eastern boundary, offering open prospects. The adjacent site to the east is zoned for mixed uses, as yet undefined. A railway line is situated close to the southern side of the site.

Design aims are as follows:
– to construct truly affordable higher-density housing
– to offer flexible, modern internal spaces, standards and services
– to deliver a durable low-maintenance home with economical servicing costs
– to provide an acceptable level of private open space
– to provide above-average levels of natural daylighting internally to each dwelling, and enhanced insulation levels throughout
– to provide security throughout
– to provide own-door access to every dwelling.
– to provide each dwelling with an adjacent visible car-parking space
– to ensure all public thoroughfares are overlooked
– to build a housing development in as short a time scale as possible without sacrificing quality
– to source, where possible, local materials, components and services solutions in the construction of the development

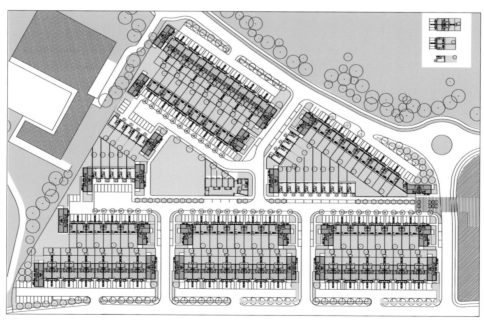

– to develop a system of building which is flexible, certifiable, durable, readily available and cost-effective within a tight programme of delivery.

design / completion – 2000–2003
client – Park Developments /
John Sisk & Sons

↖ Residential house type
↑ Corner units (duplexes over apartments)
← Site plan

height	mix	percentage	no. of dwellings	site area	density	floor area	bed spaces	site coverage	open space	car spaces	context
2-4 storey	13 x 3-bed units 286 x 2-bed units 77 x 1-bed units	100% residential	376	43,090m²	38 units/acre	24,628m²	1,077 (101/acre)	20%	2,850m²	1 per dwelling	suburban site close to railway station

Apartment Development, Loughlinstown, Co Dublin

Paul Duignan & Associates

This apartment development is divided into three individually accessed blocks, set into the hillside above a car-parking podium. The plan form of the proposed development follows the contours of the steeply sloping site and is positioned to create a large public open space above the car-park podium, which will be used as a public garden and a walkway/cycle-way adjoining the Loughlinstown river. The general orientation of the block is east-west, with the vast majority of apartments enjoying a south-easterly or westerly orientation. In addition, over 30% of the units are dual-aspect, and all apartments are above average in area terms.

The materials used on the exterior of the proposed four-storey components of the development generally consist of high-quality stone, brick/terracotta, and self-coloured render finishes, accentuating the massing elements of the building. The stepped-back penthouse level is treated with a lighter skin of glass and timber panels. Floating mono-pitched metal roofs finish the penthouse level of the blocks.

In contrast to the visually heavier four-storey components, the link blocks are differentiated with a palette of predominantly glass and timber. Large bay windows and external balconies are also a feature of the design. Natural window and timber panelling systems are used throughout.

address – St Columcille's Hospital, Loughlinstown, Co Dublin
design / completion – 2005–2009
client – Astondale Developments Ltd

↑ Front elevation to Loughlinstown river, with St Columcille's Hospital in the background
→ Location map
↓ Site plan

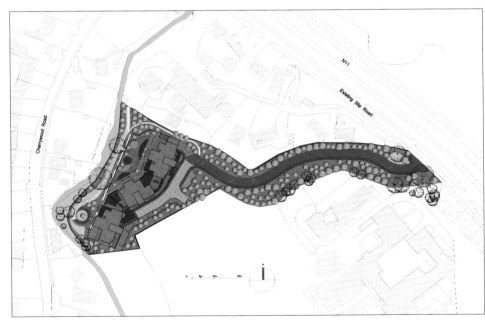

height	mix	percentage	no. of dwellings	site area	density	floor area	bed spaces	site coverage	open space	car spaces	context
4 storey over basement	6 x 3-bed apartments 34 x 2-bed apartments 21 x 1-bed apartments	100% residential	61	11,643m² (2.9 acres)	21 units/acre	5,756m²	207 (71/acre)	13%	7,023m² public 972m² private	69 (1.1 per dwelling)	outer suburban, adjacent to river

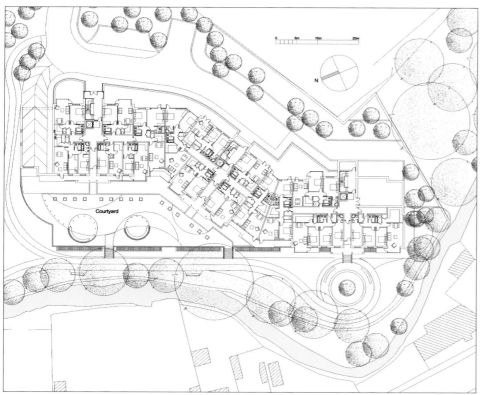

ST COLUMCILLE'S, LOUGHLINSTOWN

↑ Cross-section and rear elevation
↖ View of new development from entrance
↙ Ground-floor plan
↓ 1st-floor plan

opposite

→ View of new development from riverside walk

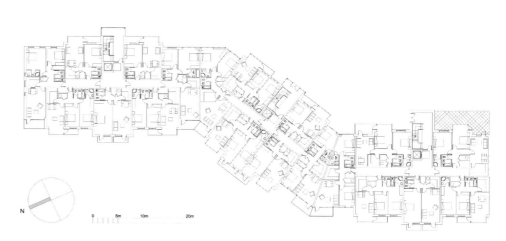

Darndale / Belcamp Village Centre, Coolock, Dublin 17

DMOD Architects

Darndale and Belcamp are two housing estates on the north-eastern periphery of Dublin, built in 1972 and home to over 3,000 people. In 1998 Dublin City Council launched an international competition for the design of an appropriate village centre for these estates.

The design objective was to create a cohesive micro-urban environment between the estates by means of a square, a street and a monument, establishing a particular identity for the community both in everyday life and in the cognitive map of Dubliners generally.

At the core of the development is the square, accessible only by means of passage through the buildings along the lines of traditional footfall over the site. Entry to each of the buildings is from this square. Separate own-door access is provided from the street to the factory units and to the apartments, which look out over the children's garden at first-floor level.

design / completion – 1998–2001
client – Dublin City Council

↗ Location map and concept study
→ Plans – ground and 1st floor

↠ opposite – Views of completed development

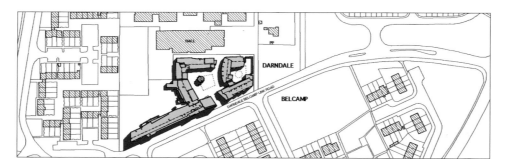

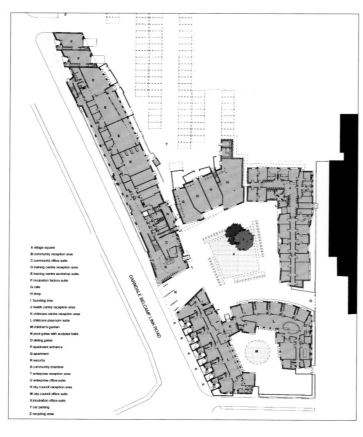

A village square
B community reception area
C community office suite
D training centre reception area
E training centre workshop suite
F incubation factory suite
G cafe
H shop
I founding tree
J health centre reception area
K childcare centre reception area
L childcare playroom suite
M children's garden
N pivot gates with sculpted bells
O sliding gates
P apartment entrance
Q apartment
R security
S community chamber
T enterprise reception area
U enterprise office suite
V city council reception area
W city council office suite
X incubation office suite
Y car parking
Z recycling area

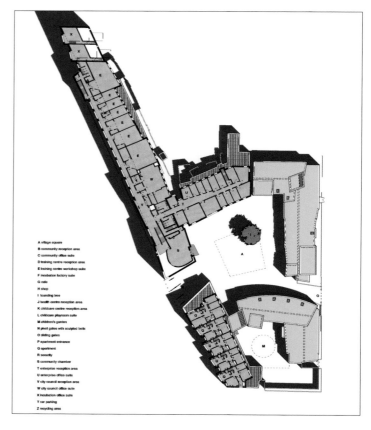

A village square
B community reception area
C community office suite
D training centre reception area
E training centre workshop suite
F incubation factory suite
G cafe
H shop
I founding tree
J health centre reception area
K childcare centre reception area
L childcare playroom suite
M children's gardens
N pivot gates with sculpted bells
O sliding gates
P apartment entrance
Q apartment
R security
S community chamber
T enterprise reception area
U enterprise office suite
V city council reception area
W city council office suite
X incubation office suite
Y car parking
Z recycling area

height	mix	percentage	no. of dwellings	site area	density	floor area	bed spaces	site coverage	open space	car spaces	context
2 storey	1 x 3-bed apartments 4 x 2-bed apartments 3 retail units, 2 factory units, community facilities (FÁS, HSE, DCC)	7% residential 93% mixed use	5	8,600m² (2.1 acres)	n/a	4,781m²	16	35%	40m² in private front gardens; 38m2 in private terraces	1 per dwelling	suburban site adjacent to main road, church and community hall

Kilkenny Western Environs Local Area Plan

O'Mahony Pike Architects

Adopted in May 2004, the Kilkenny Western Environs Local Area Plan sets out the framework for the long-term development of the western environs of Kilkenny city, comprised of 114 hectares of agricultural land. The area is one of two remaining undeveloped stretches of land within walking distance of the city centre.

The plan describes how the development of the lands will be made contingent on the necessary community facilities, roads and other infrastructure being in place in advance of or at the same time as new housing. Standards for the provision of recreational facilities – to be properly landscaped and to incorporate play areas, etc – are set out.

The aims and visions for the lands include an easily accessible village with a strong sense of community, a centre with cultural and sporting facilities which achieves a unique sense of place linked to the city, and, in so doing, ensures a sustainable community. The Local Authorities are committed to delivering a self-sustaining urban community, intimately linked to the city through pedestrian and cycle routes, public and private transport, but capable of providing for most of the needs of the community locally.

In addition to residential development, the area will provide comprehensive recreational and social facilities and employment opportunities, necessary to sustain a modern community.

The Western Environs plan was delivered as three interlocking documents:
– the statutory document which is the published LAP

↗ Aerial view of the area of the Kilkenny Western Environs LAP
➔ Extract from development criteria

264

DRAWING LEGEND

- Site Boundary
- Lower Residential
- Higher Residential
- Flexible Use
- Civic Use
- Community Use
- Developed Lands
- Public Open Space
- Local Parks
- Cemetery — Possible Location of Cemetery subject to analysis & requirements of Development Plan [C]

Parcel Name	Area in Hectares (gross)	Character of Area	The following Infrastructure must be in place before this parcel can develop	The following non-residential facilities must be in place within the plan area before housing can be developed in this parcel	This Parcel Must Contain	This Parcel May Contain
Block A	10.40	Lower Density Residential	1. Upgrade of Kilmanagh Road between Point '29' and Point '36' 2. Inner Relief Road between Point '22' and Point 29' 3. Inner Relief Road between Point '22' and Point 3'. 4. Upgrade of the Callan Rd. from Point '3' to Point '5'. 5. Upgrade of existing road between Point '27' and Point '35' 6. Water mains from Point '33' to Point '36'	A primary school. Open space area P5, with title transferred to the local authority, laid out and landscaped to the satisfaction of the planning authorities. Open Space P1 or P2, with surface	Residential development at a mean density of 29-32 residential units/hectare (11-13/acre) A crèche or other pre-school facility Open Space LP16, laid out and landscaped (incorporating a play area) and with a management agreement in place to the	Bed and breakfast/guesthouse Clinic or surgery Community facilities Convenience store(s) of not more than 100 m sq. gross floor area. Crèche and/or playgroup Halting site/group housing scheme Hotel, public house, restaurant, café

– a non-statutory urban-design document
– a non-statutory infrastructural document

The non-statutory Urban Design Guide details how a high-quality urban environment will be achieved. It was developed to accompany the LAP, addressing such issues as land-use, sense of place, permeability, sustainability, density and flexibility. It illustrates design models and treatments for specific character areas, which are seen as generators of development.

The infrastructure framework document, also included with the plan, addresses the issue of estimated costs, and sets out the infrastructure required for each development parcel.

These guides further illustrate the aims and objectives for use in the preparation and processing of development applications. This is important to ensure that the aims and objectives of the Local Area Plan are realised, and that the vision for the western environs is delivered through development proposals which are consistent with the LAP.

design / completion – 2004–2020
client – Kilkenny County Council

↗ Axonometric view of village centre
↗ Zoning-specific objectives
→ School campus
⇒ Village centre
↓ Cross-section through built form

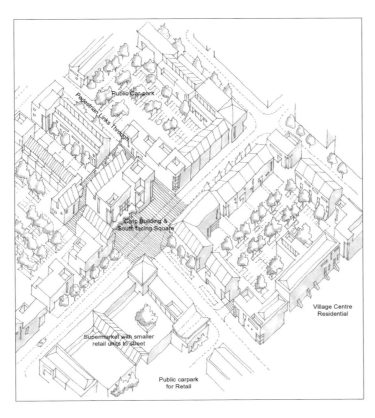

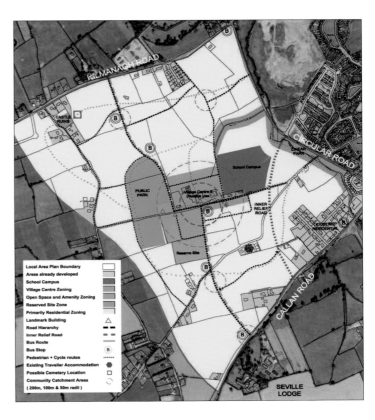

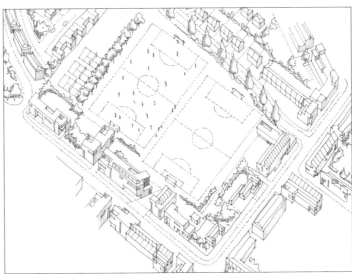

Drogheda Northern Environs Master Plan, Co Louth

O'Mahony Pike Architects

The 2004 North Drogheda and Environs Local Area Plan proposed that three new neighbourhoods, catering for a population of 20,000 people, be developed on 254 hectares north of the town. The proposed development will increase the population of Drogheda by 40%. It includes provision for three schools, community facilities and open space.

Following the adoption of the 2004 LAP, Louth County Council's consultants (OMP, Stephen Ward Town Planning Consultants, Dermot Foley Landscape Architects, Tobin Consulting Engineers) were commissioned in January 2005 to draw up a draft master plan, which was presented for public display in January 2006. The master plan would provide for the sustainable development of these lands to form three separate, but integrated, residential districts about 2km north of Drogheda town centre.

Amongst the primary elements identified by the LAP, and accommodated within the master plan, were the provision of a northern cross route, a substantial east-west linear park, and three proposed civic and commercial centres, one for each of the identified residential neighbourhoods. These would become the generators of a new integrated northern extension of the town.

The master plan is committed to the development of a self-sustaining community within the subject lands that retains strong links to the town. Among the policies that seek to establish such a development are:
– the provision of the day-to-day needs of

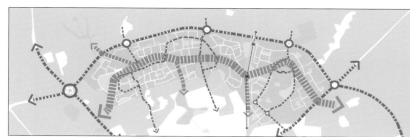

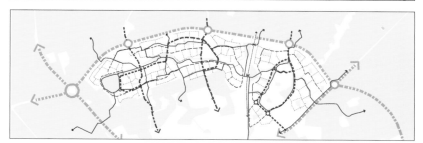

height	mix	percentage	no. of dwellings	site area	density	floor area	bed spaces	site coverage	open space	car spaces	context
2-4 storey + landmark buildings	max 30% 4 bed max 35% 3 bed min 35% 1-2 bed	n/a	5,867	628 acres (254 ha)	9.3 units/acre (23/ha) (2,180 units low; 2,301 medium; 1,386 higher)	n/a	n/a	n/a	120 acres (48.6 ha)	n/a	greenfield development along Dublin-Belfast rail corridor

the emergent community within a five-to-ten-minute walk or cycle from home – e.g. primary schools, recreational and community facilities and local shopping
– high levels of integration and connectivity between all parts of the subject lands and the urban area of Drogheda, particularly the town centre
– the creation of a well-defined urban form with a strong sense of place, with flexible and adaptable built forms.

The master plan is in compliance with the policies, objectives and development-control standards set out in the Local Area Plan, but proposes certain variations in respect of:
– civic and commercial centres, which are somewhat larger than the traditional concept of a neighbourhood centre
– the location of a new railway station, proposed for the northern edge of neighbourhood No. 3, rather than the southern edge
– a larger site-provision for each of the three primary schools, with the potential for a fourth primary school and a secondary school to be located outside of the subject lands
– detailed arrangements for phasing and implementation.

design / completion – 2005–2020
client – Louth County Council

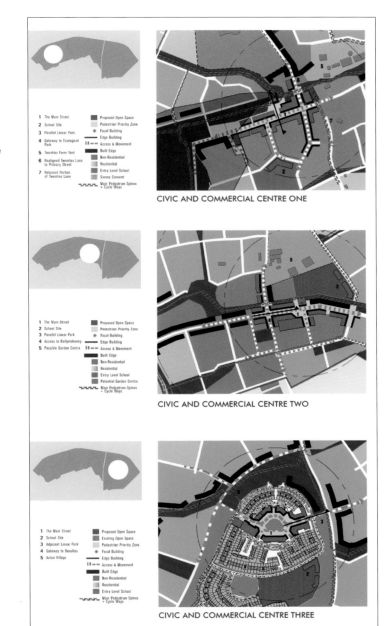

CIVIC AND COMMERCIAL CENTRE ONE

CIVIC AND COMMERCIAL CENTRE TWO

CIVIC AND COMMERCIAL CENTRE THREE

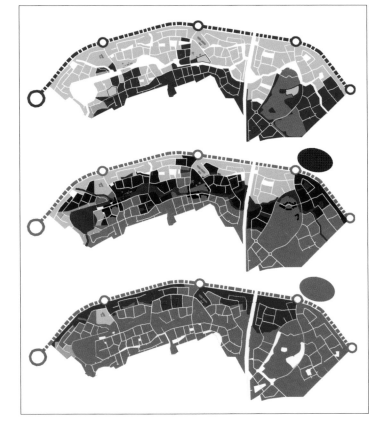

↗ Civic and commercial centres (from top) – locations 1, 2, and 3
↗ Aerial view showing extent of landscape and open space
⇥ Phasing and implementation diagrams (from top) – phases 1, 2, and 3
↘ Section showing community/civic building and street with commercial/residential on both sides

opposite

↖ Master plan
⇇ Site structure (top), and movement framework

267

Green Park, Blackrock, Cork

Reddy O'Riordan Staehli Architects

This scheme for affordable and social housing is arranged across a three-hectare pastoral site forming part of the former Mount Rivers demesne, just south of the River Lee and Blackrock Castle.

The design approach maintains, where possible, some of the character-giving site features, such as mature specimen trees and old stable buildings and walls, and reinterprets the rural vernacular tradition of the demesne into a contemporary, medium-density housing development. The scheme is broken down into a series of landscaped streets and courtyards, reducing the scale of the development and forming smaller, closer neighbourhoods, a result of which, it is hoped, will be the nurturing of a strong community.

Houses are generous in size, and have been designed to Lifetime House Standards to allow for future adaptation to the changing circumstances of residents. Room layouts provide views to front and rear gardens and to shared outdoor spaces beyond, allowing for the supervision of children.

Externally, houses are finished in self-pigmented render in a selection of traditional colours.

design / completion – 2000–2006
client – Cork County Council

↗ Site plan
→ Typical plans – 2-storey and duplex

⇥ opposite – Views of duplex courtyard (top), courtyard corner, and duplex terrace

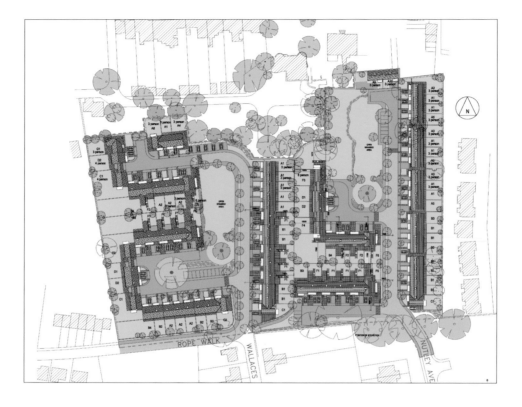

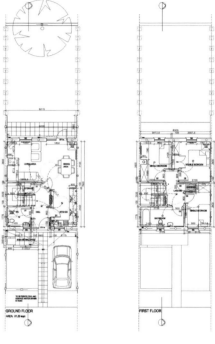

↑ Typical plans – house type B1
↙ House type D1; house type F1 ↓

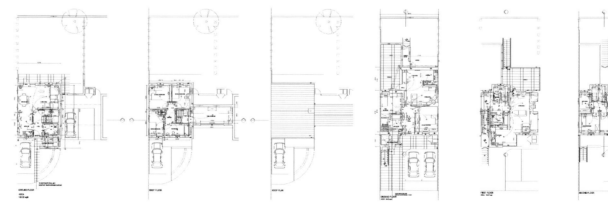

height	mix	percentage	no. of dwellings	site area	density	floor area	bed spaces	site coverage	open space	car spaces	context
1-3 storey	6 x 4-bed houses 52 x 3-bed houses 41 x 2-bed houses	100% residential	99	7.2 acres (2.9 ha)	13.7 units/acre (34.3 dwellings/ha)	8,674m²	407	16.5%	0.7 acres	124	inner suburban greenfield site – former demesne

Balgaddy C, Lucan, Co Dublin

Murray Ó Laoire Architects

Balgaddy C is the second phase of a housing development undertaken for South Dublin County Council (SDCC). It part of an overall master plan being administered by SDCC and a number of architectural practices that will provide over 600 residential units in the south Lucan area.

The intention of the integrated, overall master plan is to knit the new housing development into the existing social infrastructure, which includes St Mary's Catholic church, local primary and secondary schools, existing housing and Phase B of the housing development, which was completed in March 2003.

This scheme consists of 149 residential units arranged as apartments, duplexes and terraced houses in urban blocks. Three- and four-storey blocks give an urban edge to the development and create a sense of enclosure and protection for the one- and two-storey units inside.

The development is designed to cater for all types of residents, including single people, large families and disabled people. It will provide social housing, housing for voluntary housing associations and co-operative housing groups, and housing for private purchasers.

The basic design concept is one of densification, consolidation and urbanisation of under-utilised lands, interlacing community activities and community life within housing estates. Located centrally in the scheme is a large crèche with ample enclosed and secure play areas.

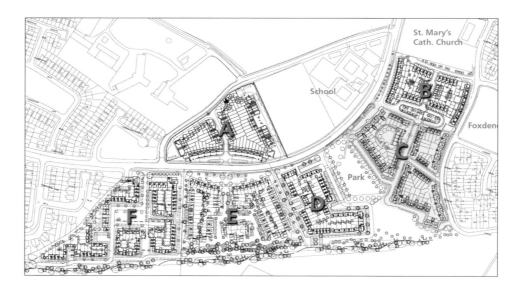

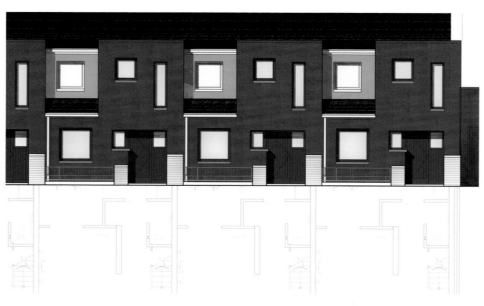

The scheme is a continuation of the urban block format of Balgaddy Phase B, with a tree-lined avenue culminating in a new landscaped park to the south. A central arboretum is included, linking the school and the adjacent Foxdene housing estates.

design / completion – 2001–2008
client – South Dublin County Council

↑ Model
↖ Master plan
← Terrace house elevation and plans

height	mix	percentage	no. of dwellings	site area	density	floor area	bed spaces	site coverage	open space	car spaces	context
2-4 storey	single and two-storey houses, apartments and duplexes; community facility and crèche	95% residential 5% communal	149	5.4 acres (2.18 ha)	68 units/acre (26 units / ha)	10,150m²	610 (113/acre)	46%	large public park and 2.5-acre arboretum; also private gardens, balconies and terraces	225	2nd phase of integrated master plan, designed to fit into existing social infrastructure

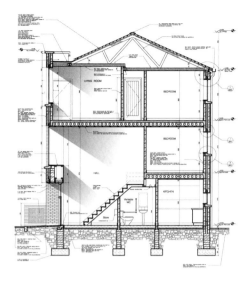

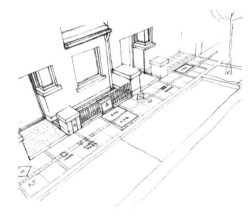

↑ Typical duplex section
↑ Typical house-entrance study
→ Views of the development as it nears completion:
  – block 2 + 3: duplex apartments and 2-storey
    housing (top)
  – block 7: duplex apartments
  – blocks 1 + 2: apartments

Prospect Hill, Finglas Road, Dublin 11

Anthony Reddy Associates

Prospect Hill enjoys a prominent location along Finglas Road, one of main transport links into Dublin City Centre.

The layout of the development takes the form of several gently curving buildings orientated around generously proportioned landscaped courtyards.

The internal layout of these apartments is unique compared to other apartments in the city. We have adapted the modern duplex apartment in a 'crossover' type arrangement allowing living accommodation and sleeping accommodation to face in opposite directions. The result is that the majority of apartments within the development are dual aspect enabling them to enjoy unparalleled access to sunlight, views and open space. Floor to ceiling glazed screens with sliding doors spanning the full width of apartments take full advantage of this ideal orientation.

A landscaped strip several metres wide separates the apartments from the pedestrian footpath along the principal boundary of the development. The easily accessed courtyards are on several levels stepping up to a newly created civic square with access to retail units, doctors surgery and crèche. Landscape Architects Brady Shipman Martin have designed the impressive landscaping including a water feature, high specification paving, timber decking and planting.

Basement level car parking is provided below the stepped podiums giving access to the principal stair cores of each block.

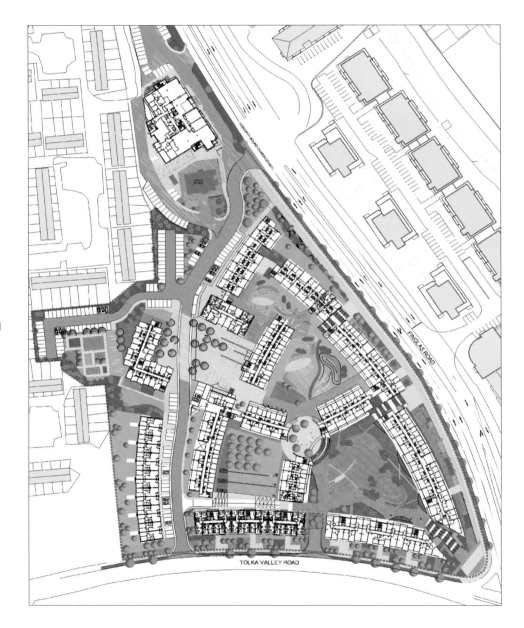

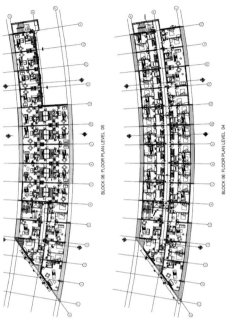

The development has evolved after considered response to local variations, orientation, movement and site forces and will aspire to create a strong sense of place for residents within this quarter of Dublin.

design / completion – 2004–2007
client – McCabe Builders Ltd

↑ Block 6 – typical floor plans
← Site plan

opposite

↗ View of development from Finglas Road
→ Block 4 – typical floor plans
↘ View of landscaped area within the developmen

height	mix	percentage	no. of dwellings	site area	density	floor area	bed spaces	site coverage	open space	car spaces	context
3-8 storey	36 x 3-bed apartments 384 x 2-bed apartments 76 x 1-bed apartments crèche, medical centre, retail	97.3% residential 1.6% commercial 1.1% communal	496	38,491m² (9.5 acres)	52 units/acre	44,250m2	952 (99/acre)	26.73%	10,690m² public; also private balconies	518 (1.04 per dwelling)	suburban site adjacent to public park and Royal Canal

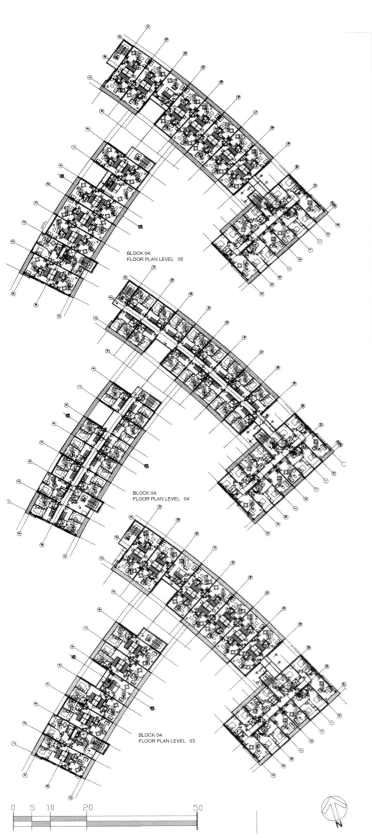

BLOCK 04:
FLOOR PLAN LEVEL 05

BLOCK 04:
FLOOR PLAN LEVEL 04

BLOCK 04:
FLOOR PLAN LEVEL 03

0 5 10   20   50

N

Former Golfcourse Lands, Dun Laoghaire

McCrossan O'Rourke Manning Architects

This new residential development with a neighbourhood centre is on a key infill site in South Dublin County, on the former golf club lands at Dun Laoghaire. At just one kilometre, the northern half of the site is within walking distance of Dun Laoghaire town centre.

The development is laid out in a series of interconnected perimeter blocks with pedestrian-friendly, attractive and traffic-calmed streetscapes. Accessibility, walkability and a high-quality public domain are key urban-design principles in this proposed development.

Two large multifunctional public parks are a major feature of the master plan. Facilities and amenities will include a lake, bowling club, sports areas and playgrounds, all set in a high-quality landscaped environment.

design / completion – 2004–2016
client – Cosgrave Developments

---

 top
– Location map
– Sketch urban-design approach
Master plan – south side
→ bottom
– Key plan – demarcation of precincts
– Material and colours 1 – primary elements
– Material and colours 2 – secondary elements
– Sample elevations

opposite

 Computer-generated views of development
→ Model

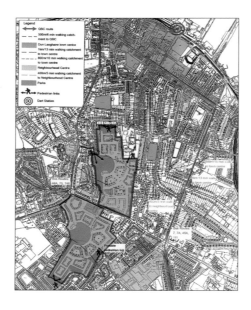
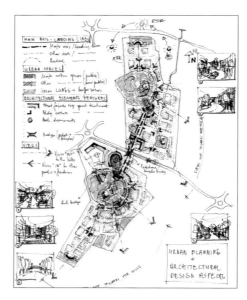
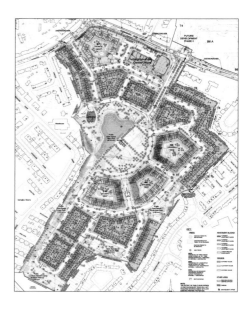
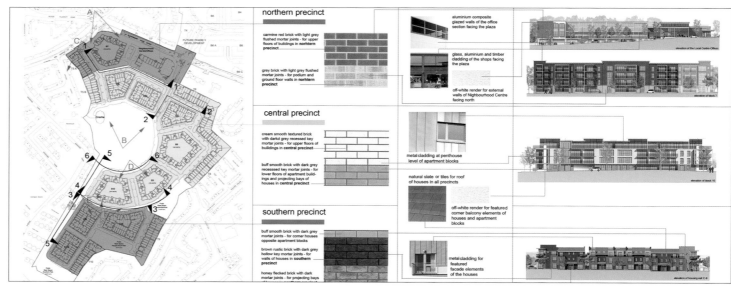

height	mix	percentage	no. of dwellings	site area	density	floor area	bed spaces	site coverage	open space	car spaces	context
2-7 storey	20% 4+-bed units 15% 3-bed units 51% 2-bed units 14% 1-bed units crèches, community centre	95% residential 5% other	1,880	32.5 ha (80 acres)	57 units/ha (23.5 units/acre)	189,750m²	c.5,500 (96/ha)	n/a	c.21%	2 per house 1.25 per apartment	suburban greenfield site 0 – former golfcourse

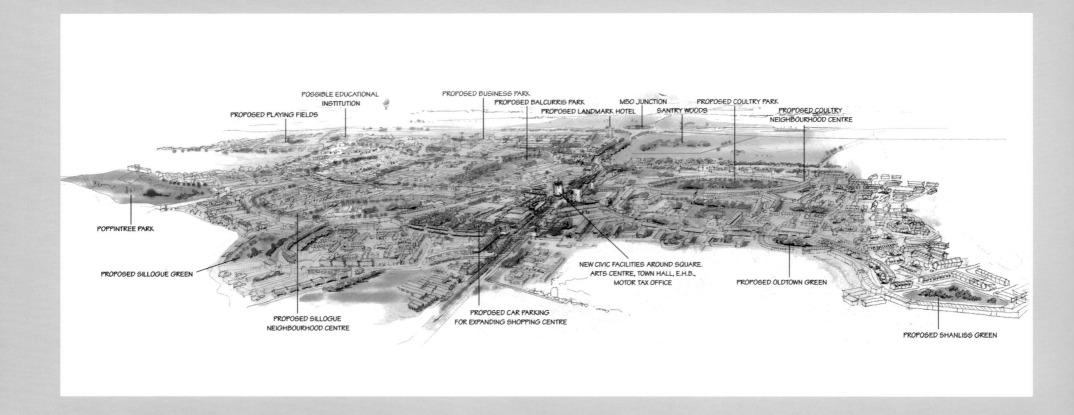

PROPOSED PLAYING FIELDS

POSSIBLE EDUCATIONAL
INSTITUTION

PROPOSED BUSINESS PARK
PROPOSED BALCURRIS PARK
PROPOSED LANDMARK HOTEL

M50 JUNCTION
SANTRY WOODS

PROPOSED COULTRY PARK

PROPOSED COULTRY
NEIGHBOURHOOD CENTRE

POPPINTREE PARK

PROPOSED SILLOGUE GREEN

PROPOSED SILLOGUE
NEIGHBOURHOOD CENTRE

PROPOSED CAR PARKING
FOR EXPANDING SHOPPING CENTRE

NEW CIVIC FACILITIES AROUND SQUARE.
ARTS CENTRE, TOWN HALL, E.H.B.,
MOTOR TAX OFFICE

PROPOSED OLDTOWN GREEN

PROPOSED SHANLISS GREEN

Ballymun – the vision at master-plan stage, 1998

Ballymun: Masterplan to Materiality

DAVID PRICHARD

Ballymun Regeneration Limited (BRL) was set up by Dublin City Council as the special-purpose vehicle to deliver the renewal of the failed 1960s high-rise estate that was home to 20,000 people. The master-plan lands, all owned by DCC, cover more than 760 acres, and the scale can be difficult to grasp except by comparison with, say, Fatima Mansions' oft-quoted eleven acres. Nearly ten years on, it is timely to reflect on the process and the product, not least in the face of the significant economic downturn. The country's unprecedented economic success to 2008 made possible the huge undertaking on this conspicuous and notorious high-rise estate. Fortunately, Ireland has only one, whereas the UK has over 200 such estates, and Europe hundreds more.

The project team's desire to understand regeneration and deliver best practice in all areas – education, employment, environment, energy, and engagement – has been helped by outreach links across Europe through programmes such as 'Image'. In turn, Ballymun is much visited by outsiders, not just for its physical regeneration (the product) but for the comprehensive processes being managed by the highly committed staff at BRL who have had to set them up – indeed, invented them – because each regeneration context requires a bespoke response.

THE PROCESS

When the team started in 1997, there were few guidance documents in master-planning, and the word 'sustainability' was just emerging. Now there are numerous books and endless checklists, and to confuse matters further, the term master plan is also often used interchangeably with vision, urban design, and development framework, and all are applied across the scale from infill schemes to whole towns. It is sometimes said master plans can be categorised as being led by vision, commerce or process. In reality, I believe all three drivers are needed, and it is the appropriate balance that matters and will avoid the document being formulaic. Without the right balance, the document will collect dust on a shelf, as many do.

The often-neglected ingredient is the role of project champions. Even with a compelling case, if the project staff are not exuding passion, conviction and

tenacity there will always be loss of focus, ambitions and time. The role calls for commitment that goes beyond the expected professional duty, and, for a decade-long project such as Ballymun, can be likened to running a marathon rather than the sprint of a usual building project.

The physical environment of Ballymun is improving. However, the community remains socially challenged. Hence, BRL continues to identify gaps in the provision of support services, developing innovative responses and forging partnerships with statutory and voluntary agencies in order to sustain such initiatives beyond the time frame of reconstruction. The palpable satisfaction expressed by residents in their new homes is matched at community level with success in the national Tidy Towns competition, which would have been impossible a few years ago.

↓ The master plan, 1998

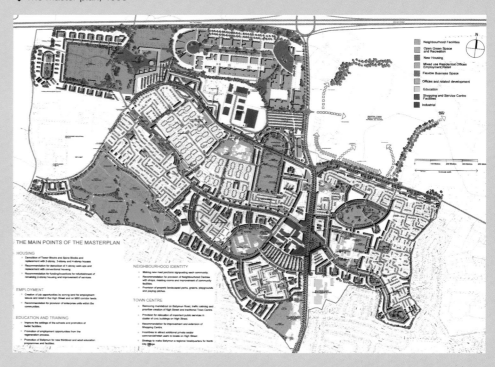

277

THE PRODUCT

The Ballymun master plan set out some simple steps to follow big ideas for the physical environment for each of the five neighbourhoods. These flowed from the critique of the alienating environment, which was conceived as a satellite dormitory with few support services or employment, severed by a fast dual carriageway. This collection of uniform buildings, accessed by cul-de-sacs, sitting in a formless, windswept, treeless context, was all space and no sense of place! Hence, the environmental agenda for each neighbourhood set out in the master plan was

– to create a distinct identity
– to provide local community facilities
– to provide new parks and play spaces
– to improve access and legibility
– to improve space and energy standards
...and achieve these with the residents' support.

These goals are being delivered, but the incremental nature of the development means the interim conditions can look quite chaotic. The puzzle pieces are revealing the bigger picture around Coultry Park, Balcurris Park and Main Street. (The latter is, in fact, the sixth community.) One of the master-plan stage ideas was that design/development parcels should straddle roads (*see illus*), thus making one designer responsible for each street becoming a place. This has been difficult for BRL to achieve because of site availability.

MASTER-PLAN EVOLUTION AND MANAGEMENT

The master plan has not been a rigid static plan. The detailed layout for each area has had to adapt to pragmatic constraints such as utility corridors, decanting priorities, land availability, funding and so forth, all of which were not known in detail at the master-plan stage. This constant evolution is what is managed by BRL's site-based team, whose role goes way beyond construction-programming, since they set and deliver the 'soft', but more difficult, non-construction projects which flow from the social, economic and environmental agendas.

The most dramatic urban-design achievement is the transformation of the dual-carriageway and roundabout into Main Street and Civic Plaza *(see figure-grounds and aerial views for 1997, 2007)*. The south end of Main Street is announced by the gate towers, which create a pinch point. The Ballymun Cross Tower lies on the bend in the street and successfully commands the north end. The character of the Civic Plaza can start to emerge now that the east side is enclosed and the tower is demolished, but the west side still awaits the start of Treasury Holdings' huge shopping centre. The plaza has an exciting art and landscape installation in hand.

Ballymun Main Street was designed in 1999 to receive the street-running Luas tram, but by 2006 the heavier metro train system was chosen, and it will run underground along Main Street. Metro is the ideal transport solution, but cut-and-cover construction will disrupt Main Street for some months.

Main Street and the plaza are home now to the Axis Arts Centre, swimming pool, Garda station, Civic Offices and hotels, all of which are northside destinations that make the public aware of the changing face of the Ballymun. The planned shopping centre and first IKEA store in the Republic will, likewise, help transform Ballymun's image and create a regional and national profile, along with much-needed local employment.

The tenure mix is shifting towards 60:40 owner:rented, from a starting point of 20:80 in 1997 when the national figure was 80:20. The increased densities resulting from Metro North will enable future sites to help deliver this change of mix more quickly. BRL has been alert to the demand for special-needs housing, and the voluntary housing sector helps to deliver this. The image of old Ballymun was high-rise, so high density was assumed, whereas, in fact, the average gross density was suburban at just twelve dwellings per acre. The swathes of formless open space provided the dilution and the sites for first-phase new homes.

↓ Ballymun 1997 (figure-ground and aerial view) – all space and no sense of place

↓ Ballymun 2007 – the hierarchy of streets and parks becomes clear

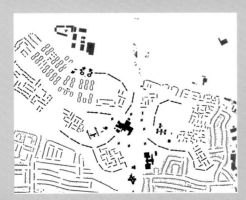

REVIEW OF PROJECTS

There are several recurring themes in the projects illustrated in this section of the book. These include sites, scheme size, community facilities, place-making, streets and homes. Each is outlined below.

Sites – Many of the sites are SLOAP (a UK 1970s expression for 'space left over after planning') and verges between the existing houses and flats. These sites are intrinsically more complex to design and develop economically, but it is this land that has enabled new homes to be built prior to demolitions, which was essential so that the community would not suffer the disruption of double-decanting.

Scheme size – The majority of the schemes are under 75 homes, which is a consequence of several factors, such as availability of sites, the phasing of demolitions, the desire for architectural variety, the construction companies' capacity and optimisation of risk-reduction. In contrast, private developers have no qualms about much bigger schemes being done by one designer.

Community facilities – Provision of these is crucial as they are the glue that holds the community together. Several schemes include meeting rooms, crèche, shops, surgery and whole neighbourhood centres. The location of these are chosen to support their commercial viability and, in the case of Shangan, to forge links to the adjacent community. The facilities reflect the fact that as more of the residents have houses with gardens to look after, their priorities and needs will change.

Place-making – Giving each community an identity was one of the key goals, and the new parks are the most dramatic win. Three parks are now in use, and their landscape needs time to become established before being photogenic and really looking the part that they undoubtedly play. The parks' management by local rangers is an essential dimension to their success because the designs are a far cry from the gang mower-friendly flat grassland of so many estates. These parks have well-equipped play areas for different ages, shelters, interesting land forms, feature lighting, swales and diverse planting, all of which require supervision and maintenance. Each park is a big investment and makes a profound impact on the neighbourhood, establishing the strong focus that unites the community and creating a good address that enhances house prices.

Streets – All the new homes are two, three or four storeys, many with monopitch roofs which help create an urban scale along with the parking, which is mostly on kerb rather than on plot. All the scheme designs place emphasis on strong corners, which this will help legibility and navigation.

Homes – All schemes provide homes with their own front door to the street. This was a major priority for residents, and largely eliminates indoor communal lobby space that needs management. Space standards and energy-saving measures are generally higher than normal, and several schemes are experimenting with solar heating and rainwater-harvesting installations.

→ Sillogue – new street frontages create pleasant courtyard approches to existing houses

→ The master-plan-stage idea that one designer should control both sides of a street

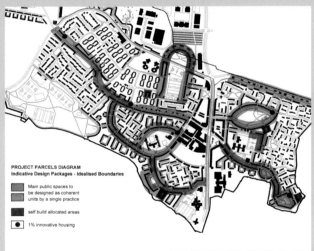

PROJECT PARCELS DIAGRAM
Indicative Design Packages - Idealised Boundaries

Main public spaces to be designed as coherent units by a single practice

self build allocated areas

1% innovative housing

→ Shangan Park – new and existing homes overlook the new park

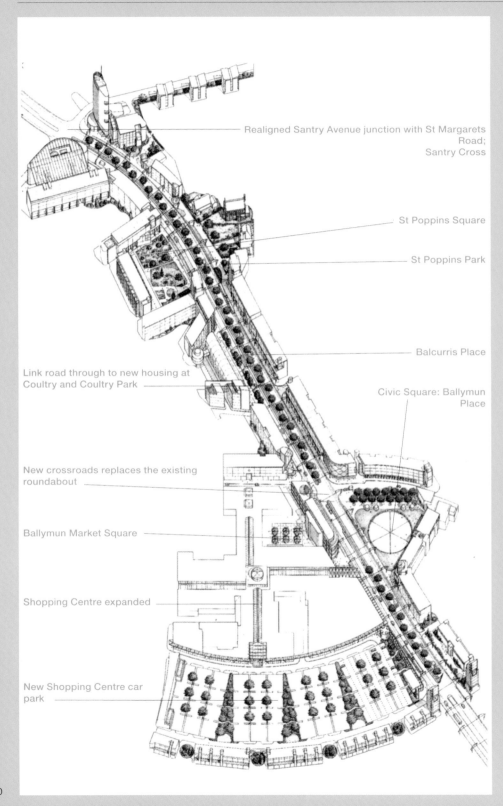

Realigned Santry Avenue junction with St Margarets Road; Santry Cross

St Poppins Square

St Poppins Park

Balcurris Place

Link road through to new housing at Coultry and Coultry Park

Civic Square: Ballymun Place

New crossroads replaces the existing roundabout

Ballymun Market Square

Shopping Centre expanded

New Shopping Centre car park

SUMMARY

The overall architectural coherence to each neighbourhood has yet to be achieved. Understandably, the current state of construction gives a patchy impression. All but two of the towers are now demolished, but most of the slab blocks are still standing and have been repainted, which presents a mixed message.

Unlike the UK development corporations of the 1970s where the chief architect dictated the colour of brick and roof tile for each neighbourhood so as to achieve an overall coherence, BRL has been more liberal and has encouraged greater diversity. No doubt for reasons of economics, the prevailing materials used are brick for front façades, with extensive use of render for other features and rear elevations. BRL's in-house landscape team have designed a town-wide palette of hard surfaces, street furniture and soft landscape, which is intended to achieve an overall cohesion.

The challenge for major projects like Ballymun is that the last phases, the last few pieces of the puzzle that make sense of the picture, must be the best. This review has been about the physical and environmental aspects of the regeneration, but the education, training, employment and community development programmes are very impressive, and it is those that deliver the socially sustainable community that new buildings alone cannot do. It will be interesting to see now what ingenuity will be brought to bear on its further evolution in light of reduced economic opportunity. The test of good planning is that it survives and thrives on questions and changes.

BIBLIOGRAPHY

Anne Power, *Estates on the Edge – Social Consequences of Mass Housing in Northern Europe* (Macmillan, London, 1999)
Ballymun Regeneration, *Ballymun Master Plan* (BRL, Dublin, 1998)
Ballymun Regeneration, Ballymun Main Street Development Framework (BRL, Dublin)
David Prichard, 'On the Edge', *City*, vol. 4, no. 1, 2000
Aibhlín McCrann (ed.), *Memories Milestones and New Horizons – Reflections on the Regeneration of Ballymun* (Blackstaff Press, Belfast, 2008)

DAVID PRICHARD lead the consultant team, working alongside BRL, who were commissioned to prepare the master plan and, subsequently, the Main Street Development Framework. He was partner at MacCormac Jamieson Prichard (MJP) until Metropolitan Workshop was established with a team of colleagues. Metropolitan Workshop is involved in various schemes in Ireland, and enjoys collaborations with several Dublin practices on architecture and urban-design commissions.

← The urban design framework for Main Street as envisaged in 1999

Balcurris Park, Ballymun, Dublin 11

WTA Landscape Architects

There are two key new parks in the master plan – Balcurris and Coultry. Balcurris, to the north-west of the town centre, has been substantially completed but awaits the demolition of the old linear blocks before completion.

The park is divided into separate areas – a major GAA pitch, an area with smaller sports facilities and children's play areas, and a semicircular area with an open lawn for informal play. Each area is surrounded by screen planting, with a variety of landscaped gardens for general amenity and relaxation.

The semicircular area, which is separated from the other areas by an access road, has not yet been completed.

The key plan shows three schemes, which are illustrated here: Balcurris 1 and 3 (by O'Mahony Pike Architects) are located either side of the south end of the park, and have been completed. Balcurris 5 (by Newenham Mulligan & Associates), to the north, has not yet been completed. Balcurris Park 2 – Balbutcher Lane (by Burke-Kennedy Doyle) forms the frontage onto Balcurris Road to the south.

client – Ballymun Regeneration Ltd

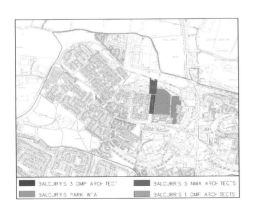

BALCURRIS 3 OMP ARCHITECTS
BALCURRIS PARK WTA
BALCURRIS 5 NMA ARCHITECTS
BALCURRIS 1 OMP ARCHITECTS

Balcurris 1 and 3, Ballymun

O'Mahony Pike Architects

PHASE 1

The project follows on from the master plan study for the regeneration of Ballymun, which OMP co-authored with MacCormac Jamieson Prichard. It forms part of the first of five phases of development. This social housing project backs onto existing dwellings at Balcurris Gardens and Ard na Meala, and faces onto the proposeed Balcurris Park. The scheme comprises a 3-storey terrace addressing the park, and two courtyards at a smaller 2-storey scale.

PHASE 2

This scheme encloses the western edge of the new Balcurris Park, containing the large, open space with a 3-storey continuous façade. The formal edge to the park is tree-lined, and front gardens are relatively shallow to increase the impact of the built edge. and to improve security on the public street. By contrast, the rear of the dwellings is the height of a typical 2-storey suburban house, increasing privacy and minimising over-looking. There are six different unit-types in the scheme.

client – Ballymun Regeneration Ltd

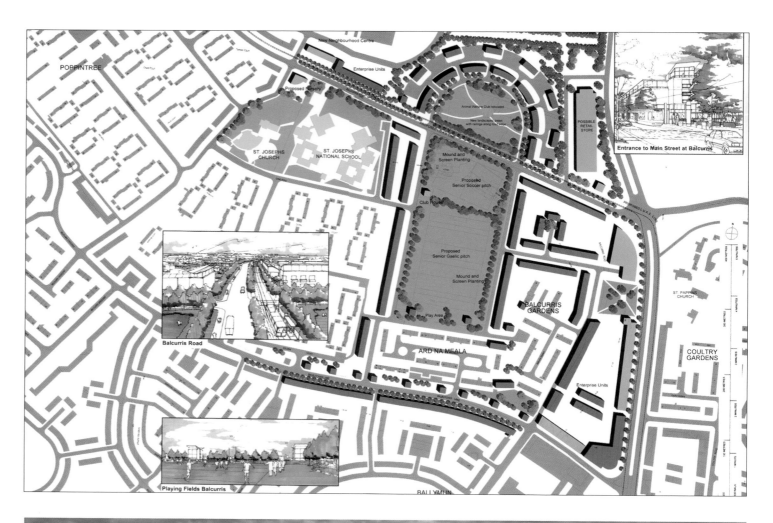

↗ Site plan showing Balcurris park and surrounding housing schemes
→ Elevation to park

opposite

↗ Views of completed development
↗ Site plans of Balcurris 1 (right) and Balcurris 3

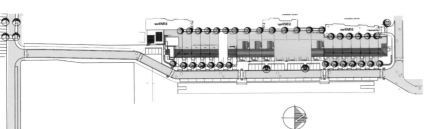
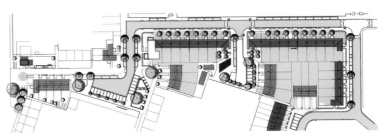

Balcurris 2, Balbutcher Lane, Ballymun

Burke-Kennedy Doyle Architects

The site development strategy for this scheme at Balbutcher Lane is informed by the master plan for the area, which defines new urban streets and pedestrian links around and through the site. The links to the existing pattern of the Sandyhill Gardens estate and the establishment of an appropriate urban scale to Balbutcher Lane are important aspects of design. The site is developed with defined edges and urban spaces, and releases a significant portion for private rear gardens – an amenity previously unavailable to the Ballymun residents.

The development along Balbutcher Lane comprises a mix of own-door apartments, duplex units and maisonettes in predominately three-storey form, with sentinel blocks of three and four storeys defining penetration areas into the site. This long, north-facing elevation is broken periodically by full-height slots, bringing sunlight to the street and containing lightweight steel staircases to access upper apartments.

All dwellings have private gardens or large private terraces, orientated towards the sun. The scale of the development is reduced to two stories within the site in deference to the scale of existing adjacent houses. Materials used include hardwood windows, self-coloured render, metal cladding, metal cills and concrete roof tiles.

design / completion – 2003–2005
client – John Sisk & Son Ltd

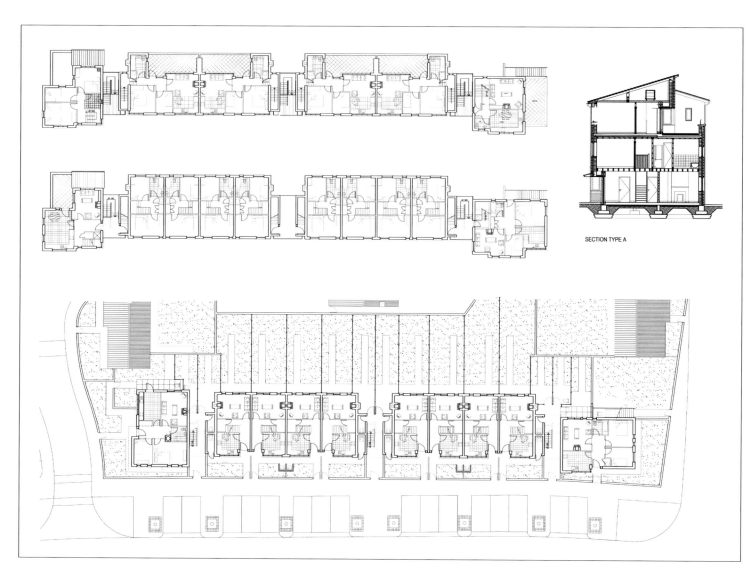

SECTION TYPE A

↑ Typical apartment / duplex plans – ground, 1st, 2nd-floor
↗ Typical cross-section

→ Main street elevation
Site plan
Balbutcher Lane, with old flats in the distance

⇥ View of gateway building
Inner courtyard

height	mix	percentage	no. of dwellings	site area	density	floor area	bed spaces	site coverage	open space	car spaces	context
1-3 storey	5 x 3-bed duplexes 20 x 2-bed duplexes 17 x 2-bed apartments	100% residential	42	12,468m² (------- acres ?)	25 units/acre	5,802m²	89	21%	5,200m²	95	infill site between existing housing

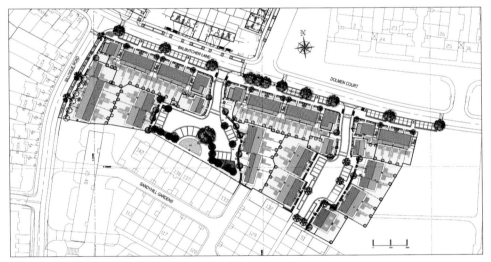

Balcurris 5, Balcurris Park, Ballymun

Newenham Mulligan & Associates

Balcurris 5 is part of Phase 3 of the implementation of the Ballymun Regeneration Master plan. The site is located on the western edge of a significant new public park. The redevelopment of Balcurris Park was identified in the master plan as both a major objective for the Balcurris neighbourhood and as an intrinsic part of the landscape strategy.

The scheme consists of 56 residential units and a boys' hostel. The design is concerned with presenting a suitable scale and presence to the edge of the park, whilst also respecting the scale of individual units.

The hostel is located at the northern end of the site in a two-storey building. This allows for the expression of this building within the overall scheme.

The design of the scheme creates an urban block surrounding internal private gardens. The side fronting the park is three-storeys high, and contains duplex units over apartments, all with private gardens.

The southern part of the scheme comprises apartments, and the western side comprises alternating two- and three-storey houses, which have private gardens. This alternating two- and three-storey form enhances the individual expression of each house whilst presenting a continuous edge.

design / completion – 2003–2006
client – Ballymun Regeneration Ltd

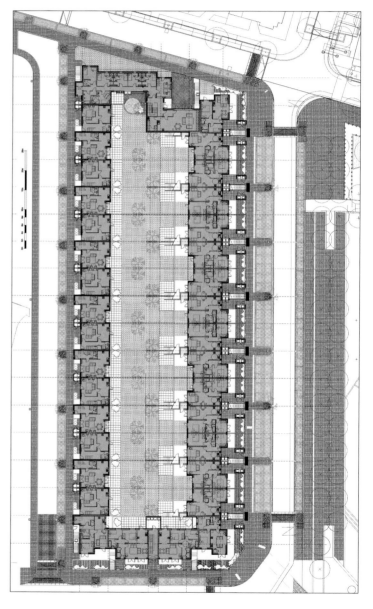

height	mix	percentage	no. of dwellings	site area	density	floor area	bed spaces	site coverage	open space	car spaces	context
2-3 storey	15 x 3-bed houses 18 x 3-bed duplex + apts 23 x 2-bed duplex + apts 7-bed boys' hostel	100% residential	56 + hostel	10,089m² (2.5 acres)	22.4 units/acre (excluding hostel)	4,825m² (including hostel)	222 (+ 7 in hostel)	23.2%	50,000m² in public park 3,063m² in private gardens 305m² in private balconies	79 (1.38 per dwelling)	3rd phase of regeneration master plan

↑ Dame Road Elevation
↗ View across Balcurris Park to East Elevation
↘ Corner of Dame Road and Balcurris Park
↓ Cross-section through block

opposite

← Ground-floor plan
⇐ Location map

Coultry Park, Ballymun, Dublin 9

This mixed-tenure Phase 1 scheme was planned in consultation with the local residents. The brief stipulated the inclusion of meeting places, which are located at ground level at the ends of terraces in such a way that they can be adapted later to a corner shop, office or apartment.

The imagery for the scheme is inspired by the architecture of Dublin. The long three-storey terraces address the new park in the manner of Dublin's 18th-century squares, and the close of houses behind the terraces, overlooking the existing school, are reminiscent of the rendered cottages in many of Dublin's side streets.

The accommodation mix required a lot of apartments, so these are interspersed along the terraces and are clustered around the open communal staircases which lead to first-floor balconies, with three front doors. It is the rhythm of these features that creates the character of the scheme. All homes have their own front door – one of the residents' main requests.

All parking is on the kerb, and front gardens are intentionally short to prevent cars parking in them. One cluster of apartments has been adapted into a day centre.

The houses are timber-frame construction, for speed and quality of construction, whereas the apartments are traditionally constructed. One house experimented with rainwater-harvesting for toilet-flushing, which has highlighted the extra management these systems require.

client – Ballymun Regeneration Ltd

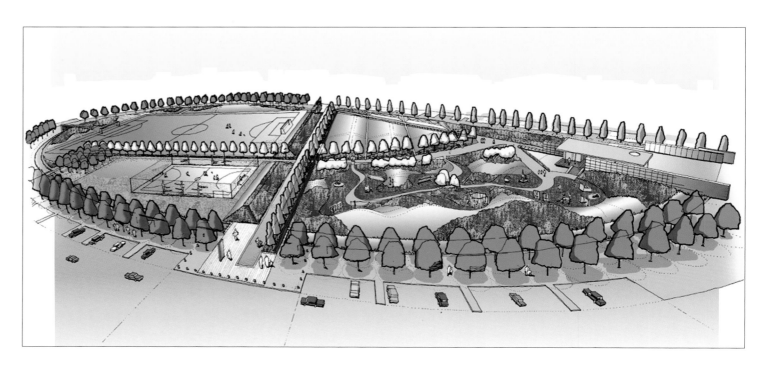

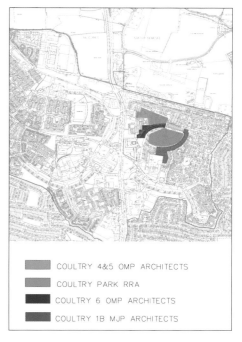

	COULTRY 4&5 OMP ARCHITECTS
	COULTRY PARK RRA
	COULTRY 6 OMP ARCHITECTS
	COULTRY 1B MJP ARCHITECTS

↗ Concept drawing
→ Aerial view of site and location map

Coultry 3, Santry Avenue, Ballymun

Ballymun Regeneration Ltd

This site for this scheme was derelict and blighted by high-voltage electric cables with a 19-bar gas mains running along its length, splitting the site into two strips. The depth of the services established the finished ground level.

The design is a response to the site restraints and several imperatives, including the provision of a complete street frontage to the new internal road and the creation of a sense of place and intimacy; and also the creation of a strong and appropriate elevation to the heavily trafficked Santry Avenue.

Three-storey U-shaped apartment buildings line the northern edge. The outer face is scaled to meet Santry Avenue, and the inner cores are facing south. Blocks are spaced to allow parking courtyards in-between. Each apartment is entered off the shared courtyard, apart from the ground-floor units, which are entered off side gardens.

Housing in terraces lines the southern boundary, responding in scale and type to the existing housing in Coultry. The mono-pitch roofscape, the use of materials, and the hard and soft landscaping layout maintain a rhythm along the internal street.

design / completion – 2000–2004
client – Ballymun Regeneration Ltd

↗ Location map and site plan
⇉ Plans of courtyard block of apartments

→ opposite – Views of the completed development

COULTRY 3 BRL ARCHITECTS   SILLOGUE 5 BKD ARCHITECTS
BALLYMUN CROSS TOT ARCHITECTS

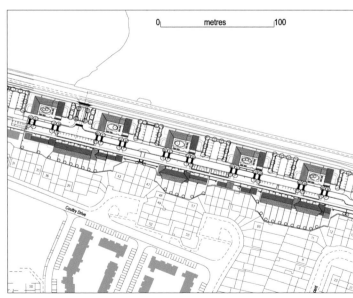

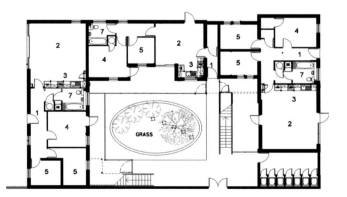

height	mix	percentage	no. of dwellings	site area	density	floor area	bed spaces	site coverage	open space	car spaces	context
1-3 storey	33 x 3-bed houses 12 x 3-bed apartment 42 x 2-bed apartment	100% residential	87	1.68 ha (4.15 acres)	21 units/acre	6,350m²	247 allocated (59 units/acre) 329 potential	22%	3,035m² in private gardens 900m² in shared courtyards 235m² in private balconies	116 (1.3 per dwelling)	edge of outer-suburban regeneration area

Sillogue 5, Sillogue Avenue, Ballymun, Dublin 11 Burke-Kennedy Doyle Architects

The Sillogue project is on a 6.3-acre site to the rear of the existing Ballymun flats. The main characteristics of the site are its linear nature, its relative independence from existing access routes, and the long exposed boundary backing onto the existing private houses.

The design response facilitates future development of the street pattern to address the main Sillogue roads when the existing blocks are demolished.

The street design is carefully considered, with shared surfaces and head-to-kerb parking generally, interspersed with trees to minimise visual impact and break up the linear nature of the layout.

Large south-west facing terraces are provided to upper-floor apartments, with smaller terraces overlooking the street activity. External steps to apartments are modelled on Georgian terraces or stoops, to provide a zone of privacy and interaction.

Pedestrian movement at all locations is direct, and overlooked by building entrances and living areas. Raised tables are provided at road junctions within and around the scheme to define areas of pedestrian priority, with raised kerbs and bollards where required.

The new Sillogue Park is centred on the development and is provided with a high-quality toddlers' playground and urban landscaping, similar to other parks proposed under the BRL play strategy.

FRONT ELEVATION (EAST)

SECOND FLOOR PLAN

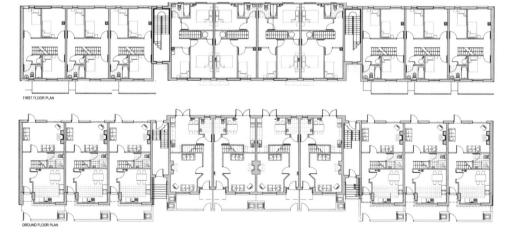

FIRST FLOOR PLAN

GROUND FLOOR PLAN

design / completion – 2003–2007
client – Ballymun Regeneration Ltd

↑ Front elevation (east)
← Typical plans – ground, 1st, 2nd floors – with 3-bedroom houses with apartments overhead in the centre of the block, and 4-bedroom houses at either end

opposite

↗ Site plan
→ Views of completed development
↘ Typical cross-sections

height	mix	percentage	no. of dwellings	site area	density	floor area	bed spaces	site coverage	open space	car spaces	context
1-3 storey	10 x 4-bed houses 2 x 3-bed houses 54 x 3-bed duplexes 29 x 2-bed apartment 40 x 1-bed apartment	100% residential	135	26,840m² (6.63 acres)	20 units/acre	12,186m² (blocks 1-11)	306 (46/acre)	16.5%	9,355m²	152 (1.1 per dwelling)	infill site to rear of flats complex

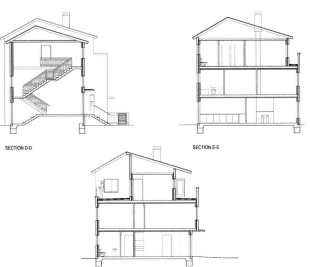

SECTION D-D

SECTION E-E

Sillogue 6, Sillogue Road, Ballymun

The site, formerly occupied by two blocks of flats, is a long, narrow strip of land between Sandyhill Gardens and the newly upgraded Sillogue Road/Marewood Crescent. The development forms a new two-to-three-storey street frontage along Sillogue Road/Marewood Crescent. Terraces of houses are 'bookended' by apartment buildings, which form the street corners.

The scale and character of Sandyhill Gardens is protected by the provision of one- and two-storey houses facing the existing 1970s housing. This pattern of development is continued along Sillogue Road, where the terrace turns at the southern end to form one side of a new park. The other boundaries of the park are formed by an existing terrace of Sandyhill houses and the new Neighbourhood Centre.

The hard and soft landscaping of the new streets ties into the environmental upgrading works of the public areas of Sandyhill Gardens, which was completed in 2007.

Considerable care has been taken to make the housing designs flexible and suitable for lifetime occupancy. Rooms can be adapted to suit changing family circumstances. Seven of the houses and ten of the apartments incorporate a bedroom at ground level, suitable for the elderly or disabled.

The buildings are insulated to a high standard, exceeding that required under

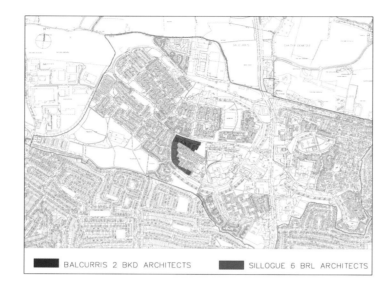

BALCURRIS 2 BKD ARCHITECTS   SILLOGUE 6 BRL ARCHITECTS

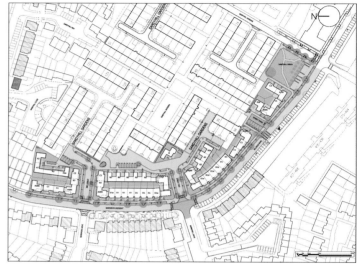

current Building Regulations. Walls are in brick and render on all main façades, and rendered on the rear elevations. High-quality timber-framed, double-glazed windows with integrated draught seals are fitted. Roofs are pitched with concrete tiles. Smaller flat roofs over bay windows, entrance canopies, etc, are clad in standing seam metal roofing to give a crisp appearance. These bays have full-height double-glazed windows facing onto the gardens. The entrance doors are in high-quality timber, with meter boxes faced in a matching timber.

design / completion – 2004–2009
client – Ballymun Regeneration Ltd

↖ Location map, site plan and bird's-eye view
→ Typical house plans and perspectives of scheme

height	mix	percentage	no. of dwellings	site area	density	floor area	bed spaces	site coverage	open space	car spaces	context
1-3 storey	22 x 3-bed houses 16 x 2-bed houses 10 x 2-bed apartments 10 x 1-bed apartments	100% residential	58	11,914m² (3 acres)	20 units/acre	4,191m²	124 (41/acre)	20%	785m² in public park; also private gardens and balconies	79 (1.36 per dwelling)	long narrow strip between existing residential areas

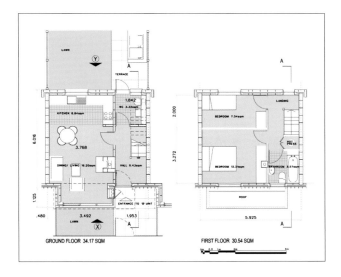

GROUND FLOOR 34.17 SQM

FIRST FLOOR 30.54 SQM

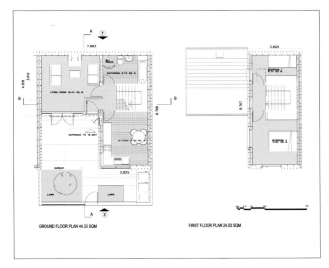

GROUND FLOOR PLAN 44.33 SQM

FIRST FLOOR PLAN 24.03 SQM

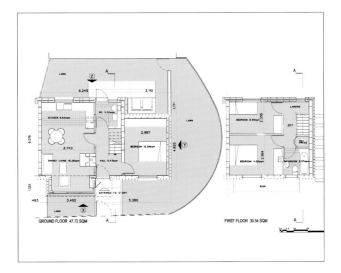

GROUND FLOOR 47.72 SQM

FIRST FLOOR 30.54 SQM

Dolmen Court, Poppintree 3, Ballymun, Dublin 11

Fionnuala Rogerson Architects

Dolmen Court was part of a scheme of over 300 courtyard houses built by Dublin Corporation in the 1970s. The layout was based on the Radburn principle, with distinct separation of pedestrian and vehicular access. The courtyards were linked by pedestrian through-routes, with vehicular access confined to the perimeter. This 'back-to-front' planning resulted in poorly supervised approaches and exposed back gardens, ultimately leading to anti-social behaviour through poor passive surveillance, and environmental neglect.

A scheme of new houses and apartments was built around the perimeter of Dolmen court on strips of unused land. A new street was created linking the existing and new development.

Designed as a home zone, shared street surfaces serve as a safe children's play area. Problematic pedestrian through-routes have been closed off, and courtyards landscaped. Each block of housing is oriented to improve security through passive surveillance of approaches.

Multiple dwelling plans were developed to cope with shallow plot depths and varying site conditions, while adaptable layouts provide the flexibility to suit various family structures.

design / completion – 2004–2009
(under construction)
client – Ballymun Regeneration Ltd

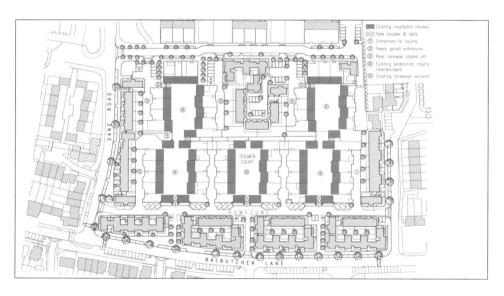

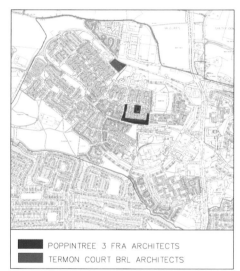

POPPINTREE 3 FRA ARCHITECTS
TERMON COURT BRL ARCHITECTS

↑ Residents of Dolmen Court, Ballymun, participate in discussions on the future design of their neighbourhood.

↑ Site plan
↗ Location map
↓ Elevation to home zone

height	mix	percentage	no. of dwellings	site area	density	floor area	bed spaces	site coverage	open space	car spaces	context
1-3 storey	31 x 3-bed houses 11 x 2-bed houses 15 x 2-bed apartments 18 x 1-bed apartments	100% residential	75	18,889m² (4.67 acres)	16 units/acre	5,215m²	268 (58/acre)	18%	200m² public 4,745m² private	1.5 per dwelling	suburban infill

↑ Elevation to Balbutcher Lane
↑ Perspective view
↓ Typical floor plans

GROUND FLOOR PLAN (Nos. 5 & 6)

FIRST FLOOR PLAN (Nos. 5 & 6)

GROUND FLOOR PLAN (Nos.10 & 11)

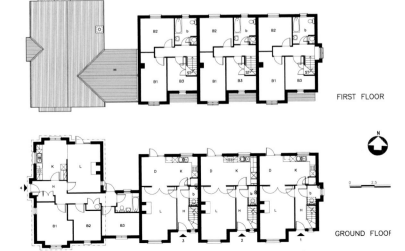

FIRST FLOOR

GROUND FLOOR

297

Termon Court, Poppintree, Ballymun

This pilot project is part of a framework plan for the improvement of the Poppintree Courts area of Ballymun.

The aim of this project is to upgrade and 'normalise' the relationship between the Courts and the surrounding street network. This is achieved by demolishing the pairs of houses at the ends of the Courts and opening up the Courts to new streets created by new houses built on poor-quality, leftover space. These houses form a street edge at the perimeter.

The project is centred on the two existing courtyards which open out to form short streets. The back lanes are gated, privatised, and continue to be used for vehicular access. New mews-type units screen exposed back-garden walls to the east and west of the site. These are arranged so that existing residents can continue to park in their back gardens, while also providing private terraces for the new dwellings at first-floor level.

A three-storey terrace comprising three- and four-bedroom houses and three 'bookend' apartment buildings front onto Balbutcher Lane North. All apartments have own-door access from street level, and communal indoor areas are eliminated. Two-storey terraces of apartments and houses form the southern edge of the project.

External materials used include brickwork, self-coloured render and fibre-cement panels, zinc or artificial slate roofs, and double-glazed softwood windows.

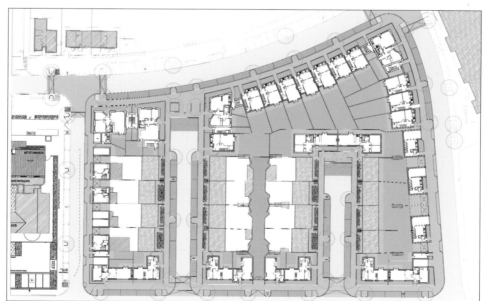

design / completion – 2005–
client – Ballymun Regeneration Ltd

↑ Model
↖ Bird's-eye view and location map
← Ground-floor plan

height	mix	percentage	no. of dwellings	site area	density	floor area	bed spaces	site coverage	open space	car spaces	context
1-3 storey	3 x 4-bed houses 12 x 3-bed houses 4 x 2-bed houses 1 x 3-bed apartment 21 x 2-bed apartment	100% residential	41 new 16 existing	10,350m² (2.55 acres)	22 units/acre	3,550m²	202 (79/acre)	34%	3,700m² in private gardens 150m² in private balconies	88 (1.5 per dwelling)	improvement and upgrading of existing 1970s housing scheme

Ballymun Cross, Dublin 9

Traynor O'Toole Architects

The design has been informed by the site context, topography, residential amenity and desired permeability of the scheme.

Accommodation is arranged around four courtyards, creating a strong perimeter to the scheme. The main courtyard is set a half-level below street level, and provides lateral penetration through the site, helping to create an intimate civic space supported by bar/restaurant, retail and leisure uses. A second courtyard, set a half-level above street level, creates a semi-private space of greater residential amenity. A health and fitness centre is provided beneath this courtyard and opens onto the civic space. The third and fourth courtyards are interconnected, and provide residential amenity and children's play areas.

Landscaping provides wide pavements, tree-planting, bicycle-parking and access to the elevated metro station. Two-storey commercial frontages provide an appropriate scale to the dual carriageway while also providing a podium for the residential floors and establishing a scale appropriate to the neighbourhood centre.

The residential units are provided over 4-5 storeys above commercial level. Typically, apartments are paired or clustered (two per lift/stair shaft per floor or four per floor where deck access is employed). The development is served by two levels of basement car-parking.

address – Ballymun Cross, Ballymun Road / Santry Avenue, Dublin 9
design / completion – 2004–
client – Genetic Developments Ltd

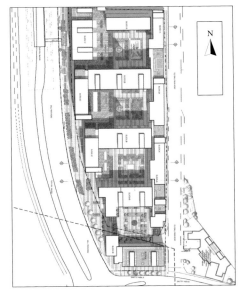

↑ Computer perspective of one of the courtyards
→ Computer perspectives of development
← Site plan

height	mix	percentage	no. of dwellings	site area	density	floor area	bed spaces	site coverage	open space	car spaces	context
3-5 storey	34 x 3-bed apartments 145 x 2-bed apartments 69 x 1-bed apartments retail, office, leisure, crèche	73% residential 27% commercial	248	13,104m² (3.23 acres)	77 units/acre	31,482m²	461 (143/acre)	55%	1,731m² public 3,513m² semi-private 388m² private	556 (1.4 per dwelling)	neighbourhood centre site in regeneration area

Shangan 5a, Shangan Avenue, Ballymun, Dublin 9

FKL Architects

The new building clearly defines the separation between public and private space, in line with the aspiration of the Ballymun master plan. The programme requires the provision of 42 dwellings, ranging from single storey one-bed apartments to three storey family units in compliance with the DoE guidelines

The concept is resolved into a singular form that responds to various site conditions and brief requirements, to provide a coherent and integrated response which embeds itself into the existing and emerging context.

The linear form twists and bends to allow for the creation of public spaces along its narrow site, and changes in section to accommodate the varying scale of units internally. The building is allowed to rise up when distant from the existing neighbours, dropping to single-storey height when the form is less than twenty metres to the rear of an existing house.

The reading of the form as a single entity is emphasised by the use of a singular colour and materiality, brick walls and concrete roof tiles.

design / completion – 2004–2010
client – Ballymun Regeneration Ltd

↗ Site plan
→ Location map
⇉ Study of materiality and concept drawing

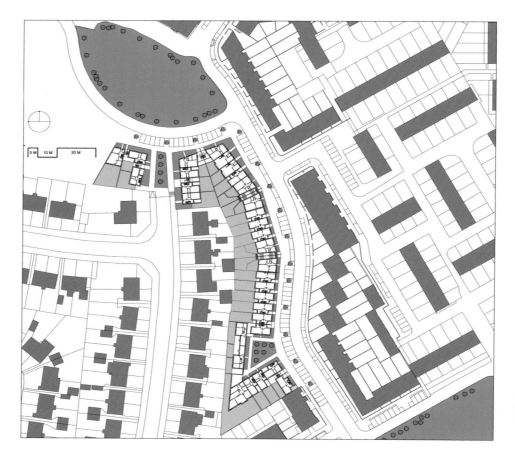

opposite

↗ Elevation to Shangan Avenue
↗ Views of model – courtyard and from north
→ Views of model – studies of form and light
→ Typical plans (ground, 1st, 2nd) and cross-section

SHANGAN 5A FKL ARCHITECTS
SHANGAN 5B M&A ARCHITECTS
SHANAGAN NC DMA ARCHITECTS

twisted form

public / private

height	mix	percentage	no. of dwellings	site area	density	floor area	bed spaces	site coverage	open space	car spaces	context
1-3 storey	2 x 4-bed houses 10 x 3-bed houses 12 x 3-bed apartments 9 x 2-bed apartments 9 x 1-bed apartments	100% residential	42	4,548m² (1.1 acres)	38 units/acre	3,180m²	159 (144/acre)	46%	2,530m² i	55 (1.3 per dwelling)	urban development site between new road and existing houses

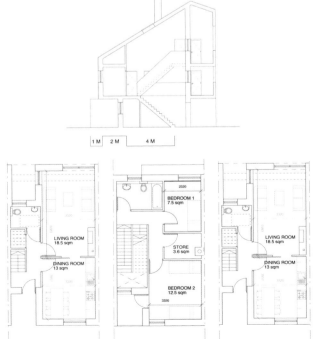

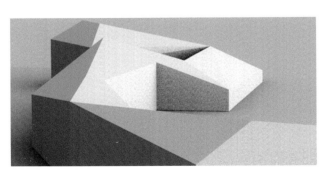

1 M   2 M   4 M

BEDROOM 1
7.5 sqm

LIVING ROOM
18.5 sqm

STORE
3.6 sqm

LIVING ROOM
18.5 sqm

DINING ROOM
13 sqm

BEDROOM 2
12.5 sqm

DINING ROOM
13 sqm

Shangan Neighbourhood Centre, Ballymun

DMOD Architects

This mixed-use development of residential and neighbourhood facilities comprises thirty one- and two-bedroom apartments, generally at first- and second-floor level, arranged in six 'houses', accessible both from the street and the rear courtyards. A seventh 'house', accessible from the street, provides office and meeting rooms for the local community forum. The street level accommodation comprises three retail units and a café, and to the rear the ancillary accommodation includes a separate laundry area for the apartments.

The site is adjacent to a proposed new village green, and the design objective was to provide a distinct edge to this green, the whole being intended collectively to form the nucleus of a new Shangan 'village'. The soft-curving frontage to the green is punctuated by a rhythm of apartment 'house' entrance cores. The community centre boldly penetrates this rhythm, and dominates it in scale and texture, being faced in natural stone and terracotta render.

design / completion – 2001–2008
client – Ballymun Regeneration Ltd

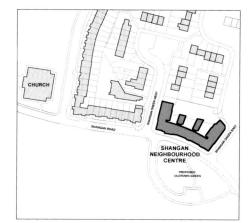

↗ Ground-level and aerial views of Neighbourhood Centre under construction
→ Typical apartment level floor plans
↠ Location maps

height	mix	percentage	no. of dwellings	site area	density	floor area	bed spaces	site coverage	open space	car spaces	context
3-4 storey	2 x 2-bed duplexes 17 x 2-bed apartments 11 x 1-bed apartments retail units, café, community rooms	72% residential 28% mixed use	30	2,100m² (0.5 acres)	60 units/acre	2,995m²	79 (158/acre)	43%	315m² in 3 courtyards	30 (1 per dwelling)	suburban site adjacent to main road and proposed new park

Shangan 5b, Social Housing, Ballymun

Mitchell & Associates

Shangan 5b housing is a scheme of 57 units – one of nine schemes in Phase 4 of the housing programme. The site is formed by the realignment of Shangan Avenue and by the existing Shangan Gardens housing units.

The scheme is designed to create a strong street edge along Shangan Avenue and to provide high-quality residential amenity in public and private open space. The massing responds to the site section, from three to four storeys on the street corridor to one and two storeys facing and adjacent to existing housing.

The development comprises 31 houses and 26 apartments. A mix of unit types, ranging from one-bedroom apartments to three-bedroom houses is proposed, and the massing responds to the site section, from four storeys on the Shangan Avenue corridor to two storeys adjacent to existing housing.

Environmental improvements to the surrounding housing is an integral part of the scheme.

design / completion – 2005–
client – Ballymun Regeneration Ltd

↗ Views of model
→ Site plan

height	mix	percentage	no. of dwellings	site area	density	floor area	bed spaces	site coverage	open space	car spaces	context
1-3 storey	50% 3-bed houses 15% 2-bed duplexes 35% 2-bed apartments	100% residential	58	12,100m² (3 acres)	20 units/acre	4,500m²	207 (69/acre)	38%	90m² private for houses 25m² private for apartments additional private balconies	73 (1.25 per dwelling)	mixture of existing and proposed social housing with parks

The New Housing 2

BUILDING BETTER COMMUNITIES

Featured Architects

CONTACT DETAILS

BALLYMUN REGENERATION
Civic Centre, Main Street, Ballymun,
Dublin 9
T 01-2225660 / F 01-8421443
E brl@brl.ie / W www.brl.ie

BURKE-KENNEDY DOYLE ARCHITECTS
6-7 Harcourt Terrace, Dublin 2
T 01-6182400 / F 01-6767385
E architecture@bkd.ie / W www.bkd.ie

DENIS BYRNE ARCHITECTS
26 North Great George's Street, Dublin 1
T 01-8788535 / F 01-8788473
E info@architects-dba.com
W www.architects-dba.com

GCA / GERRY CAHILL ARCHITECTS
24a Upper Baggot Street, Dublin 4
T 01-6676799 / F 01-6676812
E info@gca.ie / W www.gca.ie

CAREW KELLY ARCHITECTS
21-22 Grafton Street, Dublin 2
T 01-6333000 / F 01-6333001
E design@carewkelly.ie
W www.carewkelly.ie

CARR COTTER & NAESSENS
ARCHITECTS
32 South Terrace, Cork
T 021-4847123 / F 021-4847896
E info@ccnarchitects.net
W www.ccnarchitects.net

SHAY CLEARY ARCHITECTS
Mount Pleasant Business Centre, Upper
Mount Pleasant Ave, Ranelagh, Dublin 6
T 01-4125090 / F 01-4978087
E info@sca.ie / W www.sca.ie

COLLINS MAHER MARTIN ARCHITECTS
Dodder Park Road, Rathfarnham,
Dublin 14
T 01-490063 / F 01-4907633
E info@comma.ie / W www.comma.ie

CONROY CROWE KELLY ARCHITECTS
65 Merrion Square, Dublin 2
T 01-661 3990 / F 01-676 5715
E info@cck.ie / W www.cck.ie

COONEY ARCHITECTS
The Old Brewers Club, 32 The Coombe,
Dublin 8
T 01-4533 444 / F 01-4533 445
E mail@cooneyarchitects.com
W www.cooneyarchitects.com

COX POWER & ASSOCIATES
Market Lane, Bridge Street, Westport,
Co Mayo
T 098-26180 / F 098-27107
E info@coxpower.ie
W www.coxpower.ie

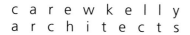

MV CULLINAN ARCHITECTS
Isolde's Tower, 2 Essex Quay,
Temple Bar, Dublin 2
T 01-6707566 / F 01-6707568
E mvarch@indigo.ie

DMOD ARCHITECTS
Cathedral Court, New Street, Dublin 8
T 01-4911700 / F 01-4911707
E mail@dmod.ie / W www.dmod.ie

DTA ARCHITECTS
22 Wicklow Street, Dublin 2
T 01-6777742 / F 01-6777713
E info@dta.ie / W www.dta.ie

Dublin City Council
Comhairle Cathrach Bhaile Átha Cliath

DUBLIN CITY COUNCIL,
CITY ARCHITECTS DIVISION
Housing & Residential Services,
Civic Offices, Wood Quay, Dublin 8
T 01-2223526 / F 01-2222084
W www.dublincity.ie

SEÁN HARRINGTON ARCHITECTS

SEÁN HARRINGTON ARCHITECTS
3rd floor, 121-122 Capel Street, Dublin 1
T 01-8733422 / F 01-8726934
E info@sha.ie / W www.sha.ie

DDA DUIGNAN DOOLEY ARCHITECTS
62 Brighton Square, Dublin 6
T 01-4900499 / F 01-4904550
E info@ddaarch.ie

HASLETTE SWEENEY ARCHITECTS

HASLETTE SWEENEY ARCHITECTS
Market Yard, Carrick-on-Shannon,
Co Leitrim
T 071-9650709 / F 071-9650710
E mail@msarch.ie / W www.msarch.ie

ELLIOT MAGUIRE LANDERS
ARCHITECTS
20 Cruises Street, Limerick
T 061-312249 / F 061-312508
E limerick@eml.ie / W www.eml.ie

40 Dame Street, Dublin 2
T 01-6707677 / F 01-6707678
E dublin@eml.ie / W www.eml.ie

HKR ARCHITECTS

HKR ARCHITECTS
5 Schoolhouse Lane, Dublin 2
T 01-6636400 / F 01-6636401
E dublin@hkrarchitects.com
W www.hkrarchitects.com

fklarchitects

FKL ARCHITECTS
Unit 19b Greenmount Lane,
Harolds Cross, Dublin 12
T 01-4736350 / F 01-4736250
E design@fklarchitects.com
W www.fklarchitects.com

iCON
Architecture
Urban Design
Conservation

ICON ARCHITECTURE
& URBAN DESIGN
Ballymurrin House, Kilbride,
Co Wicklow
T 0404-48206 / E icon@iolfree.ie

simon j kelly + partners
architects

SIMON J KELLY + PARTNERS
ARCHITECTS
Corrib Castle, Waterside, Galway
T 091-562949 / F 091-565427
E mail@sjk.ie / W www.sjk.ie

dermot foley
landscape architects

rémi salles
landscape architects

FOLEY + SALLES LANDSCAPE
ARCHITECTS
Argus House, Malpas Street, Blackpitts,
Dublin 8
T 01-4545148 / F 01-4733427
E info@dermotfoley.com
W www.dermotfoley.com
W www.remisalles.com

Westpoint, Westport, Co Mayo
T 098-24414 / F 098-24413
E mayo@sjk.ie / W www.sjk.ie

PAUL KEOGH ARCHITECTS
Cathedral Court, New Street,
Dublin 8
T 1-6791551 / F 01-6793476
E info@pka.ie / W www.pka.ie

FRAPPOLI GREEN CHATIN ARCHITECTS

FRAPPOLI GREEN CHATIN
(Aix en Provence)
c/o Wain Morehead Architects
NSC Campus, Mahon, Cork
T 021-2307150 / F 021-2307160
E wma@wma.ie / W www.wma.ie

laughton tyler
architects

LAUGHTON TYLER OWENS
ARCHITECTS
The Mash House, Distillery Road,
Dublin 3
T 01-8841470 / F 01-8841476
E info@lto.ie / W www.lto.ie

GILROYMCMAHON

GILROY McMAHON ARCHITECTS
Mill Building, Unit 10,
Greenmount Industrial Estate,
Harolds Cross, Dublin 12
T 01-4150044 / F 01-4150045
E office@gilroymcmahon.com
W www.gilroymcmahon.com

MCCROSSAN O'ROURKE MANNING

McCROSSAN O'ROURKE MANNING
ARCHITECTS
Block E, Iveagh Court, Harcourt Road,
Dublin 2
T 01-4788700 / F 01-4788711
E arch@mcorm.com / W www.mcorm.com

MAGEE CREEDON KEARNS
ARCHITECTS
11 North Abbey Street, North Gate
Bridge, Cork
T 021-4932702 / F 021-4932704
E mail@mageecreedonkearns.com
W www.mageecreedonkearns.com

ROBIN MANDAL ARCHITECTS

ROBIN MANDAL ARCHITECTS,
The Meeting Hall, 73 George's Avenue,
Blackrock, Co Dublin
T 01-2786164 / F 01-2836923
E rma@meetinghall.ie
W www.meetinghall.ie

MCO | PROJECTS

MCO PROJECTS
121-122 Capel Street, Dublin 1
T 01-8870630 / F 01-8874330
E info@mco.ie / W www.mco.ie

Metropolitan Workshop
Architecture and Urban Design

METROPOLITAN WORKSHOP
14-16 Cowcross Street,
London EC1M 6DG, UK
T 0044-(0)20-75660450
F 0044-(0)20-75660460
E info@metwork.co.uk
W www.metwork.co.uk

MITCHELL + ASSOCIATES

MITCHELL & ASSOCIATES
Fumbally Court, Fumbally Lane, Dublin 8
T 01-4545066 / F 01-4545065
E info@mitchellassoc.net
W www.mitchellassoc.net

Unit 24, Webworks, Eglinton Street, Cork
T 021-4250662 / F 021-4250665

MJP
ARCHITECTS

MJP ARCHITECTS
9 Heneage Street, Spitalfields,
London E1 5IJ, UK
T 0044-(0)20-73779262
F 0044-(0)20-72477854
E mjp@mjparchitects.co.uk
W www.mjparchitects.co.uk

Richard Murphy
Architects

RICHARD MURPHY ARCHITECTS
15 Old Fishmarket Close,
Edinburgh EH1 1RW, Scotland
T 0044-(0)131-2206125
F 0044-(0)131-2206781
E mail@richardmurphyarchitects.com
W www.richardmurphyarchitects.com

murrayōlaoire architects

MURRAY Ó LAOIRE ARCHITECTS
Fumbally Square, Fumbally Lane,
Dublin 8
T 01-4537300 / F 01-4534062
E dublin@murrayolaoire.com
W www.murrayolaoire.com

Merriman House, Brian Merriman Place,
Lock Quay, Limerick
T 061-316400 / F 061-316853
E limerick@murrayolaoire.com

3 Victoria Road, Cork
T 021-4967777 / F 021-4924800
E cork@murrayolaoire.com

NMA
Newenham Mulligan & Associates
Architects / Project Managers / Interior Designers

NEWENHAM MULLIGAN
& ASSOCIATES
11-12 Baggot Court, Dublin 2
T 01-6767400 / F 01-6767280
E info@nma.ie / W www.nma.ie

NJBA ARCHITECTURE
& URBAN DESIGN
4 Molesworth Place, Dublin 2
T 01-6788068 / F 01-6788066
E njbarchitects@eircom.net

O'DONNELL
+ TUOMEY
ARCHITECTS

O'DONNELL + TUOMEY ARCHITECTS
20a Camden Row, Dublin 8
T 01-4752500 / F 01-4751479
E info@odonnell-tuomey.ie
W www.odonnell-tuomey.ie

35 Grand Parade, Cork
T 021-4271600

● **MAHONY PIKE**
Architects / Urban Design / Sustainability

O'MAHONY PIKE ARCHITECTS
The Chapel, Mount St Annes, Milltown,
Dublin 6
T 01-2027400 / F 01-2830822
E admin@omp.ie / W www.omp.ie

60 South Mall, Cork
T 021-4272775 / F 021-4272766

oms
architects

OMS ARCHITECTS
Columbia Mills, 14-15 Sir John
Rogerson's Quay, Dublin 2
T 01-6773490 / F 01-6774849
E architects@oms.ie / W www.oms.ie

ANTHONY REDDY ASSOCIATES
Dartry Mills, Dartry Road, Dublin 6
T 01-4987000 / F 01-4987001
E info@anthonyreddy.com
W www.anthonyreddy.com

41 Dean Street, Kilkenny
T 056-7762697 / F 056-7763699
E kk@anthonyreddy.com

**REDDY O'RIORDAY STAEHLI
ARCHITECTS**
Schoolhouse Studio, Carrigaline Road,
Douglas, Cork
T 021-4362922 / F 021-4363048
E info@rorsa.ie / W www.rorsa.ie

FIONNUALA ROGERSON ARCHITECTS
Ardtona House, Lower Churchtown
Road, Dublin 14
T 01-2984261 / E info@rogerson.ie

SHAFFREY ASSOCIATE ARCHITECTS
29 Lower Ormond, Dublin 1
T 01-873 5602 / F 01-8725614
E studio@shaffrey.ie / W www.shaffrey.ie

MIKE SHANAHAN + ASSOCIATES
O'Rahilly Street, Clonakilty, Co Cork
T 023-33353 / F 023-33489
E msa1@eircom.net

**SHERIDAN WOODS ARCHITECTS
& URBAN PLANNERS**
42 Arran Street East, Dublin 7
T 01-878 0403 / F 01-878 0532
E info@sheridanwoods.ie

Thompson's ARCHITECTS + DESIGNERS

**TRAYNOR O'TOOLE
Architects**

WAIN MOREHEAD ARCHITECTS
ARCHITECTURE, INTERIOR DESIGN & PROJECT MANAGEMENT

WEBER & COMPANY
ARCHITECTS

A & D WEJCHERT & PARTNERS ARCHITECTS

TAYLOR ARCHITECTS
Breaffy Road, Castlebar, Co Mayo
T 094-9021988 / H 094-9022840
E info@taylorarchitects.ie

JOHN THOMPSON + PARTNERS
Ballinacurra House, Ballinacurra,
Limerick
T 061-227755 / F 061-2277377
E info@thompsonsarchitects.ie
W www.thompsonsarchitects.ie

TRAYNOR O'TOOLE ARCHITECTS
48-49 Upper Mount Street, Dublin 2
T 01-7037800 / F 01-6610551
E info@totarch.ie / W www.totarch.ie

67-69 South Mall, Cork
021-4806458 / F 021-4254980

WAIN MOREHEAD ARCHITECTS
NSC Campus, Mahon, Cork
T 021-2307150 / F 021-2307160
E wma@wma.ie / W www.wma.ie

WEBER & COMPANY ARCHITECTS
715 South 3rd Street, Philadelphia,
PA 19147, USA
T 01-215-9222499 / F 01-215-9222598
E aweber@weberandcompany.net
W www.weberandcompany.net

**A & D WEJCHERT & PARTNERS
ARCHITECTS**
23 Lower Baggot Street, Dublin 2
T 01-6610321 / F 01-6610203
E mail@wejchert.ie / W www.wejchert.ie

Featured Architects

PROJECTS LISTING

_____

alphabetical listing by surname – above
– for thematic listing of featured projects – see pages 7-9
– for contact details for featured architects – see pages 306-309